The
Colonel Peter Vroman House
A House with History

Berna Heyman

Schoharie, New York
Covered Bridge Books
2018

Published by
Covered Bridge Books
Schoharie, New York
covered.bridge.bks@gmail.com

Cover art by John Wilkinson. The Colonel Peter Vroman house is the yellow house on the lower right. Also pictured is the covered bridge over Fox Creek. The white house, built in 1791, is the original parsonage for the Dutch Reformed Church. The Old Stone Fort Museum and its annex buildings are pictured in the background. The Old Stone Fort was the Dutch Reformed Church and became a fort during the American Revolution.

Cover design by Michael J. Silber.

Photography by Joseph Heyman. The documents and maps have been color-corrected to enhance clarity and readability.

Text embellishments derived from one of Mildred Vrooman's hand-painted egg designs.

ISBN 978-0-578-44163-4 (hardcover)

Berna and Joseph Heyman bought the Colonel Peter Vroman property in 2013. They modernized the interior and updated the infrastructure while preserving as much as possible. They treasure the history of the property and the people who lived there. This work has been compiled and written to honor them and to provide others with a well-documented record of one place during many times.

Very special thanks to Joseph Heyman for providing continual encouragement and support throughout this project. He also used his fabulous skills as a photographer and Photoshop expert to take or correct the photographs in this book. But most of all thanks for more than 50 years of wonderful adventures.

"Excuse all faults of grammar, punctuation, spelling and sense on the score of telegraphic haste."

— William James

CONTENTS

List of Figures

LIST OF MAPS

Timeline of the Colonel Peter Vroman Property

The individuals indicated by bold print are directly related to Colonel Peter Vroman either through birth or marriage. The house was in the Vroman family for more than 145 years and the Stevens family for 82 years. The house is filled with the history of the Vromans of Schoharie, of New York, and of the Nation. It is hoped that this work will help to keep that history alive in the years to come.

To 1700s	Mohawk Iroquois
1714	Myndert Schuyler
1752	John Eckerson
1785?	**Colonel Peter Vroman**
1793	**Angelica Vroman (daughter of Col. Vroman) and Peter A. Vroman. The property passed to their children and grandchildren**
1832	Jacob Fisher
1844	John P. Griggs
1856	Benjamin Griggs (son of John P. Griggs)
1860	Simeon Fairlee
1863	Samuel B. Stevens
1877	Charles B. Stevens
1912	**Louise Stevens Vrooman (daughter of Charles B. Stevens)**
1945	**Charles S. Vrooman (son of Louise Stevens Vrooman)**
1956	**Cora W. Vrooman and Mildred Vrooman (Cora's daughter)**
2013	Joseph and Berna Heyman

The heading dates in the text designate the years of individual property ownership.

The Colonel Peter Vroman House and Property

Historic Homes are not merely old homes with a construction year brass plaque. Behind that front door there are interesting stories of the people who lived there. Some of those people leave good hints about their lives and make it easier to connect the dots. Others leave us with mysteries that just beg to be solved. And when you visit an historic home, don't you always want to peek into the closets and see what's behind that locked door? This work on the Colonel Peter Vroman house and property in Schoharie, New York provides the history and background of the interesting people who have made this house their home, with special emphasis on Colonel Peter Vroman. And after you read about the people and the times in which they lived, you will get to look into the house and go behind the doors and even behind the walls.

The Colonel Peter Vroman house is located in Upstate New York in the Town of Schoharie, west of Albany. The name Schoharie comes from a Mohawk word meaning "floating driftwood."

To 1714 -- The Mohawk Iroquois Nation

The Mohawk Iroquois were the earliest occupants of the Schoharie Valley, during the Late Woodland Period (ca. 300 to 1000 AD.). Arthur C. Parker, a noted authority on Native American culture, identified sites within the Vroman property in a 1922 archeological study of New York[1]. His map *(Map 1)* identifies the location of an American Indian village and burial site, marked #9. The map does not provide sufficient detail to accurately identify the exact location. An Indian village and burial site, marked #10, were on a site near the Vroman property.

Map 1. Detail from Arthur C. Parker's "Archaeological History of New York," New York State Museum Bulletin (1922): 693.

#9 = Native American village on Vroman property. = Burial site on the Vroman property.

#10 = Native American village, Snyder farm = Burial site, Snyder farm south of Vroman property.

Without a written record, our knowledge of the Mohawk Iroquois is primarily through the artifacts they left behind. A 1995 reconnaissance survey produced 130 artifacts, 28% of which were identified as prehistoric. These artifacts included various flakes, chert, and bones. Preliminary observations from that test study suggest, "This site appears to have been a temporary camp where people manufactured stone tools from nearby chert sources. More data are needed in order to determine site boundaries, date of occupation, and the actual use of the site."[2] A follow-up dig was done in 1998. The New York State Department of Transportation and the Federal Highway Administration excavated a section of the Vroman property prior to a proposed road reconfiguration. Christina B. Rieth, the principal investigator for the 1998 archaeological dig, reported that a small American Indian burial site and a village were located on the Vroman property. The site is "located along a prehistoric footpath [the present Route 443 roadway] that followed the north bank of Fox Creek over the Helderberg Mountains into western Albany County … the footpath was probably also an important transportation route between the Hudson and Schoharie valleys."[3] The dig tested a limited area on the east and north sections of the property, along Covered Bridge Road and Rt. 443. Five unit and eight shovel test pits were excavated for the project. One Woodland-like projectile point tip was recovered as were 956 prehistoric artifacts, 1,359 historic artifacts, and 73 unidentified artifacts. Mildred Vrooman, the property owner at the time, reported finding other projectile points and prehistoric artifacts.

Rieth concluded, "Given the large number of artifacts that have been recovered from the site and the research potential of the site, the site is recommended to be eligible for the National Register of Historic Places under Criterion D as a property that has yielded or may be likely to yield, information important in prehistory or history."[4] No action was taken at the time of the archaeological dig to place the property on the National or State Registers of Historic Places but the house and property were approved for the National and State Registers of Historic Places in 2018/2019. Further archaeological work still needs to be done to tell the story of the Mohawk Iroquois on the property.

Fig. 1. Artifact from 1998 archaeological dig on the Vroman site conducted by Christina B. Rieth. Photograph taken at the New York State Museum, Archaeology Collections.

Fig. 2. Artifact drawer from 1998 archaeological dig on the Vroman I site conducted by Christina B. Rieth. Photograph taken at the New York State Museum, Archaeology Collections.

1714-1752 Myndert Schuyler and Others (The Old Schoharie Patent)

The first known non-native landowners were Dutch aristocrats from Albany: Myndert Schuyler (1672-1755), Peter van Brugh, Robert Livingston, Jr., John Schuyler, Peter Wileman, Lewis Morris, Jr., and Andrus Coeman. In 1714, they received a patent for 10,000 acres in Schoharie from the Governor of the Province of New York, Robert Hunters. The land grant is known by several different names including the Old Schoharie Patent, the Huntersfield Patent, and the Seven-Partners Patent.

Myndert Schuyler was a member of the prominent Dutch Schuyler family of New York. He was a successful trader, merchant, and contractor with extensive real estate holdings throughout the region. Major Schuyler held several appointed and elected government offices, including Mayor of Albany and member of the New York General Assembly. He had vast real estate holdings in Schoharie, Normanskill, and Schaghticoke. But he never lived on the land in Schoharie; he made his home in Albany.

The other patentees included Peter Van Brugh (1666-1740), a member of the Albany aristocracy and a Mayor of the City of Albany. Robert Livingston, Jr. (1688-1775) was a member of the New York Colonial Assembly. John Schuyler (1697?-1746?) was another member of the important Schuyler family. There were several John Schuylers around the same time and it is difficult to differentiate between them. There appears to be little information about Peter Wileman except that he was a land speculator.

Lewis Morris, Jr. and Andrus Coeman were employed by the five original patent owners (Myndert Schuyler, Peter van Brugh, Robert Livingston, Jr., John Schuyler and Peter Wileman) to survey and divide the land *(Map 2)*. Lewis Morris, Jr. (1726-1798) signed the United State Declaration of Independence as a New York delegate to the Continental Congress. Andrus Coeman was a land speculator. Following is the early Schoharie historian Jeptha Simms's description of the original patent:

> Finding the flats along Foxscreek, and a large piece at Kneiskern's dorf, near the mouth of Cobelskill, were not included in that patent [e.g. the original patent]; lost no time in securing them. Those several patents often ran into each other, and in some instances were so far apart as to leave a gore between them…. Finding much difficulty in dividing their lands – they so often intersected – the first five purchasers and their surveyors, Morris and Coeman, whose right in the Schoharie soil was proportionably [*sic*] valuable, agreed to make joint stock of the three patents. Since that time they have been distinguished as the lands of the *seven partners*. Patents and deeds granted at subsequent dates, for lands adjoining those of the seven partners, were, in some instances, bounded in such a manner as to infringe on those of the latter, or leave gores between them … proved a source of litigation for many years.[6]

In the early 1700s, the German Palatines became the first Europeans to settle in the Schoharie Valley. The Palatines were refugees from religious warfare along the border of Germany and France. They first fled to England and stayed there until 1709-10, when Queen Anne of Great Britain granted them land to settle in America. The Palatines were guaranteed the land as long as they produced naval supplies, such as ship parts and tar, for England. They first settled in the Hudson Valley. Many did not like the work they were given and felt they were poorly treated in the Hudson Valley. Several families decided to seek a better life and moved to Schoharie to farm the land. The Palatines cleared the fertile land and established farms in an area then considered the wilderness.

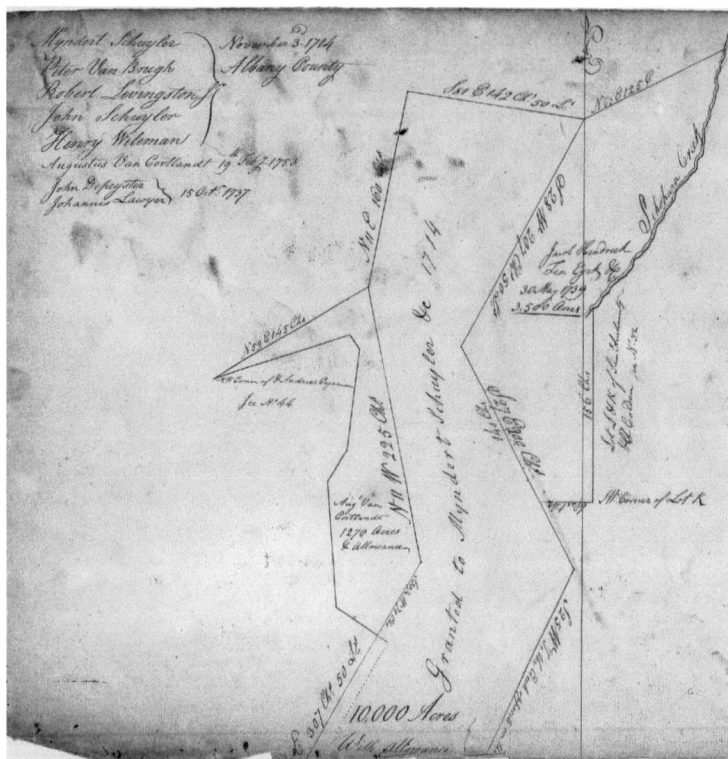

Map 2. (1714) Survey of Land for Myndert Schuyler et al. Retrieved from the New York State Archives, "Survey maps of lands in New York State," Series A0273-78, map #613.

The Palatines settled in seven dorfs or villages led by William Fox, Conrad Weiser, Hartman Winteker [Windecker], John Hendrick Kneiskern, Elias Garlack, Johannes George Smidt, and probably John Lawyer. Each dorf was named for its leader so Fuchsendorf was the area settled by William Fox. Fuchsendorf was also called Foxendorf, Fox's Dorf, Fox Town, and Foxestown. Foxendorf included the property now incorporating the Old Stone Fort Museum and the Colonel Peter Vroman house. Foxendorf was in existence by 1728[7] when the High Dutch Reformed Church was formed or perhaps even as early as 1718.

Foxendorf was the site of one of the earliest roads in Schoharie. The first settlers likely traveled that road from Albany, over the Heldeberg Mountains through Foxendorf and then down the stream into Schoharie. About 1762, a new road opened from Foxendorf through Duanesburg to Schenectady. And by 1817, turnpikes with tolls replaced the old Indian roads. There was a plank road with Toll Gate No. 1 near the Fox Creek Bridge. The plank road was a single-track road using eight-foot long planks to form a flat surface. The planks were usually made of hemlock to resist warping. From that area, there was another plank road that led to Schenectady. The main road led to Gallupville, up Kings Creek to Township in the town of Knox, then on to Altamont. These roads provided access to other settlements thus encouraging trade. Foxendorf was considered the center of the Palatine settlements. It was both a commercial center and a gathering place for prayer. The early Schoharie historian, John M. Brown, noted that Fox Creek supported a good deal of business on the water. Fox Creek, not named for William Fox, flows into the Schoharie Creek near Vroman Corners, the intersection near the Colonel Peter Vroman house. It then flows into the Mohawk River and is part of the Hudson River watershed.

4

The Palatines believed this was the land promised them by Queen Anne. But it appears they did not have clear title to all the lands they inhabited in Schoharie. Supposedly, Queen Anne commissioned an agent, Nicholas Bayard, to give each householder a deed and title to the land if the householder would describe the boundaries of their land. The Palatines were suspicious of outsiders like Bayard so he was rebuffed and run off the land. Consequently, in 1714, Bayard sold the entire tract to the seven Dutch investors noted previously (Schuyler, van Brugh, Livingston, Schuyler, Wileman, Morris, and Coeman).

These seven partners then insisted that the Palatines lease or buy the land they were living on or leave. The Palatines were offered free rent for ten years and then a modest quit-rent after that. But the Palatines insisted that the land was theirs. After several skirmishes, William Fox, the founder of the dorf, and several other Palatine families, decided to leave Schoharie. Some Palantines stayed in Schoharie while others settled in Stone Arabia, Canajoharie, Herkimer, Palatine Bridge, Palatine, and German Flats as well as Berks County in Pennsylvania. Those who stayed in Schoharie lived separately from the Dutch but the families eventually intermarried and the distinction between the two groups diminished.

> The German and Dutch races long remained distinct. The Dutch were generally wealthier than the more hardy and laborious Germans, and preferred to contract marriages with their own class in the older Dutch settlements. They often kept slaves, while the Germans seldom had further assistance than such as their own households, of both sexes, might afford. The Germans, by intermarriage, became a "family of cousins," and many ties of common interest united them. Industry and frugality gradually brought them to a level, and long acquaintance has almost entirely obliterated these hereditary distinctions of society.[8]

Notes: Schoharie was a district of Albany County from 1772 until 1795 when it achieved independence. Albany County originally consisted of a huge area of land including Schenectady, Schoharie, Saratoga, Rensselaer, Greene, and Columbia. The City of Albany in the mid-18th century consisted of about 1,500 to 2,000 inhabitants, mostly Dutch and English. Because of its location on the Hudson River, Albany served as a major center for trade and transportation for agricultural goods, timber, and furs going to New York City. Albany also was a center of trade for the French and Indians to the north. Schoharie was considered the western wilderness.

Within the County of Schoharie, there is also the Town of Schoharie and the Village of Schoharie. Sections of Foxendorf on the south bank of Foxes Creek became part of the Village of Schoharie, previously called Fountain Town. The north bank of Foxes Creek became part of the Town of Schoharie. The Peter Vroman home is located in the Town of Schoharie in Schoharie County, New York.

1752-1785 John (Johannes) Eckerson; Thomas Eckerson

It is unclear whether John Eckerson or Thomas Eckerson was the next property owner. An online transcription of a handwritten deed in the Old Stone Fort entitled *A Deed from Myndert Schuyler to John Eckerson for Lands att Schoharie 1752* suggests John Eckerson as the subsequent owner. However, an 1899 Old Stone Fort Donation Inventory includes listings for two original manuscripts given by Henry Cady: (1) *Deed from Johannes Veeder to Thomas Eckerson, 1752;* and (2) *Deed from Thomas Eckerson to Adam Vrooman in 1785.* Neither of those documents is currently available to determine their relevance. Therefore, we are proceeding under the assumption that John Eckerson is the next owner of the property based on the fully transcribed document accessible through ancestry.com (See Appendix A)

The Eckersons were among the early Dutch settlers in Schoharie. Thomas Eckerson (1669-1735) and his second wife Elizabeth Slingerland (1672-1735) had several children including: John Eckerson (1701-1776?), Thomas Eckerson (1713-1790), and Annatie (Eckerson) Ziele (1702-1747). "The Eckersons were a business family and were connected with several different kinds of branches of industry that were started in the valley, as well as foremost in the church. They were large land owners and when the Revolution commenced were wealthy for the people of the frontier." [9]

According to the transcribed deed previously cited, John Eckerson (1701-1776) bought land and water creek rights from Myndert Schuyler on March 7, 1752 for 65 pounds. John Eckerson is described in the deed as a blacksmith. The deed includes several tracts of land both south and north of Foxes Creek, consisting of about twenty acres. The land included parts of the original Lot 51 of the Schoharie Patent. A section of the deed reads:

> …two Equall Seaventh part of four Acres of-Land Lying a Lidle blow the bridge on foxes Creek, to the north of Said Creek, Which was Reserved by the owners of Schoharie for a mill place, together With the two Seventh part of the Stream-of water in foxes Creek from the bridge to Schohary River. [10]

It is particularly interesting to note that the deed specifically mentions that the land was intended for a mill and that a bridge already existed over Fox Creek. According to the deed, John Eckerson was required to pay a yearly quick rent of nine pence.

The Eckerson family and Colonel Peter Vroman were closely connected. Thomas Eckerson Junior (1713-1790), the brother of John Eckerson, was a Major under Col. Vroman. And John Eckerson's sister, Annatie Eckerson married Pieter Ziele. The Ziele's daughter, Janneke Ziele (1735-1811), married Colonel Peter Vroman's brother, Adam B. Vroman (1740-1823). The marriage took place on May 15, 1761, the same day that Col. Vroman married Engeltie Swart.

In 1752, John Eckerson donated some of his land to build the Dutch Reformed Church, now known as the Old Stone Fort Museum. His name is inscribed, along with other early Dutch settlers, in the stone façade of the building *(Fig. 3)*.

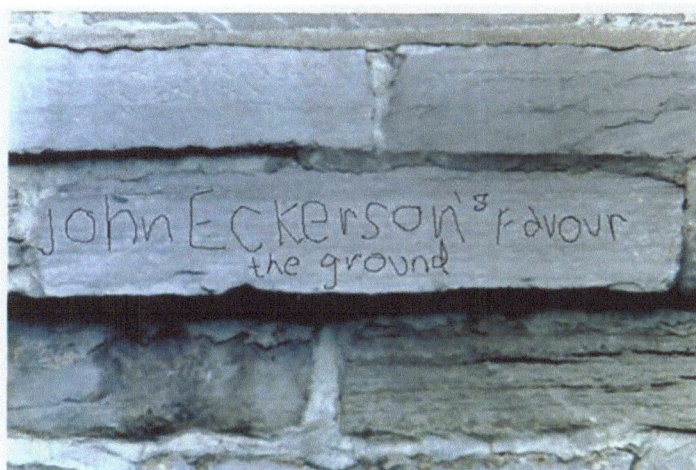

Fig. 3. John Eckerson's name etched near the top of the Old Stone Fort. The inscription reads: "John Eckerson's favour the ground."

A 1758 map *(Map 3)* shows Foxes Town on the north side of Foxes Creek. A road leads to Albany, 30 miles away. The map includes at least 5 houses in Foxes Town. In addition, there is a sawmill along with two other structures on the north bank of Foxes Creek. A church (the Old Stone Fort) is shown on the south bank of Foxes Creek. Some of the structures were likely the property of John Eckerson. The mill attracted other business to the area and Foxes Town was supposedly the envy of several of the other dorfs. According to Sias, the first blacksmith in the area set up shop in the small settlement at Fox's creek.[11] Perhaps Eckerson was that blacksmith since the deed stated he was a blacksmith. But we cannot verify that he opened a blacksmith shop in addition to the mill. The area around Fox's Dorf purportedly also housed a tavern and trading post. According to John M. Brown, in 1752 Schoharie had about 101 houses with 875 people, mostly Palatine Germans with about one third Low Dutch. [12]

Captain William Gray's Oct. 1778 map of "Schohara" (Map 4) was drawn while he was with Major General John Sullivan's expedition to the Indian Country. Rufus Alexander Grider[13] copied the map drawn for that expedition. Rufus Alexander Grider (1817-1900) created numerous pen-and-ink sketches and watercolors of places and objects related to New York State history. Many of his works are contained in nine albums of drawings and sketches housed in the Manuscripts and Special Collections of the New York State Library. Volume 8 (created 1887-1888) primarily relates to Schoharie history. Many maps and documents copied by Grider are the only versions now available. He intended the volume as a "collection of illustrations old and new and of objects possessed by inhabitants of that region ... of what exists and what formerly existed there." He drew landscapes and Indian relics and then traced rare documents making a "complete duplicate of the original." His works were invaluable to this book.

Gray's map used double dotted lines for wagon roads and single lines for paths. While no houses are shown, the map includes the High Dutch Church (the Lower Fort), Fox Kill (Foxes Creek) and the roads to Albany, Schenectady, and Duanesburg. The roads intersect at about the location of the Eckerson/Vroman property. A mill on the map is identified as the *old oyl mill*.[14] This map was part of the Sullivan-Expedition, which was an extended systematic military campaign against the Tories and the four nations of the Iroquois that had sided with the British. The campaign, ordered by George Washington, intended to put an end to the Loyalist and Iroquois attacks that occurred in 1778 around Cobleskill, Cherry Valley, and Wyoming Valley. The expedition was successful in severely damaging the Iroquois' infrastructure.

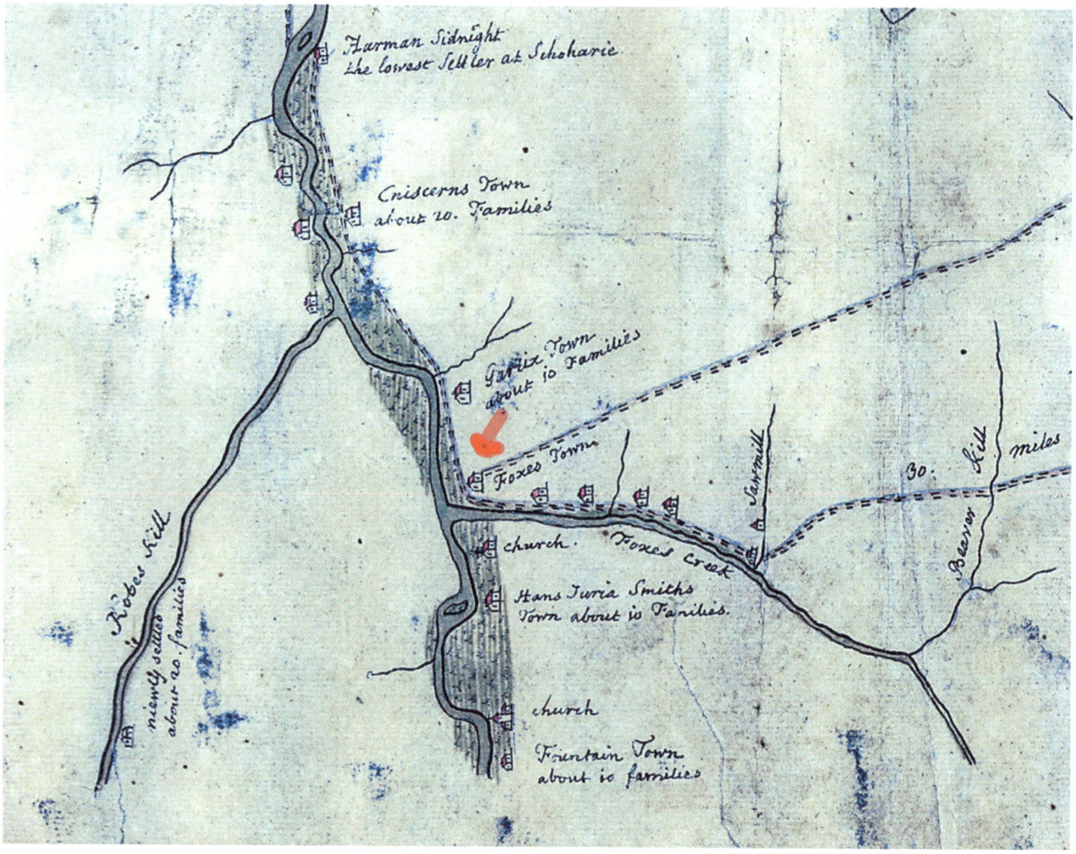

Map 3. (1758?) Detail from: "Map of the Northern Parts of New York." Retrieved from the Library of Congress.

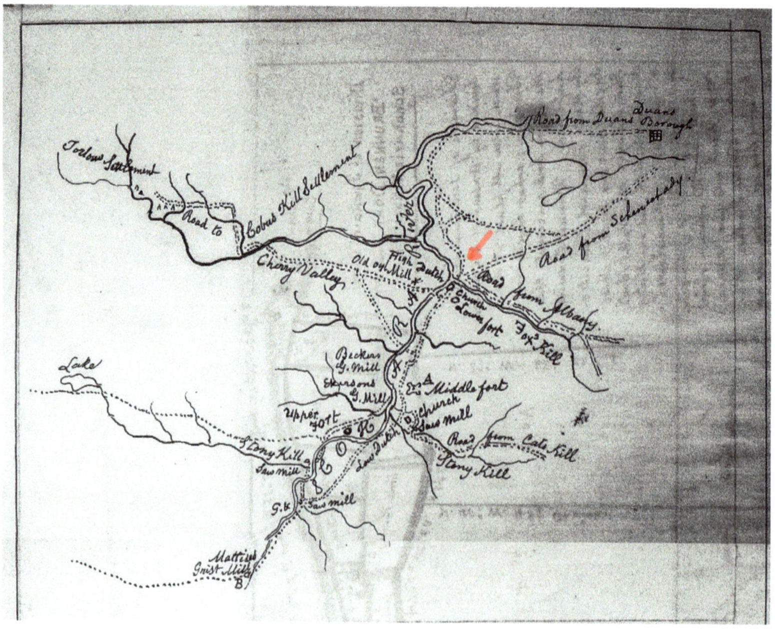

Map 4. (1778-/1888) Detail from William Gray's "Map of Schohara." Copied by Rufus Aleander Grider.

Map 5. (1779) Detail from Claude Joseph Sauthier and William Faden's "A Chorographical Map of the Province of New-York in North America, 1779." Retrieved from the Library of Congress.

The 1779 Sauthier map[15] *(Map 5)* shows Foxestown with at least five structures, likely homes, clustered together. It appears that the structures near the sawmill on the 1758 map *(Map 3)* also exist on this map. There is a road to the north of Foxes Creek as well as a road that crosses Foxes Creek. The map includes the following names around Foxestown: Sternberg, G. Zimmer, Lawyer, Morris but not John Eckerson, as might have been expected.

The first gristmill at Foxestown was likely built by William Fox and was operational by 1718. It was supposedly about a mile east of the Old Stone Fort Museum. Evidently, that mill couldn't keep up with demand so the community needed a larger mill. Several members of the Eckerson family owned mill properties. Tunis Eckerson, a relative of John Eckerson, built a trading post, a tavern, and then ca. 1740 a gristmill, dam, and flume in Middleburgh. That mill was burned during Johnson's 1780 raid on Schoharie. Tunis Eckerson was a Major in the 15th Regiment under the command of Col. Vroman. The T. Eckerson shown in the southwest quadrant of the 1779 map *(Map 5)* might have referred to either Tunis Eckerson or Thomas Eckerson.

The second gristmill in Foxes Town was built ca. 1760 by John Eckerson (1701-1776), That grist mill was described as consisting of "two or three run of millstones, had a good sized overshot water wheel and continued in operation, serving the settlers of that locality as the 'Stevens Mill'...."[16] The wheel would have been about 12 to 15 feet in diameter and required a fall of water of from 15 to 20 feet.[17]

John Eckerson married four times: (1) Elizabeth Slingerland, (2) Margrietje Viele in 1733, (3) Maria Catharina Borst in 1735, and (4) Maritie Vedder in 1748. He had children with each wife but many of the children died young. One of his sons, Thomas Eckerson (1750-1817), was the miller at his father's mill when it was attacked during the 1780 Johnson raid on the Lower Fort. Thomas Eckerson married Elisabeth Ecker in 1779.

Roscoe writes, "Thomas Eckerson a nephew of Major Thomas Eckerson, of Middleburgh, settled after the Revolution, upon the farm now [1882] occupied by Alexander Hays. He held a commission as Major after that war, and was a very sagacious and energetic man. He early enrolled himself in the Colonial cause and was the miller of the present Stevens mill, near the lower fort, during the Revolution. He was a son of John Eckerson, and nephew of Thomas Jr., the major under Colonel Peter Vroman of the 18th regiment."[18]

The Schoharie Valley was the site of several skirmishes during the American Revolution. It was a strategic site, particularly as a grain provider for the Continental Army and for other colonies. George Washington stationed troops in the Valley to protect one of the main sources of food for his army. The mills ground flour for the settlers but also provided bread flour for New England.

During the Revolution, the High Dutch Reformed Church near the old Foxes Town, was converted to a stockade fort. The fort served as a refuge for the nearby inhabitants. During one skirmish in 1780, a Loyalist and Indian party attacked the Eckerson mill and partly destroyed it. But the mill was soon repaired and put back into operation.

Several accounts of that raid suggest that the homestead near the mill was not burned during the fighting. Simms (1845) writes: A dwelling and grist mill standing near the fort, (where those of Griggs now are), were set on fire, but extinguished after the enemy left."[19] Simms attributes this account of events to P. M. Snyder, Major P. Vrooman and Jacob Becker. Major P[eter] Vrooman was Col. Peter Vroman's son-in-law and his nephew. Major Vrooman married Colonel Vroman's daughter, Angelica, who inherited the house, giving considerable credibility to Simms account.

Roscoe, in his *History of Schoharie County* (1882) writes,

> The old grist-mill that was built by Johannes Eckerson about 1760, stood between the old house and the creek, and was set on fire, but making little progress before the enemy disappeared it was soon extinguished, and stood for many years after, and was owned by Colonel Peter Vroman, who settled there at the close of the war. Thomas Eckerson, son of Johannes, was the miller at that time, and he with his wife [Elisabeth] had just returned on foot from Schenectady as the enemy set fire to the mill. Upon his entering the building, an Indian raised his rifle and fired upon him, when a Tory of the neighborhood standing near threw up the muzzle of the gun, and the charge went over him. As he struck the gun, he exclaimed, 'If you shoot him we can't get any more flour!'[20]

Nelson Greene in his *History of the Mohawk Valley* (1925) writes about the 1780 raid:

> The Indians advanced to the opposite side of Fox Creek [opposite the Old Stone Fort, e.g. north side of the Creek] and entered the mill there standing. While supplying themselves with flour and meal they were discovered by Mr. and Mrs. Eckerson. They ran to the fort and were soon followed by a negro in their employ. The Indians gave chase and captured him but the guns of the picket guards covered the Eckersons and they escaped. Upon reaching the fort, Mrs. Eckerson stationed herself at the circular window in the tower and while watching the movements of the Indians and expecting every minute to see the flames destroy her home, an Indian fired and sent a bullet in the casement only an inch from her head.[21]

There were at least two New York State historical markers for the Eckerson Mill and Colonel Vroman property. According to a *Survey of Historical Sites in MVLA Area* there was a New York State marker that read:

> Site of Eckerson Mill on the North side of Fox Creek near the Old Stone Fort circa 1760. This mill was partly destroyed by the forces of Sir John Johnson in 1780. In 1785 Col. Peter Vrooman, commander of the 15th Ret. Albany County Militia bought this property (after the Peace of Paris[22]) and restored it to usefulness. [23]

Fig. 4. Major Eckerson's Mill marker originally placed on Rt. 30.

No photographs have been found of the MVLA historical marker that was likely placed on the property ca. 1933. A marker for the Eckerson mill *(Fig. 4)* was placed on the property by the Schoharie County Bicentennial in 1995. That sign disappeared from the property in 2015.

1785-1793 Adam B. Vroman, Colonel Peter Vroman
ca. 1792 house built and occupied

Note: The Vroman surname is variously spelled, Vroman and Vrooman. Even the same individuals did not use consistent spelling. Given names in the Vroman family are repeated, sometimes making it difficult to differentiate one individual from another.

Most secondary sources and local lore suggest that the Colonel Vroman home was built in 1785. Research found no justification for that assumption. Vroman's home in Vroman's Land was destroyed in the 1780 Johnson/Brant raid so it seemed reasonable to expect that he would build a new home shortly thereafter. John Eckerson bought the property in 1752 and held it until 1785. The Old Stone Fort inventory of 1899 lists a 1785 deed between Thomas Eckerson and Adam Vroman as well as another 1785 deed between Adam Vroman and his brother, Peter Vroman. The actual documents, originally donated by Henry Cady, no longer seem to exist but the 1899 inventory listing suggests the possibility that Eckerson sold the land to Adam B. Vroman and then Adam B. Vroman conveyed the property to his brother, Peter B. Vroman, in 1785 and that is perhaps the previous basis for dating the house '1785.'

The Vroman Family Early Years

Peter Vroman, a.k.a. Peter B. Vroman (1735-1793) was the great grandson of Adam Vroman (1649-1730), the original claimant to a large parcel of land in the upper Schoharie Valley, now part of Middleburgh. Adam Vroman was born in Holland and came to New York in 1664, along with his father, Hendrick Meese Vroman (1618-1690) and his grandfather Pieter Vroman (1590-1647). Adam bound himself for two years to Cornelis Vanden Bergh to learn the millwright's trade. He was to receive 80 guilders in silver and a pair of new shoes in his first year of service, and 120 guilders in silver the second year. In 1683, Adam built a mill in Sand Kill, near Schenectady. He was living in Schenectady in 1690 when his home was attacked and burned by the French and Indians.

> They first set fire to the house of Adam Vroman, who when he offered resistance was shot through the hand. After several shots had been fired, his wife, hoping to find an opportunity to get away, opened the back door, whereupon she was immediately shot dead and devoured by the flames.... His eldest daughter...had her mother's child on her arm.... Asked...whether the child was heavy...she said yes, whereupon [one of the invaders]...took the child from her and taking it by the legs dashed its head against the sill of the house, so that the brains scattered over the bystanders.... The women and children fled mostly into the woods, almost naked and there many froze to death...[24]

Two of Adam Vroman's sons, Barent and Wouter, were taken captive to Canada. Adam Vroman journeyed to Canada and arranged the release of these sons. Another son, Pieter Vroman (1684-1771), who survived the attack, was Col. Peter Vroman's grandfather.

In 1714, Adam Vroman obtained a patent for 1,400 acres in Schoharie and settled there in 1715. The land surrounded a mountain known to the Native Americans as Mt. Onistagrawa or 'Corn Mountain.' Many of Adam's descendants owned this land and the mountain became known as Vroman's Nose and the area as Vroman's Land (Vromansland).

Vroman's Nose is connected to several tales about local Revolutionary War hero Timothy Murphy. It is said that Murphy had encounters with the Indians and the British on or near Vroman's Nose. The mountain also figures in modern history. During World War II, Dr. Vincent Schaefer and his team of General Electric scientists used Vroman's Nose and the Schoharie Valley to test an artificial fog generator aimed at screening troops and cities from air attacks. [25]

"Vroman's Nose is a local jewel that contains a portion of the Long Path trail, sweeping views of the Schoharie Valley, nesting peregrine falcons and a unique geology that makes it one of the most recognizable landscapes in the area"[26] according to New York State Department of Environmental Conservation Regional Director Keith Goertz. In 1983, a small group of Adam Vroman's descendants banned together to purchase the property and create the Vroman's Nose Preservation Corporation (VNPC) to manage the area for public use. In 2017, the VNPC donated Vroman's Nose to the State of New York to preserve the historic and scenic property for the good of the public.

The Vroman family was reportedly the first Dutch settlers in Schoharie Valley. The settlement included "a bold, high and rocky headland, called Vroman's Nose, jutting out into the Flat and dominating the valley for miles, both south and north." [27] The map of Vroman's Land *(Map 6)* shows the many acres owned by members of the Vroman family dating back to 1716. The house of P. Vrooman near the top of the map was likely Colonel Peter Vroman's grandfather's home.

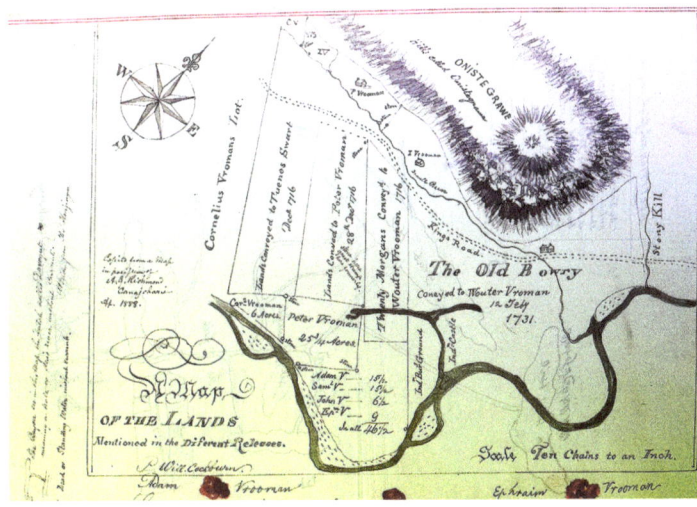

Map 6. 1731/1888) Detail from Will Cockburn's 1731 "Map of the Lands Mentioned in the Diferent Releases."
Copied by Rufus Alexander Grider, 1888. Grider's Albums. Courtesy of the New York State Library, Manuscripts and Special Collections.

Adam Vroman and his sons were building the second story of a stone house in Vroman's Land when Conrad Weiser, one of the original Palatine settlers, and other neighbors, attempted to drive them away by demolishing Vroman's house and by steering their horses over his cultivated fields. Adam traveled to Schenectady and petitioned the governor for redress. The governor ordered the arrest of Weiser and that appeared to resolve the opposition to Vroman cultivating his land. In 1726, Adam Vroman received an additional patent for 1,400 acres, described by Brown as the "best lowland in all Schoharie."[28] Adam died on his farm at Vroman's Land in Schoharie in 1730. He was a large landowner and he and his brother also inherited all the considerable land owned by their father. Adam had a total of 13 children from his three marriages and there are numerous Vroman descendants, some still living in the area.[29]

Adam Vroman's original 1718 Dutch bible *(Fig. 5)* descended through the family from Adam to his son Pieter, to his son Barent, and then to Col. Peter Vroman. In 1899, Henry Cady donated the Bible to the Old Stone Fort Museum and it is on display there. Peter's grandfather also willed him his silver watch, his writing desk, his silver-headed cane, and all of his apparel.[30]

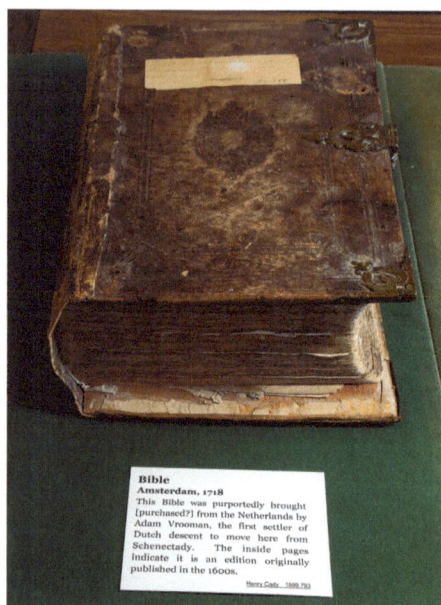

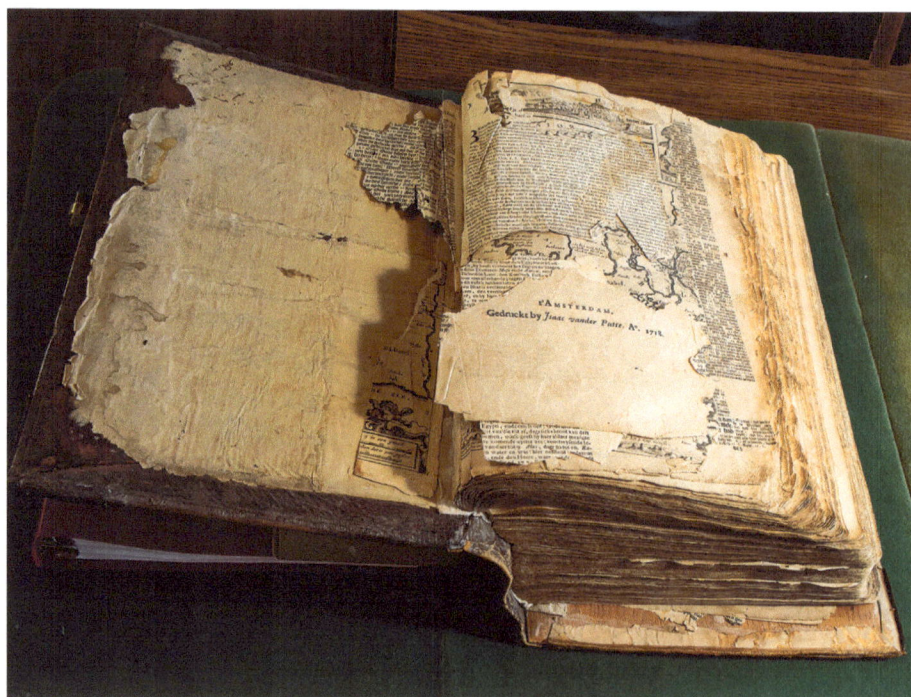

Fig. 5. 1718 Dutch Bible of Adam Vroman (1649-1730) passed down to his grandson Barent Vroman (1709-1782) and then bequeathed to Barent's son, Col. Peter Vroman (1735-1793). On display at the Old Stone Fort, Schoharie, New York.

Peter B. Vroman — Early Military Career

Pieter Vroman was the third surviving son of Adam Vroman. He lived in Vroman's Land and had seven sons and five daughters. His son Barent Vroman (1709-1784) married his first cousin, Engeltie Swart, the daughter of Christiana Vroman and Teunis Swart. In 1735, their son, Peter B. Vroman, was born in Vroman's Land. George Washington was three years old when Peter B. Vroman was born. Vroman "under his father's guidance [e.g. Barent] … learned frontier farming and land acquisition. He was entrusted with much property and had accumulated such a quantity of his own that his father found it unnecessary to provide for him in his will."[31]

Peter B. Vroman began his military career with an appointment from Governor James DeLancey of the British Province of New York. He was commissioned a Lieutenant of the Militia in 1759. Vroman had several responsibilities during his time in service. He oversaw the building of a road from Oswego to Three Rivers. And while at Oswego, Lt. Vroman was ordered on June 30, 1759 "to sit immediately at the Presidents Tent, to try all prisoners brought before them." [32]

Vroman observed and participated in the Battle of Niagara during the French and Indian War when he was 19 years old. According to Sir William Johnson's *Papers*, Vroman was assigned night detail of "50 men to parade at 5 o'clock to receive their directions of Engineer Williams, for this duty Captain VanVaughten and Lt. Vrooman."[33] On July 11, 1759, Vroman was assigned night duty to guard the trenches, along with Captain Visher. The Battle of Niagara was a major defeat for the French and they were forced to surrender. Lieutenant Peter Vroman's *Account Book* (Figs. 6-7) includes his description, in Dutch, of his daily military activities from leaving Oswego through the end of the Battle of Niagara.

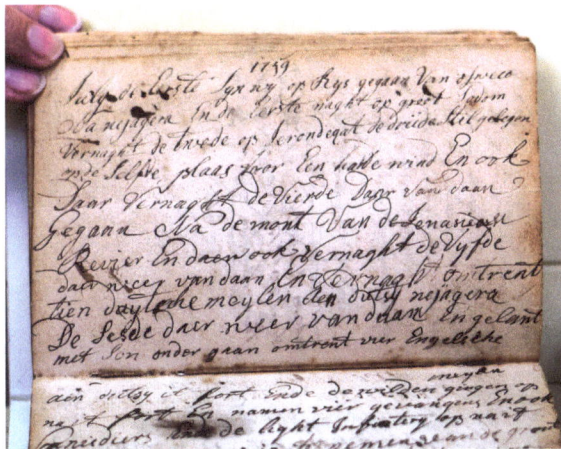

Fig. 6. Original Dutch pages of Peter Vroman's "Account Book" on the Battle of Niagara.

Fig. 7. Leather cover of Peter Vroman's "Account Book" with original buckle closure. Courtesy of the New York State Library, Manuscripts and Special Collections.

Following is a translation[34] of Peter Vroman's account of the Battle of Niagara. Explanations or definitions are shown in *<brackets>*. Vroman was among the over 3,500 men Brigadier General John Prideaux and Sir William Johnson (the British Indian agent who commanded Iroquois and Colonial militia forces) led from Fort Oswego to battle at Fort Niagara.

July 1.   The first of July we started the journey from Osveld <*Oswego*> to Niagara and the first night we stayed on/at big Sadem <*Sodus Bay*>

July 2.   The second on Sevendegat <*Irondequoit Bay*>

July 3.   The third remained on the same spot because of a half wind and also stayed the night there.

July 4.   The fourth gone from there to the mouth of the river Senasiase <*Genesee*> also stayed the night.

July 5.   The fifth gone from there and stayed the night about ten Dutch (or German) miles at/or south of Niagara.

July 6.   The six from there and landed at sun set circa four English miles at the south side of the fort. And the savages went up to the fort and (we) made four prisoners. And also the Grenadiers and the light infantry (went) to the fort to observe the ground/field.

July 7.   The seventh we brought the Cur-pieces <*artillery*> on the ground/land.

July 8.   The eighth we all went well

July 9.   The ninth we made Cabions <*gabions=cage or box of rocks*> and fasenen <*bundle of rods bound together and used for fill or to strengthen trenches*> and we started also to actrensen <*dig trenches*>.

July 10. The tenth the same.

July 11. And the eleventh we started to throw bombs.

July 12. The 12th the shooting went on from both sides.

July 13. And the 13th the same.

July 14. The 14th the same.

July 15. The 15th the same.

July 16. The 16th the same.

July 17. The 17th in the morning our Curstucken <*artillery*> started to shoot at/to the fort.

July 18. The 18th the same.

July 19. The 19th the same.

July 20. The 20th the same. And also at the end of the afternoon between 4 and 5 hour our Lieutenant Colonel Thody[36] was hurt <shot in the leg> and half an hour after seven our Colonel in chief[37] <Col. John Johnson> was shot dead and around nine o'clock general Frida[38] <Brigadier General John Prideaux> was shot dead by our own bombs <he was killed when a shell fragment from one of his own guns hit him>.

July 21. The 21th, 22nd, 23rd, 24th a group French and savages of 13 hundred men came again ? from Ohio[39] <Ohio Valley, also known as western Pennsylvania> but we defeated them all and made a lot of them prisoner and also shot a lot of them dead and the same day the French abandoned the fort.

July 22. <Battle>

July 23. <Battle>

July 24. <Battle>

July 25. And the 25th we went in the fort. <Captain Pouchot[40] surrendered Fort Niagara>

In 1761, Volckert Petrus Douw[41] sent a letter (*Fig. 8)* written in Dutch and addressed to Lieutenant Peter Vrooman enquiring whether Vroman intended to continue in military service. Grider copied the letter and provided the following translation: "Inquiring whether he intended entering the service again this year – let us know by the 6th what you intend to do. I send greetings & remain your obedient Volkert P. Douw." It is interesting to note that even within this one document, the surname is spelled both Vroman and Vrooman.

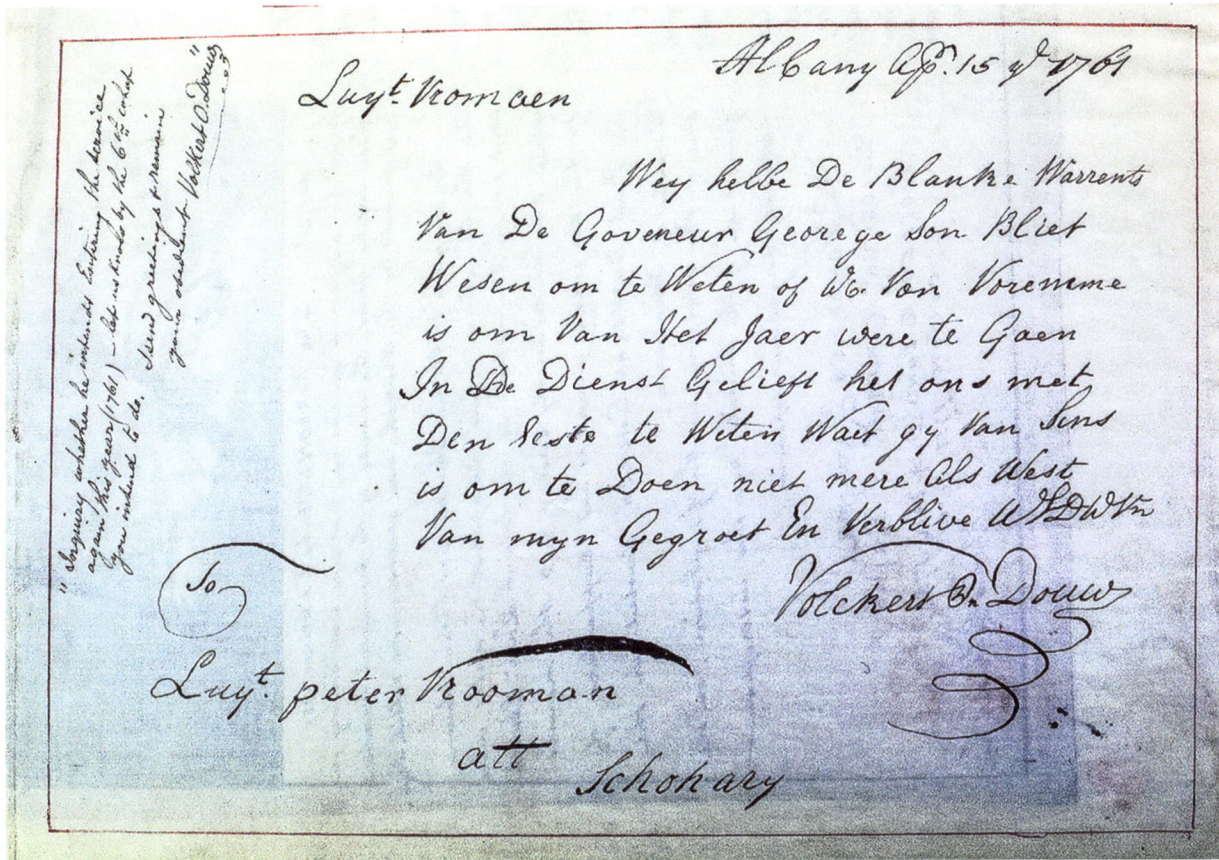

Fig. 8. *Letter from Volkert Petrus Douw to Peter Vroman, 1761. Copied in 1888 by Rufus Alexander Grider. Grider's Albums. Courtesy of the New York State Library, Manuscripts and Special Collections.*

Peter B. Vroman — Pre-Revolution

Peter B. Vroman married Engeltie Swart (his first cousin), the daughter of Josias Swart and Jannetie Vrooman, on May 15, 1761 in Schenectady, New York. They had four children: Jannetie (Oct. 31, 1764-Nov. 13, 1764), Angelica [a.k.a. Angeletie, Anna] (May 22, 1766-Aug. 14, 1839), Josias (Aug. 19, 1769-?), and Barent (Aug. 9, 1775-?). Angelica was the only child to live to adulthood. It is unknown when Peter's wife Jannetie died or where she is buried.

The years after the French and Indian War were fairly calm and prosperous years in Schoharie. The people were independent and able to raise sufficient animals and crops to satisfy most of their needs. Peter Vroman farmed, owned land, and served as a merchant. He sold and shipped wheat, corn and 'pease' (e.g. peas). He also sold cloth, paper, and tea to local settlers as well as to customers in the cities. He drew wills, bonds, mortgages and deeds and continued to do so throughout his life. He occasionally went to Albany and

Schenectady to do business so probably was well versed on the various British Acts that were opposed by many colonists. Vroman was an educated man; he spoke and wrote Dutch, English and probably German. He was a respected member of the community and often called upon for service.

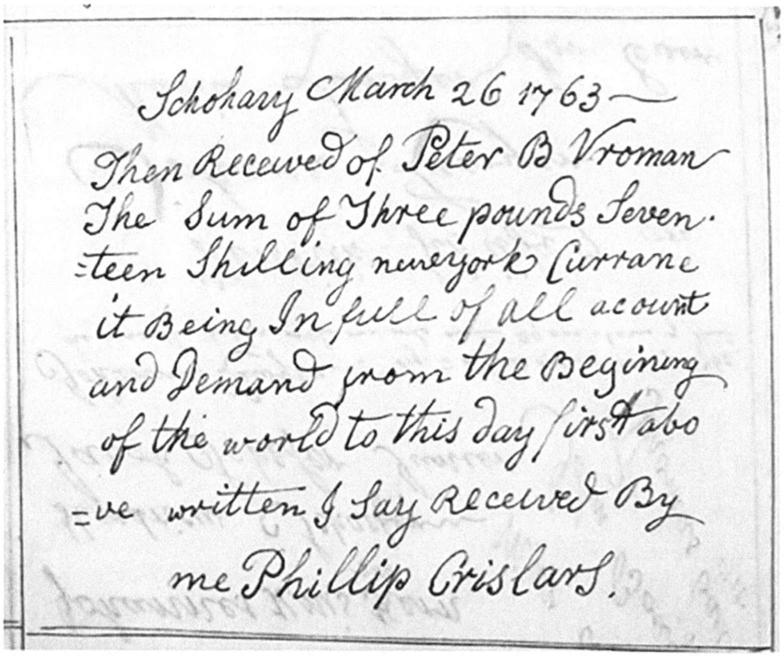

Schohary March 26 1763 —
Then Received of Peter B Vroman
The Sum of Three pounds Seven=
=teen Shilling newyork Currane
it Being In full of all acount
and Demand from the Begining
of the world to this day first abo
=ve written I Say Received By
me Phillip Crislars.

Fig. 9 Account note between Philip Crysler and Peter Vroman, 1763. Copied by Rufus Alexander Grider. Grider's Albums. Courtesy of the New York State Library, Manuscripts and Special Collections.

Peter Vroman's *Account Memorandum Book, 1759-1792*, is housed in the New York State Library. There are also a few other existing documents on Vroman's financial activities. Grider hand-copied a document showing that Vroman paid '3 pounds 17 shillings New York' to Phillip Crislars (Crysler) in 1763 to settle his accounts "from the Beginning of the world to this day."*(Fig. 9)* Crysler joined the British during the Revolutionary War and Simms attributes some major Schoharie attacks to Crysler and his brothers. After the War, Crysler immigrated to Canada.

Sir William Johnson probably thought highly of Peter Vroman's service with him during the French and Indian War. In 1769, Johnson wrote: "The Regiments in the forming of which I had a particular hand were those this way, of these the Schohare Regt wants still a Major occasioned by Sr Harrys death, for this majority I recommended & take the Liberty to recommend to you Peter B. Vroman."[42] Vroman was promoted to Major in 1770, at the time, he was known as Peter B. Vroman likely to distinguish himself from relatives similarly named. The middle initial "B" might also have been intended to identify himself as the son of Barent. Later Peter dropped the middle initial "B" possibly to make it more challenging for the British to recognize him during the Revolution since he had used the name 'Peter B. Vroman' while serving in the British Army and might have been charged with desertion if captured by the British.

Peter Vroman was purported to have extensive land holdings. According to a typescript copy of a 1770 indenture *(Fig. 10)*, Vroman "had long been high in the confidence of Sir William Johnson who had appointed [him] captain and served [with him] during the French Wars; highly recommended by Sir William to Governor [Cadwallader] Colden to be promoted as major…"[43] Another token of Johnson's esteem is the 300 acres he conveyed to Peter B. Vroman. The land was formerly part of a tract of land containing 18,000 acres granted to Michael Byrne and adjoined the Adam Vroman land on the north. The land was conveyed to Sir William Johnson by letter patent from His Majesty King George III. In this land transfer, Vroman conveyed 100 acres of his 300 acres to Cornelius Vroman for 50 pounds. This is an example of part of Peter Vroman's estate prior to the Revolution. The Cornelius Vroman named in the land transaction was likely related.

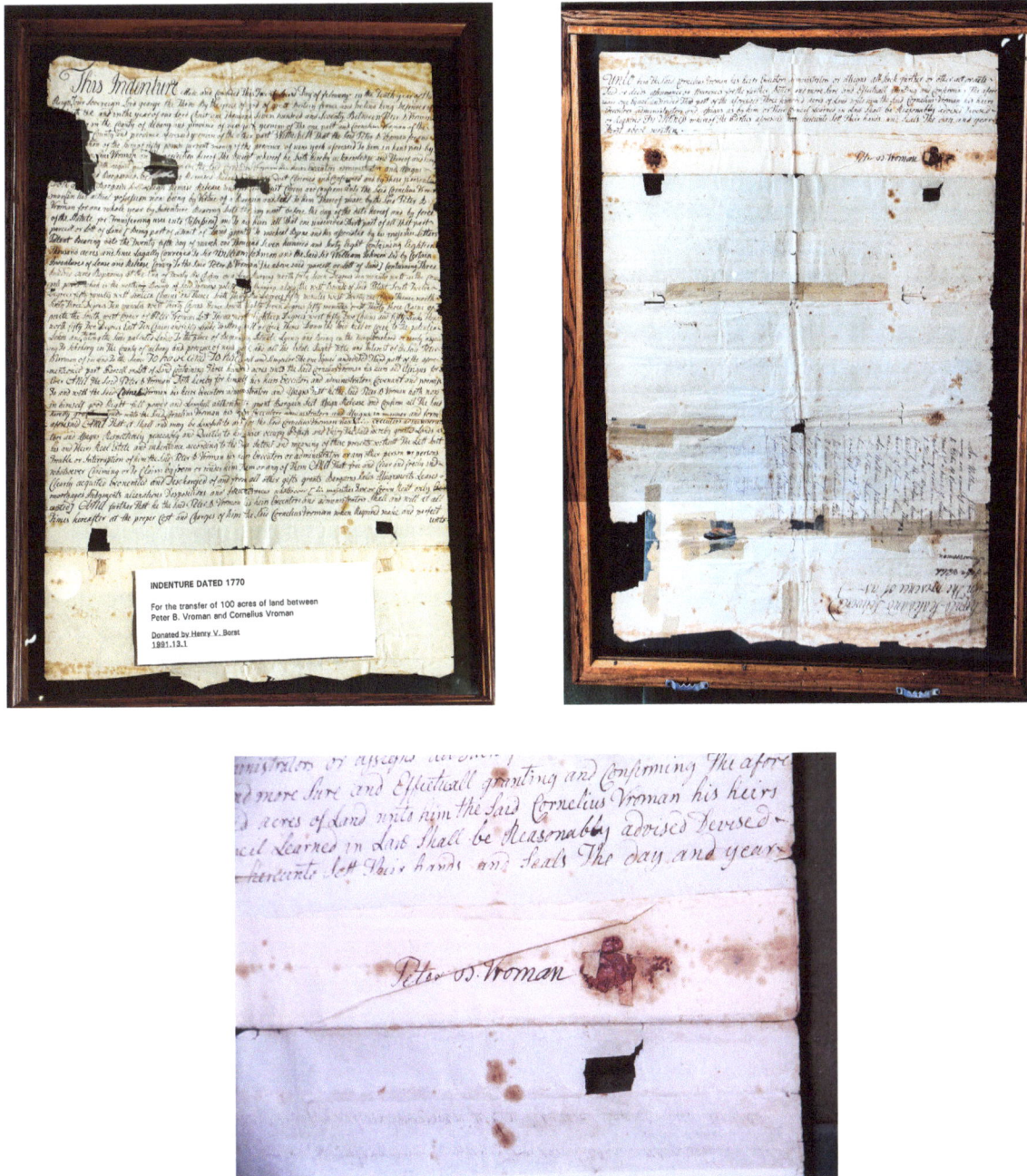

Fig. 10. *Indenture Peter B. Vroman and Cornelius Vroman, 1770. This original indenture is located in the Old Stone Fort. Appendix B includes a transcript of the indenture.*

Colonel Peter Vroman — Revolutionary War Years

Peter Vroman played an important role for his community during the American Revolution. Committees of Correspondence were formed to send and receive news of common concerns among the colonies. This extra-legal group began the transition from colonial to state government. In Albany the committee was known as the Committee of Safety and Correspondence. In 1774, a Committee of Safety was chosen for the Schoharie District of Albany County. Committees of Safety at first were charged with keeping watch on the distrusted royal government. By 1775, the Committee of Safety became the operating provisional local government. Peter Vroman was one of six members of the Schoharie Committee of Safety. He was elected their 'penman' or secretary and was credited with writing their proceedings. The Committee supposedly met in secret, sometimes at Peter Vroman's house, sometimes at a house north of the Lower Fort, and sometimes supposedly in a cave across the river from the Middle Fort. The Committee was primarily concerned with military issues but it also tried to regulate such things as tavern owners' sale of whiskey to Indians. And the Committee sought to detect and examine people thought to be Loyalists, occasionally jailing them as enemies of the state.

In some communities, the Committee of Safety was viewed with great fear and trepidation. There is no indication this was so in Schoharie but there is at least one report of a disgruntled Schoharie Loyalist. After the war, Alexander Campbell made a claim to the British Parliament due to the 'late unhappy dissentions in America' (e.g. The American Revolution) for actions on "June 3, 1775, for losses sustained by Peter Vrooman, Esq.[44], Johannes Ball, Thomas Eckerson, Peter W. Ziele, and Daniel Budd, Committee men, and one hundred and four others, assembled in a mob when he [Alexander Campbell] was obligated to leave the District of Schoharie with his Family and Effects [and to go] to Schenectady with an order never to return. Losses were £37 N. York Currency."[45] Campbell made several other claims for loss of land and property. The British Parliament rejected some of his claims.

Members of the Schoharie Committee of Safety took the following oath:

> You shall swear by the holy evangelist of the Almighty God to be a true subject to our continental resolve and Provincial Congress and committees in this difficulty existing between Great Britain and America and to answer upon such questions as you shall be examined in, so help you, God."
> —Schoharie Committee Chamber, July 17, 1777[46]

The New York Historical Society reports receiving a "Revolutionary broadside printed in New York by John Holt containing 'Instructions for the inlisting of Men,' issued by the Provincial Congress at New York, June 1775 and signed by Peter Van Brugh Livingston, President of the Provincial Congress. It is addressed to Peter B. Vroman, offering him a captaincy if he can enlist seventy two 'able bodied sober Men, of good Reputations.' The back of the broadside indicates that Vroman declined and suggested Barent Ten Eyck."[47] Ten Eyck accepted the commission and either resigned or was discharged in 1778.[48]

The Committee of Safety passed a resolution in October 1775 that "Peter Vrooman be authorised to receive from Leondard Gansevoort Treasurer to this Board [Committee of Correspondence] the Money due on the Account heretofore allowed and ordered to be paid to Doc[r] Budd, for and on behalf of the said M[r] Budd, and that he the said Vrooman furnish this Board with a Receipt from him for the said Sum within one fortnight."[49] Dr. Daniel Budd was a member of the Schoharie Committee of Safety. Perhaps this was a repayment to Dr. Budd for money (£6.13.6) he paid to the Oneida and Mohawk Indians per an order of the Schoharie Subcommittee[50] of the Committee of Safety.

On October 20, 1775, the Provincial Congress of New York appointed long-time resident and "well-established gentleman farmer," Peter Vroman as Colonel of the 15th Regiment of the Albany County Militia. Lieutenant Colonel Peter U. Ziele was appointed his assistant commander and both Thomas Eckerson, Jr. and Joseph Becker were appointed majors. Vroman commanded three companies formed in the Schoharie District: the Upper Fort, the Middle Fort and the Lower Fort. So it appears that Vroman turned down a position as Captain in June 1775, as noted previously, and then accepted the position of Colonel just a few months later. It is unknown if he considered Captain too low of a rank or if he wanted to stay close to home or if he perhaps just changed his mind.

Colonel Vroman and his troops were active in Schoharie as well as in other regions. In October 1776, the Committee of Correspondence ordered Col. Vroman to send 50 men to the Coxackie District, along with Coxackie District Captain Bratts' Rangers, to apprehend and take suspected "enemies of this state" into "safe custody" until further orders were received.[51] The Committee also ordered a payment of £68.14.6 to Col. Vroman's Regiment for the "late alarm in Tryon County."[52]

In 1777, the Committee expressed concerns about actions taking place in the Helderbergs. "In order to prevent practices so detrimental to the safety of the State and to support in those parts the Friends to the Country in the enjoyment of their liberty and property"[53] the Committee ordered Vroman to draft 50 men from Schoharie and to immediately march to the house of Captain Jacob Van Aernam to be joined by 100 other militia. Van Aernam was a Captain in the 3rd Albany Regiment under Col. Philip B. Schuyler and served as the leader of patriot forces in the Helderberg region. While the Helderberg area did not have any major battles against the British, the area did have internal threats and Van Aernam's major charge was to root our Tories.

Colonel Vroman appeared before the Albany Committee of Safety in July 1777 to report the defenseless condition of Schoharie and request more aid. His plea was relayed to Major General Schuyler who sent John Ten Broeck, Henry Bleecker, and John Tillman to Schoharie to confer with people of the district and "endeavor to revive their Spirits and arouse them for their State of Supineness, as nothing can more effectually tend to save their Country from Rapine and devastation as a Vigorous exertion of their own Strength."[54] The Committee's investigation perhaps suggested that more than encouraging words were needed because three Schoharie forts were created to increase Schoharie defenses by fall 1777. The Upper Fort at Fultonham was the most impregnable. The Fort at Middleburgh, called the Middle Fort, enclosed the stone house of Johannes Becker (Colonel Peter Vroman's brother-in-law) and was considered the Headquarters because the officer in charge of the military had his residence there. Before it took the name of Middle Fort in 1778, it was known as Fort Defiance. And the Stone Dutch Church at Schoharie was palisaded and became known as the Lower Fort.

Col. Vroman was paid for helping support the Garrison of Fort Defyance (Defiance) in 1777. Existing records indicate, for example, he was paid 1£ 16 shillings for 12 skip (about ¾ of a bushel) of oats at 3/ for the Light Horse.[55] So it is likely Vroman's farmland helped feed the mobile cavalry troop.

Col. Vroman's reports on the deteriorating condition of the 'Western Frontier' were sent to Militia Brigadier General Abraham Ten Broeck and forwarded to George Clinton, eventually to be transmitted to George Washington. On July 17, 1778 Vroman wrote asking for reinforcement "without Delay" in light of information gathered from an Indian "spy of the Enemy … that the Enemy are on their Way coming up the west branch of Delaware River to this place [Schohaire]" and "that they had made a wide Road … to bring field Pieces … their number is great."[56]

On July 24, 1778 Vroman wrote:

> Capt. Harper a Gentleman of varicity gives me Intelligence that the Enemy are at Unidilla, very Strong [150] amounting to nigh Three Thousand, and by one of my Scouts which arrived this afternoon brings Intelligence, that they saw four Indians within fourteen miles of this place, going from this which they supposed to be a Scout, and I believe it is very Likely, the Scout also Informs me that they staid last night in sight of one Services, a great Enemy to the Country upon the Susquahanna where they heard frequent Yellings of the savages.[57]

During the Revolution, an attempt was made to take Colonel Vroman prisoner and a reward was offered for his capture. "A meeting of the council of safety was to take place at his home and supposing he would remain home, several of the enemy secreted themselves, intending to secure his person when the rest of the committee retired. But it became necessary for him to leave home with his guests and the intention of the foe was thwarted."[58]

On August 9, 1780, some Tories and Indians raided Vroman's Land and destroyed Colonel Peter Vroman's home (described by Simms as a "good brick tenement"). They burned his house and buildings, all of his animals were slaughtered, and 600 skipples of grain, along with hay, flex, and hemp, were burned. The Colonel's favorite dog was reportedly shot, ripped open with a knife, and thrown into a well next to Vroman's burning home. Fortuitously, Colonel Vroman's family was in Middle Fort at the time.

Johannes Becker's 'mansion' and three acres of his land were barricaded and served as the Middle Fort, the Headquarters for the Schoharie Militia. On October 17, 1780, Loyalist Sir John Johnson and Mohawk Chief Joseph Brant conducted a raid on the Middle Fort. The officer in charge, Major Woolsey, wanted to call a truce whereupon Colonel Vroman assumed command. With supplies running low, Colonel Vroman carefully distributed the meager gunpowder supplies so the soldiers at the Fort wouldn't know the extent of the shortage. "Needing an additional supply, Angelica Vrooman [Col. Peter Vroman's daughter], as she informed the author [Simms], took [Timothy] Murphy's bullet mould, lead, and an iron spoon, went to her father's tent, and there moulded a quantity of bullets for that fearless ranger [Murphy], amidst the roar of cannon and musketry.[59] The Colonel's daughter, Angelica Vrooman, was reported to have said about her father, "more than once when he went for powder … did his hair rise on his head, not from fear of the enemy, but lest the small supply of ammunition should be completely exhausted, and the foe, becoming conscious of it, storm their works."[60] Roscoe in his history of Schoharie called Col. Peter Vroman "the hero of the middle fort."[61]

Colonel Peter Vroman — After the Revolution

Some time after his home was burned and sacked in the 1780 raid, Vroman purchased the Eckerson property and mill on Fox Creek as his new homestead. According to an article by Louise Vrooman, her grandfather (Samuel B. Stevens) had old Eckerson deeds, which were placed in the Old Stone Fort Museum. Those deeds indicate that the purchase gave Col. Vroman water rights as well as rights to own and operate a mill.[62] The land transfer might have occurred in 1785.

The Eckerson sawmill was likely a very profitable endeavor for Col. Vroman because so many homes, barns, and other structures had to be repaired or built anew from the damage or destruction of the Revolutionary War. "It is said that 134 buildings were burned in Schoharie during the war … The citizens were living in good frame houses and had large barns well filled with grain. Schoharie had not only supplied her own citizens and soldiers, but also had furnished large quantities of grain for the troops at other stations. Such was the destruction that the most rigid economy would scarcely enable them to subsist on what remained, until the next year's harvest."[63] The gristmill continued to be essential for all the grain farming in the area. It is interesting to note that Col. Peter Vroman's great-great grandfather was also a mill owner.

Fox's Dorf was a popular community after the Revolution and many notable individuals, besides Col. Vroman, lived there. Dr. Daniel Budd (1750-1815), a Princeton and University of Edinburg graduate, was on the staff of Col. Goose Van Schaick, 1st Regiment. He served with George Washington and was with Washington at Valley Forge. He was taken prisoner by the British in 1779 and then exchanged, serving until the end of the War. It was previously noted that Col. Vroman had dealings with Dr. Budd, who was also a member of the Schoharie Committee of Safety. Dr. Budd was married to Rebecca Lawyer (1752-1824), the daughter of Johannes Lawyer, Jr. (the owner of substantial lands in Schoharie) and Cathrina Sternberg of Schoharie. Rufus Grider wrote that Rebecca was a beautiful woman. The couple "went to Albany in a carriage with outrider after marriage & thence to NY by vessel, which took two to three weeks. They lived several years in New Jersey and then resided opposite the Lower Fort, he was a leading Whig & a Patriot."[64] Budd is listed in the Town of Schoharie in the 1790 United State Federal Census along with one male under 16 and two free white females.

George Tiffany, an ancestor of the well-known Tiffany family and an attorney from New York City, also lived in the area and had an office in the George Mann Tavern building. Capt. Jacob Snyder, Johannes Ball, and Col. William Dietz were others living in Fox's Dorf, which was considered the 'Fifth Avenue' of Schoharie. Roscoe claims that "the busiest part of the town was at Fox's dorf, and at this place the aristocratic portion of the town settled."[65]

Simms shared the following story Angelica Vroman told about her father, Col. Vroman. The Colonel was attending a party in Poughkeepsie during a session of the State Legislature. He spotted Major Woolsey across the room. This is the same Major Woolsey who was ready to surrender during the 1780 Johnson/Brant attack on the Middle Fort. Col. Vroman did not plan to surrender and consequently relieved Woolsey from command. At the party, Vroman thought he would be sociable and went to talk to Woolsey, only to find that Woolsey had already made a hasty exit from the house. Woolsey likely wished to avoid any type of encounter with Col. Vroman.[66]

Colonel Peter Vroman — Church

There are numerous indications that Col. Vroman was a dedicated member of his community and his church. The Reformed Church at Schoharie was organized as a High Dutch Church but it soon came under the control of the Low Dutch. The Low Dutch included the Vromans, the Eckersons, the Zielies, and the Beckers. The Low Dutch Reformed Church was burned and destroyed in the Oct. 17, 1780 raid by Johnson and Brant. After that date, services were performed at the Middle Fort until peace was proclaimed and the inhabitants could rebuild.

In 1784, Vroman petitioned the New York Legislature *(Fig. 11)* on behalf of the Low Dutch Reformed Church of Schoharie.[67] Damage to the Church was estimated to be 500 pounds. Vroman writes, "we are distress to the utmost degree and not able to build for themselves instead of a Church altho it should ben the first thing done to worship the almighty."[68] The letter demonstrates Vroman to be a defender of the people of Schoharie and a pious man devoted to his Church.

Rufus Alexander Grider also copied a letter *(Fig. 12)* found among the effects of Col. Peter Vroman. Grider declares that the undated letter is in Vroman's handwriting. The letter is a forceful lament on the condition of Schoharie following the Revolution but made even more perilous by a major flood that caused extensive damage as well as the death of people and livestock. Vroman pleas for help from the State, specifically asking them to come view the damage and requesting a tax exemption for the people of Schoharie. This letter is an example of Vroman's dedication to and empathy with the community around him. The letter was written on the back of a 1760 deed but its contents indicate it was written after the Revolutionary War. Grider copied the original letter that was in the possession of Chaplin R. R. Hoes (Roswell Randall Hoes, 1850-1921) of the U. S. Navy.

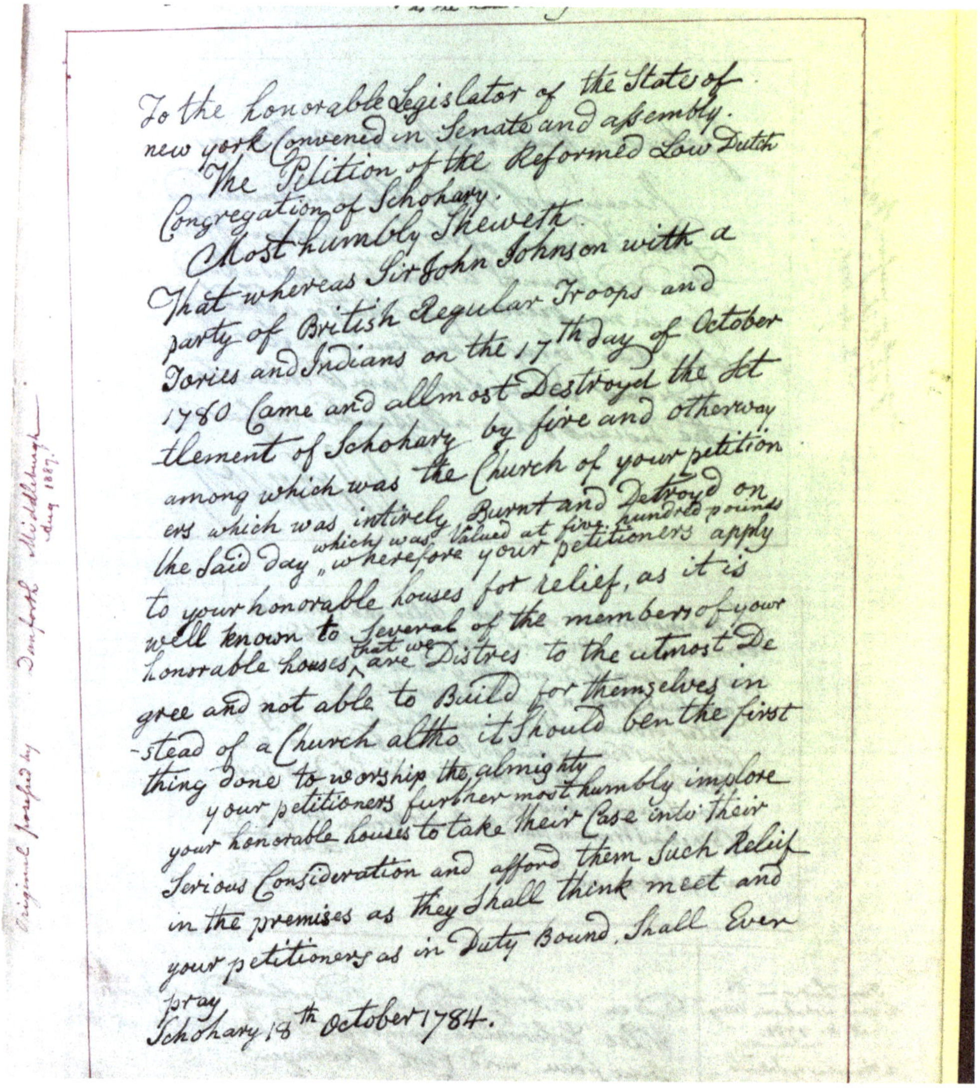
To the honorable Legislator of the State of
new york Convened in Senate and assembly.
The Petition of the Reformed Low Dutch
Congregation of Schohary.
Most humbly Sheweth
That whereas Sir John Johnson with a
party of British Regular Troops and
Tories and Indians on the 17th day of October
1780 Came and allmost Destroyed the Set
tlement of Schohary by fire and otherway
among which was the Church of your petition
ers which was intirely Burnt and Destroyed on
the Said day, which was Valued at five hundred pounds wherefore your petitioners apply
to your honorable houses for relief, as it is
well known to Several of the members of your
honorable houses that we are Distres to the utmost De
gree and not able to Build for themselves in
-stead of a Church altho it Should ben the first
thing done to worship the almighty
your petitioners further most humbly implore
your honorable houses to take their Case into their
Serious Consideration and afford them Such Relief
in the premises as they Shall think meet and
your petitioners as in Duty Bound Shall Ever
pray
Schohary 18th October 1784.

Original possessed by Danforth Middleburgh Aug 1887.

Fig. 11. Vroman's petition to the New York State Legislature on behalf of the Low Dutch Reformed Church, 1784. Copied by Rufus Alexander Grider. Grider's Albums. Courtesy of the New York State Library, Manuscripts and Special Collections.

In 1785, Peter Vroman was listed as an elder of the Schoharie Low Dutch Reformed Congregation. In the same year he wrote a letter *(Fig. 13)* soliciting funds from others to help rebuild the Church that had been destroyed during the American Revolution.

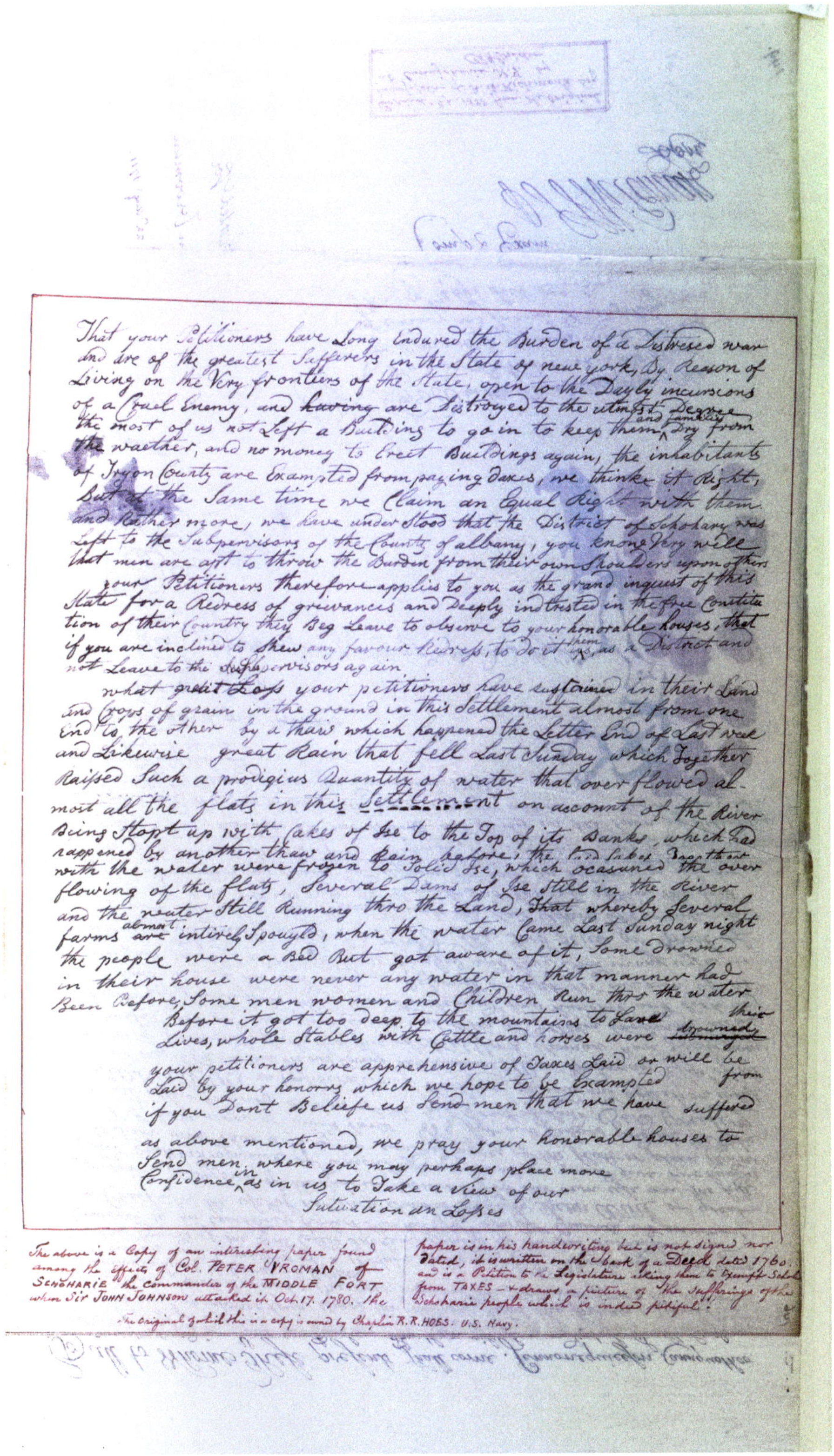

That your Petitioners have Long Endured the Burden of a Distresed war and are of the greatest Sufferers in the State of new york, by Reason of Living on the Very frontiers of the State, open to the Dayly incursions of a Cruel Enemy, and having are Distroyed to the utmost Degree the most of us not Left a Building to go in to keep them and familie Dry from the waether, and no money to Erect Buildings again, the inhabitants of Tryon County are Exampted from paying Taxes, we think it Right, But at the Same time we Claim an Equal Right with them and Rather more, we have under Stood that the District of Schohary was Left to the Subpervisors of the County of albany, you know Very well that men are apt to throw the Burden from their own Shoulders upon others

your Petitioners therefore applies to you as the grand inquest of this State for a Redress of grievances and Deeply indtrested in the free Constitution of their Country they Beg Leave to observe to your honorable houses, that if you are inclined to Shew any favour Redress, to do it them as a District and not Leave to the Subpervisors again

what great Loss your petitioners have sustained in their Land and Crops of grain in the ground in this Settlement almost from one End to the other by a thaw which happened the Letter End of Last week and Likewise great Rain that fell Last Sunday which Together Raised Such a prodigius Quantity of water that over flowed almost all the flats in this Settlement on account of the River Being Stopt up with Cakes of Ise to the Top of its Banks, which had happened by another thaw and Rain before, the [illegible] together with the water were frozen to Solid Ise, which ocasuned the over flowing of the flats, Several Dams of Ise Still in the River and the water Still Running thro the Land, That whereby Several farms almost intirely Spoygld, when the water Came Last Sunday night the people were a Bed But got aware of it, Some drowned in their house were never any water in that manner had Been Before, Some men women and Children Run thro the water Before it got too deep to the mountains to Save their Lives, whole Stables with Cattle and horses were drowned

your petitioners are apprehensive of Taxes Laid or will be Laid by your honorrs which we hope to be Exampted from if you Dont Beliefe us Send men that we have suffered as above mentioned, we pray your honorable houses to Send men where you may perhaps place more Confidence in as in us to Take a view of our Situation an Losses

The above is a Copy of an interesting paper found among the effects of Col. PETER VROMAN of SCHOHARIE the commander of the MIDDLE FORT when Sir JOHN JOHNSON attacked it Oct. 17. 1780. The paper is in his handwriting but is not signed nor dated, it is written on the back of a Deed dated 1760. and is a Petition to the Legislature asking them to Exempt Schoharie from TAXES — & draws a picture of the Sufferings of the Schoharie people which is indeed pitiful!

The original of which this is a copy is owned by Chaplin R. R. HOBS. U.S. Navy.

Fig. 12. Letter written by Peter Vroman requesting a tax exemption for the people of Schoharie. [n.d.] Copied 1888 by Rufus Alexander Grider. Grider's Albums. Courtesy of the New York State Library, Manuscripts and Special Collections. Transcription of letter (Appendix C).

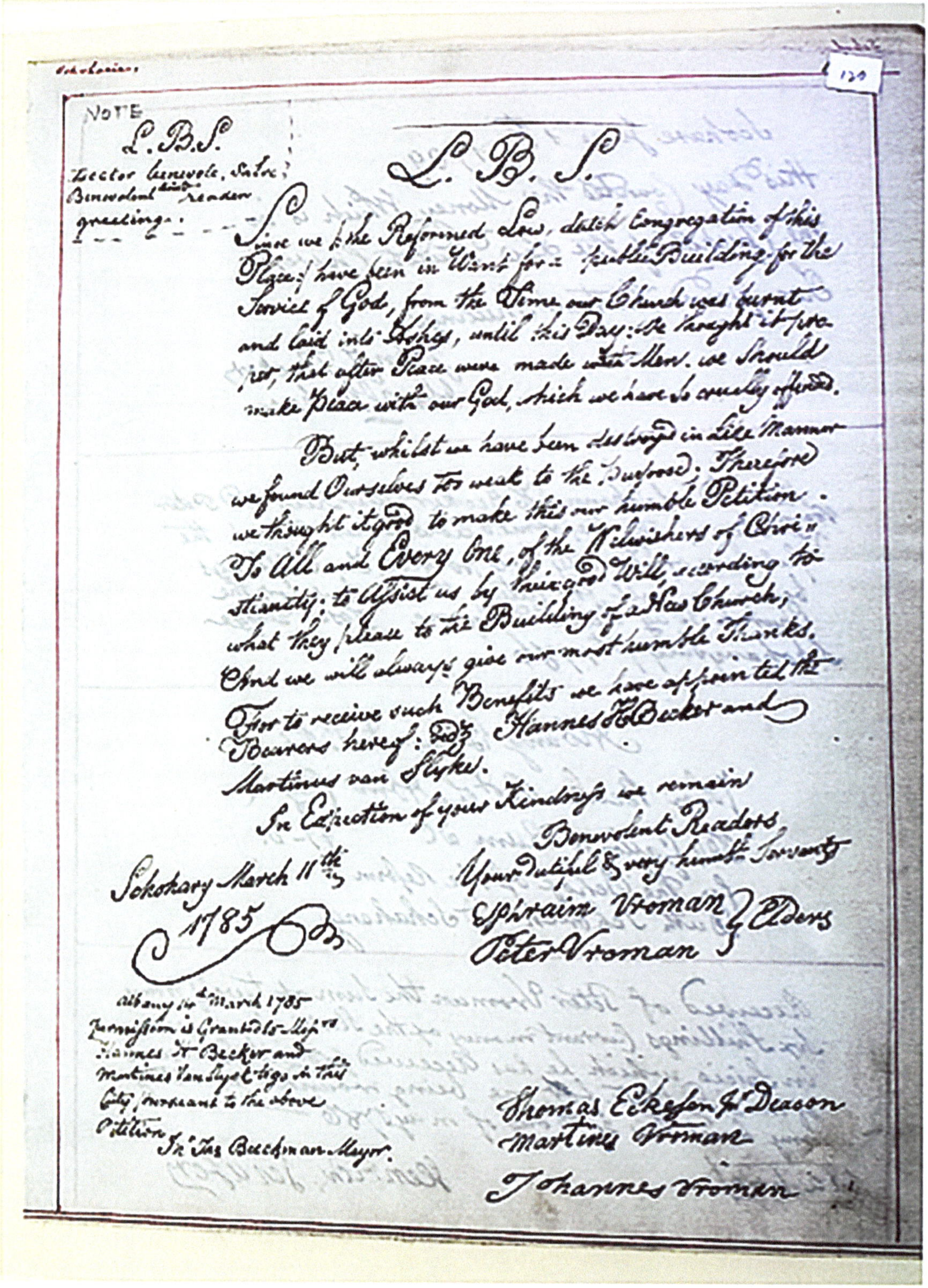

Schoharie

NOTE
L.B.S.
Lector benevole, Salve;
Benevolent kind reader
greeting.

L. B. S.

Since we, the Reformed Low dutch Congregation of this Place, have been in Want for a publick Building for the Service of God, from the Time our Church was burnt and laid into Ashes, until this Day: We thought it proper, that after Peace were made with Men, we Should make Peace with our God, which we have so cruelly offended.

But, whilst we have been destroyed in like Manner we found Ourselves too weak to the purpose. Therefore we thought it good to make this our humble Petition. To All and Every One, of the Welwishers of Christianity: to Assist us by their good Will, according to what they please to the Building of a New Church, And we will always give our most humble Thanks. For to receive such Benefits we have appointed the Bearers hereof: viz. Hannes H. Becker and Martinus van Slyke.

In Expectation of your Kindness we remain
Benevolent Readers
Your dutiful & very humble Servants

Schohary March 11th 1785

Ephraim Vroman } Elders
Peter Vroman

Albany 14th March 1785
Permission is Granted to Messrs Hannes H. Becker and Martinus Van Slyck to go in this City, pursuant to the above Petition.
Jn. Jas Beekman Mayor.

Thomas Eckerson Jr. Deacon
Martinus Vroman
Johannes Vroman

Fig. 13. Petition to raise funds for the Low Dutch Reformed Church, Peter Vroman, elder, 1785. Copied by Rufus Alexander Grider. Grider's Albums, Courtesy of the New York State Library, Manuscripts and Special Collections. Transcription of letter (Appendix D).

Roscoe writes that Col. Vroman was the treasurer for the Low Dutch Reformed Church when it was rebuilding after being burned in 1780. He was responsible for paying for the necessary project materials and expenses. He approved bills for rum for the workers but he refused to allow reimbursement for '18 drinks.' Rum was the most popular liquor in colonial America. Water was believed unhealthy so rum and other alcohol were safer choices. Rum was also inexpensive to make and the ingredients were readily available. Colonial Williamsburg historians estimate that American men drank an average of three pints (six cups) of rum every week. It is unknown if those 'drinks' were cider, beer, or maybe distilled spirits.

In 1786, Vroman was serving as a Trustee of the Low Dutch Reformed Church in Schoharie. Peter Vroman, Johannes H. Becker and Peter Ziely, were paid 22 pounds, ten shillings by Josiah Dodge to cut timber for the Church *(Fig. 14)*. It took almost three years to rebuild the Church and it was finally completed during the summer of 1787. Roscoe writes that work on the Church was "performed by the people of the vicinity, under Philip Schuyler, carpenter and joiner. Tradition tells us the iron figures '1786,' placed upon the front of the belfry, were the work of one Lutwig Schneider, a blacksmith, who also made the 'stays' placed in the brick walls."[69] Perhaps Vroman cut the lumber for his house from the same woods used for the Church. And perhaps he even used the same carpenter and blacksmith to build the house. Those are intriguing possibilities but unknowns at this time.

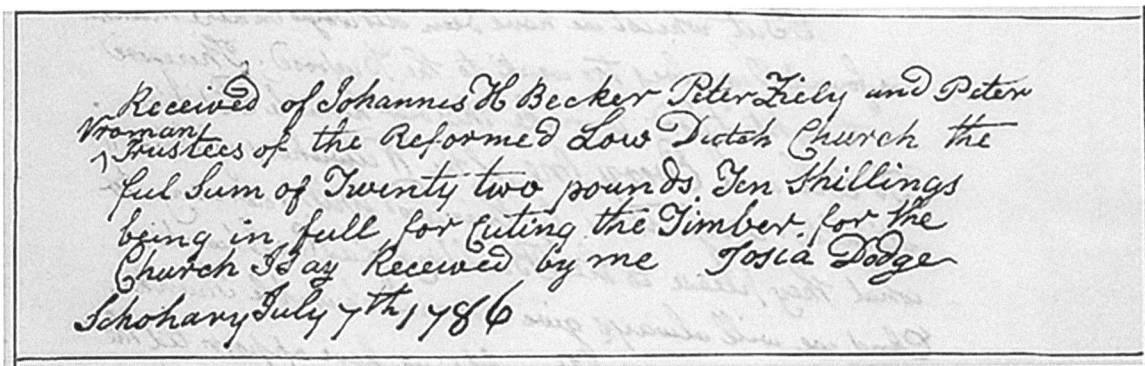

Fig. 14. Receipt to Peter Vroman and others for cutting timber for the Low Dutch Reformed Church in Schoharie, 1786. Copied by Rufus Alexander Grider. Grider's Albums. Courtesy of the New York State Library, Manuscripts and Special Collections.

Colonel Peter Vroman — Native Americans

There are a few existent documents giving information on Colonel Vroman's dealings with Native Americans. A 1770 memorandum *(Fig. 15)* details Peter and Cornelius Vroman's deliveries to and dealings with Indians. The document lists several deliveries totaling nine quarts of rum for 180 pounds. But then in 1775 Vroman expressed concern about tavern-keepers who sold liquor too freely to the Indians 'from which evil consequences often happen.' This actually led the Committee of Safety to adopt a resolution recommending that tavern-keepers in Albany County sell spirits to the Indians as sparingly as possible to prevent drunkenness.[70]

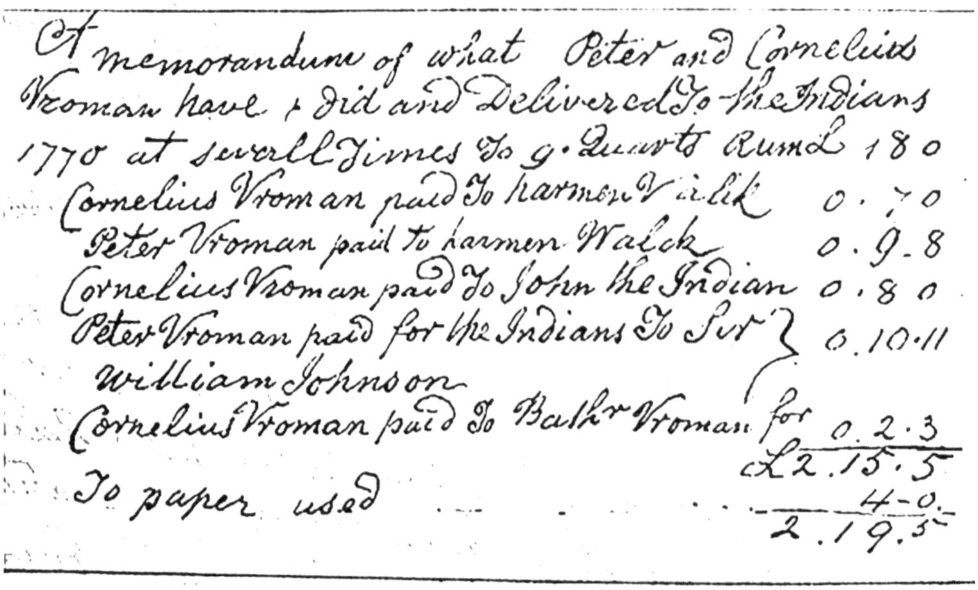

A memorandum of what Peter and Cornelius
Vroman have + did and Delivered To the Indians
1770 at severll Times To 9 Quarts Rum £ 1 8 0
Cornelius Vroman paid To harmen Valik 0 . 7 0
Peter Vroman paid to harmen Walck 0 . 9 . 8
Cornelius Vroman paid To John the Indian 0 . 8 0
Peter Vroman paid for the Indians To Sir 0 . 10 . 11
William Johnson
Cornelius Vroman paid To Bathr Vroman for 0 . 2 . 3
£2 . 15 . 5
To paper used 4 - 0
2 . 19 . 5

Fig. 15. Memorandum of Indian accounts of Peter Vroman and Cornelius Vroman, 1770. Copied by Rufus Alexander Grider. Grider's Albums, Courtesy of the New York State Library, Manuscripts and Special Collections.

Transcription of document *(Fig. 15):*

A memorandum of what Peter and Cornelius
Vroman have paid and Delivered To the Indians

1770 at several Times To 9 quarts Rum	£ 180
Cornelius Vroman paid To Harmen Valik	0.70
Peter Vroman paid to Harmen Walck	0.98
Cornelius Vroman paid To John the Indian	0.80
Peter Vroman paid for the Indians to Per William Johnson	0.10.11
Cornelius Vroman paid to Barh^{lr} Vroman for	<u>0.2.3</u>
	£ 2.15.5
To paper used	<u>4.0</u>
	2.19.5

In 1771, Sir William Johnson of Johnson Hall received 400 pounds from Bartholomew and Peter Vroman for a tract of "low land bought by them of the Schohare Indians which sum I (William Johnson) to deliver to the Indians when assembled in Council." *(Fig. 16).* The documents suggest that Vroman had regular dealings with Native Americans.

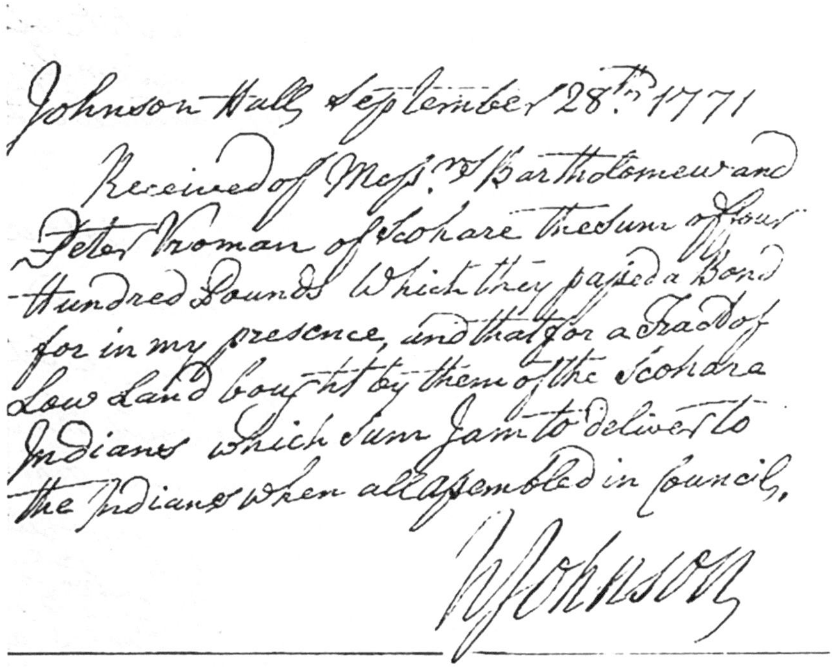

Johnson Hall September 28th 1771

Received of Messrs. Bartholomew and Peter Vroman of Schohare the Sum of four Hundred Pounds Which they passed a Bond for in my presence, and that for a Tract of Low Land bought by them of the Schohare Indians which Sum I am to deliver to the Indians when all assembled in Council,

W Johnson

Fig. 16. Receipt for Indian land bought by Bartholomew Vroman and Peter Vroman from Sir William Johnson, 1771. Copied by Rufus Alexander Grider. Grider's Albums. Courtesy of the New York State Library, Manuscripts and Special Collections.

Colonel Peter Vroman — Governance

Colonel Vroman took an active role in governance during and after the Revolution. He served in the 1st New York State Legislature as one of ten representatives from the Albany District from September 9, 1777 to June 30, 1778. He also served in the 2nd New York State Legislature from October 13, 1778 to March 17, 1779. His correspondence during those periods of service suggest that he was extremely concerned and distressed while awaiting reinforcements and supplies during the raids from 1777-1781 upon the Schoharie Valley. As a delegate to the New York Assembly both in 1777 and 1779 it must have been terribly disconcerting to request aid and feel that the cry went unheard."[71] After a break of a few years, Colonel Vroman returned to the New York State Legislature for the 9th and 10th sessions in 1786 and 1787.

Vroman also participated in local issues. In January 1784, a petition was presented to the Assembly of the State of New York from Peter Vroman and other inhabitants of Schoharie "complaining that the Supervisors of the County assign to that District too large an Apportionment of the Taxes of the County, and praying redress, was read and referred to Mr. Yates, Mr. Veeder and Mr. Sears."[72] It is unknown, what, if any, actions might have been taken.

Colonel Vroman was one of sixty-one delegates elected to represent citizens at the New York State Ratifying Convention held in Poughkeepsie from June 17, 1788 to July 26, 1788. He was part of the seven-man Albany County delegation to the Convention and he was 'Anti-Federalist.' The Anti-Federalists thought the Constitution would destroy state government and end up creating an aristocracy. The Convention was charged with deciding whether New York would ratify the Federal Constitution. There was considerable opposition to the Constitution, particularly by the river communities like Albany. Many in the Albany delegation held the opinion:

......that the delegates had exceeded their authority ... that the government was consolidated, not federal; that its powers were too great; that the representation was too small; that the Senate was too powerful; the Congressional control of elections; that Congress had the power to levy taxes and to create federal tax-collectors; that federal law superseded state law; that slaves were counted in representation; that state bills of credit were prohibited; that a standing army in peace time was created; that Congress had power over the militia; that the government controlled salaries and immigration; that freedom of religion was not expressly guaranteed; that the powers of the President and of the Supreme Court were too extensive; that freedom of the press and trial by jury were not assured; that federal officers might be appointed in the states; that the scheme would involve great expense; that the ratification by nine states only would cause a schism; that there was no bill of rights; and finally, that the whole thing was the product of secret, and therefore, suspicious deliberations.[73]

These opinions elicited some angry discussion at the Convention. Of the fifty-seven members present for the final vote, thirty voted for ratification and twenty-seven voted against. The seven-member delegation from Albany had four votes against adoption of the proposed Constitution and three members (including Vroman) abstained or did not vote. Vroman evidently was not present for the vote. Linda Grant De Pauw speculates that Vroman might have left the convention early.[74] While Vroman was identified as Anti-Federalist (as were all of the Albany County delegates), it is intriguing to consider whether he refrained from voting after recognizing that the majority of other representatives would be voting in favor of adopting the Federal Constitution or if there was another reason for his absence.

A year later, in 1789, Peter Vroman wrote a letter to Gerard Bancker Esq., the Treasurer of the State of New York, requesting that his wages earned as a member of the Constitutional Convention be made payable to John N. Bleecker Esq.[75] Evidently Bleecker served as Vroman's solicitor and they had several dealings with one another, including Vroman's purchase of wallpaper for his home. *(Appendix F)*

Factions and divisions remained after the Revolution. Vroman likely was considered a conciliatory member of the community. For example, an announcement was made on April 18, 1791 that Peter Vroman was chosen as one of seven candidates nominated for the New York Assembly "in order to prevent the continuance of the animosities and divisions which have lately prevailed in the politics of this county."[76]

Col. Vroman was also involved in the early attempts to establish a College in Schenectady. Beginning in 1779, a group worked to obtain land and funding for such a College. One of the requirements for the incorporation of a College was the creation of a Board of Visitors. In 1792, Colonel Peter Vroman was named as one of the trustees for the proposed College. The proposal was not approved at that time but it demonstrates the regard others had for Colonel Vroman. The efforts to establish a College continued and in 1795, after Vroman's death, a charter was granted and Union College was created in Schenectady.[77]

In 1790, Vroman was one of seven electors chosen to represent the Western District of Albany in determining New York's representatives to the United States House of Representatives.[78] He also served as the Chair of the Freeholders of the Town of Schoharie in 1792 when the town succeeded in nominating George Clinton for governor and Pierre Van Cortlandt for lieutenant governor.[79] Clinton and Van Cortlandt were the successful candidates and served from 1777 to 1795, 1801-1804. Clinton later served as Vice President of the United States (1805-1812) under both Presidents Thomas Jefferson and James Madison.

Colonel Peter Vroman — Hero or Not?

Early writings about Colonel Vroman range from laudatory to rather dismissive. The earliest writings include William Campbell's *Annals of Tryon County* (1831), William Stone's *Life of Joseph Brant* (1838), and Jeptha Simms' *History of Schoharie County* (1845). All of these secondary resources were written almost 40 to 50 years after Colonel Vroman's death.

William Wallace Campbell (1806-1881), born in Cherry Valley, was an American author, historian, lawyer, and politician. Campbell, encouraged by others to write the history of Cherry Valley, authored *The Annals of Tryon County* (1831). He begins a chapter on Schoharie with the notation, however, that the 'facts [for that chapter] were principally furnished by a friend.' Campbell writes:

> The following account is given by the Rev. Mr. Fenn, the former clergyman of Harpersfield, who received the information from Col. Harper.
>
> In the year 1778 ... Col. Vrooman commanded in the fort at Schoharie at this time: they saw the enemy wantonly destroying every thing on which they could lay their hand. The garrison were so weak, that they could spare no men from the fort to protect the inhabitants, or secure the crops. – 'What shall be done,' says Col. Harper. 'O, nothing at all,' says Col. Vrooman, 'we be so weak we cannot do any thing.'[80]

This is not a first-hand account. Campbell was not born until after the Revolution. So Campbell's retelling of this story began when Colonel John Harper conveyed a story to Rev. Mr. Fenn and Fenn told that story to Campbell for inclusion in the book. Colonel Harper is the hero of this account and we must keep in mind that he is the one originating the story. In addition, the narrative was relayed through more than one person, making it a bit less reliable. Colonel Vroman in 1778 praised Harper as a man of 'varacity' [sic] so he must have held him in some respect even if that respect was not reciprocated.

Campbell also tells of Major Woolsey's inclination to surrender the Middle Fort and indicates that the officers of the militia prevented surrender. Colonel Harper, a Tryon landowner, rode from Middle Fort to Albany to request assistance. Burgoyne was on the move and the forces in Albany couldn't be spared to assist Schoharie. But Harper persuaded a troop of Sheldon's Second Continental Light Dragoons to divert to aid Schoharie. And this intervention crushed the attack at Middle Fort. Campbell does not mention Colonel Vroman's apparent role in Harper's dash to Albany to request assistance or how Vroman took control and played a major role in defending the fort.

William L. Stone (1792-1844) was an influential journalist, publisher, and author. His early years were spent in Cooperstown and Albany so he was acquainted with the Schoharie area. Stone authored books on various topics including the American Revolution. In his *Life of Joseph Brant* (1838), Stone writes:

> The little fortress of Schoharie was occupied by a small garrison, commanded by Colonel Vrooman – one of that class of men who, though officers, are certain never to be called soldiers. They saw the ravages of the enemy – the conflagrations by night rendering visible the acts of outrage committed by day – but from their own weakness dared not to venture forth, or make a show of opposition. The brave Colonel Harper was in the fort with Vrooman, and was little satisfied with the course of that officer. Leaving the fort, therefore, himself,

he succeeded in making his way through the enemy, mounted his horse, and started express for Albany.[81]

It is unknown, but certainly possible, that Stone's account is based on William Wallace Campbell's writing. Contemporary primary documents about the defense of the Middle Fort consist of existing letters and military communiqués. None of those documents suggest that Vroman was derelict in his duty. And it should be noted that Vroman's contemporaries thought highly enough of him to elect him to the legislature as well as to the New York State Ratifying Convention after the Revolution. In addition, Vroman had a successful military career during his service in the French and Indian War so he did have experience as a true soldier.

Jeptha Root Simms (1807-1883) was an American historian best known for chronicling the settlement of Schoharie. He interviewed many of the oldest surviving residents of the area, including Col. Vroman's daughter Angelica and her husband Lt. Peter Vroman. Simms used the interviews in writing his *History of Schoharie County and the Border Wars of New York* published in 1845. Simms writes about the "services of that brave man [Col. Vrooman] were to be spared to his country."[82] Simms describes Vroman as "a portly figure directing and encouraging his soldiers in his melodious Low Dutch notes…From what has appeared in several publications, a belief has gone abroad that Col. Vrooman was a cowardly, weak man. The impression is very erroneous, he was far otherwise, as the author has had *indubitable and repeated evidence.*"[83]

Simms writes about the attack on the Middle Fort:

> The Middle fort, at this, time was under the command of Major Woolsey, a continental officer, unfitted for the important duties of the station he held, who is said to have been a *broken officer* before going to Schoharie. Col. Vrooman was fortunately in the fort, as were Lieut. Col. Zielie and Maj. Thomas Ecker … Captains Lansing, Pool, Hall, Miller and Richtmyer …men of real courage.[84]

> The cellar under the kitchen part of the [Middle Fort] dwelling [where the women and children were confined] was occupied as a magazine, and Col. Vrooman, to conceal the deficiency of powder, brought it himself when wanted … As powder was needed Col. Vrooman laid down his gun and sword and went to get it. Near the cellar door he encountered Maj. Woolsey, who had just left the presence of the women, as may be supposed, not in very good humor. 'Maj. Woolsey is this your place,' interrogated the brave colonel, 'who are placed here to defend this fort?' He replied, half dead through fear – 'Col. Vrooman, the men will not obey me, and I give up the command to you.' …

> The fire of the Dutch colonel [Vrooman] was instantly ignited at the indifference and filthy expression of the commandant [Woolsey], and speaking in his usually quick manner, he rejoined – 'Maj. Woolsey, had I my sword I would run you through with it.'[85]

Interestingly, Simms delivers critiques of Stone's *Life of Brant* and Campbell's *Annals of Tryon County*. Simms states that Stone made several errors including the date of the attack on the Middle Fort. He goes on to comment that "Campbell, who wrote [*Annals of Tryon County*], at an earlier period has given its true date, and so far as it goes, a much more authentic account of the invasion. Stone blended part of the invasion in August, with that in October, and incorporated several popular errors in the narrative."[86]

Simms states, "If not as energetic as some officers, he [Col. Vroman] was far from being as pusillanimous[87] as represented in the *Annals of Tryon County*, or Stone's *Life of Brant*. The old soldiers who served under him, represent him as having been a bold and determined man, and his conduct on several occasions during the war, gave good evidence of that fact."[88]

The Stone and Simms accounts also differ regarding the role of Colonel Harper. Stone suggests that Col. Harper, unsatisfied with Col. Vroman's actions, left on his own to seek assistance from Albany. Simms, on the other hand, writes that Col. Vroman first sent Mr. Swart and then Capt. Hager and Henry Becker to Albany to request assistance. On the same day that Hager and Becker left, Colonel John Harper arrived in Schoharie and consulted with Col. Vroman and others. They expected the enemies to arrive in Schoharie the next day so time was critical. Col. Harper, according to Simms, then volunteered to leave immediately and ride to Albany. We do not know which version is more accurate.

Individuals who were present at Middle Fort during the siege contributed to Simms's writings about Vroman and the events in the region. Angelica and Lt. Vroman (Col. Vroman's daughter and son-in-law) and Henry Hager shared their stories with Simms. Henry Hager was a Schoharie County judge. He provided Simms with a manuscript of stories relating to Schoharie. His grandfather (also named Henry Hager) participated in the events. It is unknown if these firsthand retellings, though many years after the fact, are more or less accurate than the earlier authors cited. But the earlier unflattering descriptions of Col. Vroman are at least partially suspect.

Solomon Sias in his *A Summary of Schoharie County* (1904) describes Vroman as "a prudent but a bold and determined man as his conduct at the Middle Fort during Johnson's raid in 1780 demonstrated."[89] In 1907, Alfred Abrams writes, "Although most of the early writers and some of the more recent ones accuse Colonel Vrooman of weakness and indecision, the charge seems wholly unsupported by evidence. He continued in command of the local forces through the war when a ranking officer was not present. He seems to have had at all times the confidence of the people, and certainly rendered the settlements and the cause of liberty valuable service."[90] Taking all of these historians into account, it appears that Colonel Vroman can certainly be credited with loyal and continuing service to his local and regional communities.

Colonel Peter Vroman — Possessions

Vroman correspondences, land dealings, account book, and artifacts are scattered among various depositories including the New York State Archives, the New York Public Library, the Albany County Records Department, and the Old Stone Fort. The Old Stone Fort Museum has several Colonel Peter Vroman artifacts on display. Most of these items came through donations from Henry Cady, the adopted son of Col. Vroman's granddaughter and the first archivist at the Old Stone Fort. Since there are no known portraits of Vroman and few descriptions of him as a person, these artifacts give us a bit of a glimpse into the man. Possessions are often a window into the lives of the people who possessed them. Beneath the surface of the possessions one can sometimes find commentary not only of the people but also the major social, economic, and political issues of the time.

The Vromans owned a foot stove, also called a stoof (in Dutch). This foot stove was a decorative pierced wooden box with a metal container that held heated coals or bricks inside. Some Dutch foot stoves, including this example, used elaborately ornamented metal (likely tin) as well as intricate carvings and piercing. It is a wonderful piece of folk art. These foot warmers would often be used in unheated churches or in carriages.

Rufus Alexander Grider's drawing of the Colonel Peter Vroman family foot stove *(Fig. 17)* is part of the Grider *Albums* located in the New York State Library. The drawing includes the following information:

Label: Foot warmer of the Col. Peter Vroman family of wood painted d[ar]k brown, it was used in Church & in sleighs & wagons heated with bricks width at top 10 in.height 8" drawn ½ size
Pos{sessed]by Henry Cady at Schoharie

Fig. 17. Drawing of a foot warmer belonging to the family of Col. Peter Vroman. Drawn by Rufus Alexander Grider. Grider's Albums. Courtesy of the New York State Library, Manuscripts and Special Collections.

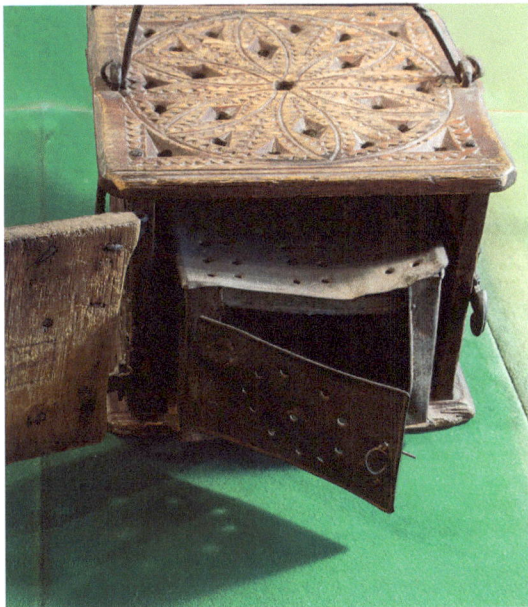

Fig. 18. Foot warmer on display at the Old Stone Fort Museum; very likely the same foot warmer drawn by Grider (Fig. 17)

Comparisons of the Grider drawing with photographs of a foot warmer in the Old Stone Fort Museum *(Fig. 18)* suggest they are one and the same. Note specifically the heart-shaped carving, the decorative 6-point star top, the metal handle, the hinges, and the closure mechanism. According to the information label accompanying the Old Stone Fort piece, this "fine specimen of beauty and function … is painted red and decorated with chip carving that incorporates hearts and *sechssterne* (six pointed stars). A pierced, sheet iron firebox inside the wooden case holds hot coals from the fireplace. This object was exhibited at the 1939 World's Fair in New York City."[91] At the time of the drawing, August 1887, the foot warmer was in the possession of Henry Cady. Cady's connection to the Vroman family makes the Vroman provenance of the Old Stone Fort object much more likely.

35

The decorated chest *(Fig. 19)* is purported to come from the Vroman family of Schoharie County. It is a wonderfully decorative folk art landscape chest, probably from the colonial period. This photograph is reproduced from an article that included reference to the piece and noted that it is "significant as example[s] of American landscape deriving from a period hitherto considered to have been almost exclusively devoted to portraiture... The same sort of landscape, typical of the itinerant, was occasionally used on furniture as well as for panel decoration."[92] Unfortunately, the chest does not depict the Peter Vroman house and the small Fox Creek certainly could not sustain a large sailboat. It may have been owned by another branch of the Vroman family or it could have been part of Col. Vroman's property.

Photograph courtesy of "The Esther Stevens Brazer Guild of Early American Decoration."

Fig. 19. Decorated chest from the Vrooman family of Schoharie County. Photograph from Nina Fletcher Little's "Itinerant Painting in America, 1750-1850," 1949.

Rufus Grider drew several objects, purported to be the property of Col. Peter Vroman *(Fig. 20)*. The drawing includes: a silver-headed cane, a snuff box, two Masonic badges, a pewter plate, two silver spoons with engraved initials, and a representation of Peter Vroman's tombstone.

The silver-headed cane, with "Col. Peter Vroman" engraved on the handle, might have been the cane bequeathed to Colonel Vroman in his grandfather's will (Pieter Vroman). Canes were a token of social stature during the 17th and 18th centuries. It was not unusual to have canes encrusted with jewels and precious metals. The silver-head is simple but has decorative details. If the pictured cane is the one bequeathed to Colonel Vroman, his grandfather must have thought it fairly valuable.

Grider identified the small snuffbox as being the property of Colonel Vroman's wife, Engeltie Swart Possibly, one of the initials represented her maiden name. Colonel Vroman's wife is somewhat of a mystery. There is little mention of her in any records, no death documents have been found, and her place of burial is unknown.

The Masonic badge on the left of the drawing was perhaps the property of Peter A. Vroman, also known as Peter Vroman, Jr., the husband of Col. Vroman's daughter. Peter A. Vroman was a member of the St. George Masonic Lodge of Schenectady which is the organization represented on that badge. Roscoe also reported that Peter A. Vroman was a member and treasurer of the Schoharie Union Lodge.

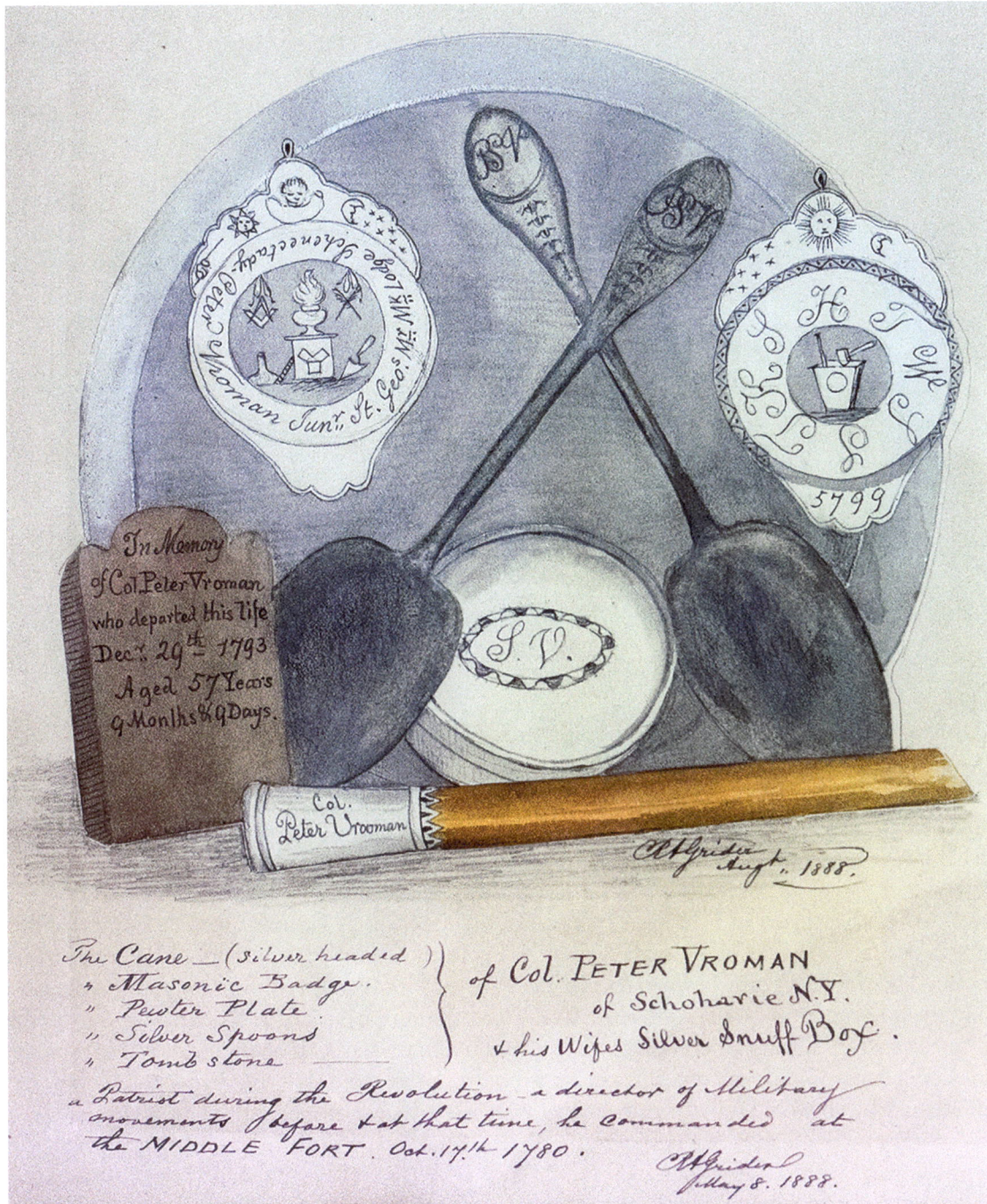

Fig. 20. Vroman artifacts. (Drawn by Rufus Alexander Grider).
Grider's Albums. Courtesy of the New York State Library, Manuscripts and Special Collections.

Colonel Peter Vroman — Slavery

The Vromans were part of the Dutch slave system. "The Dutch regarded slavery as an economic venture and did not equate slavery with social organization or race control."[93] It has been suggested that religious discrimination was more prevalent among the Dutch than racial bias. The Dutch slaves were given some personal liberties in exchange for their labor. Perhaps they were treated humanely but they were still slaves. According to Roscoe, the Vroman Family was responsible for introducing slavery to Schoharie settlements.

Several documents directly connect the Vromans to slavery. In 1736, Pieter Vroman (Col. Vroman's grand-father) signed a 'bill of sale'[94] for a Negro slave bought from Storm Becker.[95] The document reads:

> Hunterfield, July the fifteenth Day, one Thousent, Seven hundred and Tharty sex. Then Bouth of Storm Becker a negor man, and the said Storm Becker Grant the Said negor unto Peter Vroman for his one lawful saruant fore forty two pount Corrant Lawful money of the province of new York. Wetness my hand and the present of
>
> Storm Becker
>
> Cornelius Vroman
> Martines Vroman

> July 15, 1736
> Then received of Peter Vroman the Just and ful sum of twenty pounds one shilling, Corrant Lawful money was received by me.
>
> Storm Becker

Col. Vroman's father, Barent Vroman, certainly had slaves. Barent willed Peter a young slave boy named Zoda[96] upon his death in 1782. Zoda may be one of the 3 slaves listed in Colonel Vroman's household in 1790. Records also indicate Peter Vroman purchased a young male slave named Henry on January 16, 1788 from John Price of Albany, New York. *(Fig.21)*. Henry was 17 years old at the time and Vroman paid 90 pounds. The 90 pounds would translate to about $13,000 in 2018 funds.

There were 152 slaves listed in Schoharie by the 1790 United States Federal Census. The readable sections of that schedule list at least 34 Vroman-related slaves in the Town of Schoharie. Col. Vroman has three slaves while his brother, Adam B. Vroman has eight slaves. Compared to Southern slaveholders, they held relatively small numbers of slaves. And while Col. Vroman might have suffered financially during the Revolution, he still had sufficient funds available to buy and maintain slaves. It is unknown if the Vroman's slaves lived in the house or in separate quarters on the property. There were slave quarters on the property during the 19th century but it would only be conjecture to suggest when those separate slave quarters were erected.

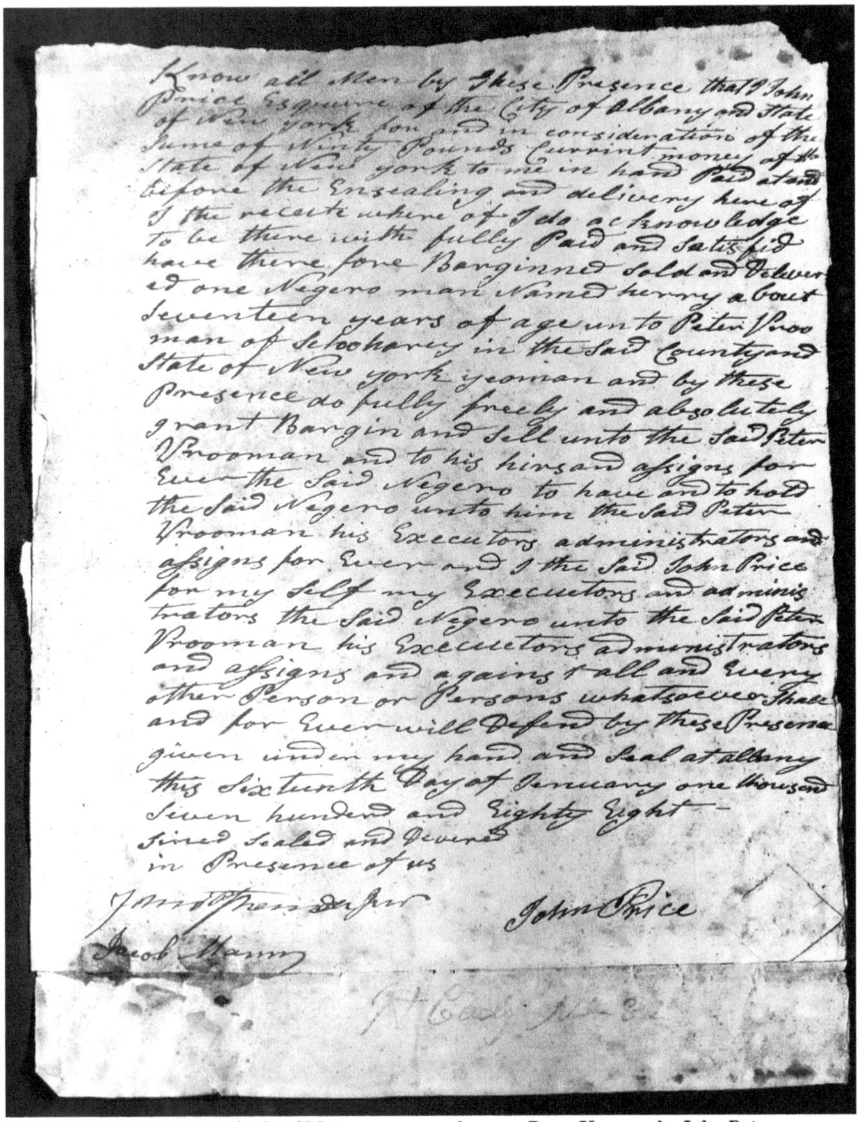

Know all Men by These Presence that I John Price Esquire of the City of Albany and State of New York for and in consideration of the Sume of Ninty Pounds Currint money of the State of New York to me in hand Paid at and before the Ensealing and delivery here of I the receite where of I do acknowledge to be there with fully Paid and Satisfid have there fore Barginned Sold and Delivered one Negero man Named henry about Seventeen years of age unto Peter Vrooman of Schoharey in the Said County and State of New York yeoman and by these Presence do fully freely and absolutely grant Bargin and Sell unto the Said Peter Vrooman and to his hirs and assigns for Ever the Said Negero to have and to hold the Said Negero unto him the Said Peter Vrooman his Executors administrators and assigns for Ever and I the Said John Price for my Self my Executors and administrators the Said Negero unto the Said Peter Vrooman his Executors administrators and assigns and against all and Every other Person or Persons whatsoever Shall and for Ever will Defend by these Presence given under my hand and Seal at albany this Sixteenth Day of Janewary one thousand Seven hundred and Eighty Eight —
Sined Sealed and Deliverd in Presence of us

John Price

Fig. 21. Document of sale of Henry, a young slave, to Peter Vroman by John Price, 1788. Original in the Old Stone Fort Museum.

Colonel Peter Vroman — House

It is unknown where the Colonel and his family lived after the destruction of his Vroman's Land home in 1780 and before the construction of the Colonel Peter Vroman house in ca. 1792. Several secondary sources suggest there was an old 'homestead' on the Eckerson property. Perhaps, Vroman and his family lived in that old homestead while building the new house but we have not yet found any substantiating documentation.

The 1790 United State Federal Census indicates Peter Vroman was head of household and living somewhere in Schoharie, New York along with 11 other people. The household consisted of three free white males over 16 years of age, one free white male under 16 years old, four free white females, and three slaves. It was thought, possibly, that Col. Vroman's married daughter and only living child, Angelica, and her family might have been living with her father but there are separate 1790 census listings for Col. Peter Vroman and Peter A. Vroman (his son-in-law). So, we are unable to determine definitively the 11 people in the 1790 Col. Peter Vroman household or where that household was located. If his daughter and her family were living with him, the composition of the household might have looked like this:

1790 United State Federal Census, Schoharie, New York	
	'POSSIBLE' IDENTITIES
3 free white males over 16	Colonel Peter Vroman (b.1735), head of household; Major Peter A. Vroman (his son-in-law, b.1763); Unknown
1 free white male under 16	Adam Vroman, Jr. (grandson of Col. Vroman, b.1786)
4 free white females	Angelica Vroman (daughter of Col. Peter Vroman, b.1766); Sara Vroman (granddaughter of Col. Vroman, b.1788); 2 Unknown <have been unable to identify when Col. Vroman's wife died>
3 slaves	Zoda, Henry, Unknown
11 total residents	

Only four people would have been 'unknown' if this configuration is accurate. The unknown free white male might very well have been an employee. The two slaves might have been Zoda (bequeathed from Peter Vroman's father) and Henry (purchased by Peter Vroman in 1788). But these projections are merely conjecture since the two separate listings must be acknowledged and cannot be explained.

Col. Peter Vroman's daughter, Angelica, married Major Peter A. Vroman in 1784 and they had a son in 1786 and a daughter in 1788. So, their household in 1790 would have consisted of at least 4 people. There is a separate listing in the 1790 United State Census for a Peter A. Vroman with one free white male 16 or older, one free while male under 16, and two free white females. This matches the information we know about Angelica Vroman and her family.

The 1790 Census does not provide addresses for the individuals listed, it only indicates they lived in Schoharie, Albany County, New York. The census enumerator could arrange the records as he pleased so individuals were not necessarily canvased by neighborhood. The original document is difficult to read because several names are obstructed.

Many secondary sources suggest the Colonel Vroman house was built in 1785, while a few sources suggest even earlier construction dates. For over a century, the local population traditionally accepted 1785 as the construction date for the Colonel Vroman house. When Louise S. Vrooman added the dormer windows ca. 1930s, she even added the date '1785' to a space between the dormers.

In order to accurately determine when the house was built, the Heymans contracted to have a dendrochronology study done. Dendrochronology is the scientific method of dating tree rings to the exact year they were formed. The dendrochronology study provided statistically very significant evidence that the house beams were cut from November 1791 to February 1792. The beams were worked soon after cutting in keeping with historical woodworking and carpentry techniques making them easier to work with and ensuring the structure tightens as it dries. The beams are suggestive of a first growth forest that was likely located in Schoharie, perhaps the forest was even on land owned by Col. Vroman. The beams are of high quality and were chosen very deliberately; the entire project was well planned and executed. Although the house might not be particularly large or ornate, its construction was up to the standards of a 'rich' man's project.

The Dendrochronology report states:

> The degree of chronological congruency in the collective datings of the selected cellar oak and attic pine timbers indicates that a significant construction phase for the Vroman House began with the laying down of the cellar oak timbers, conceivably performed during the clement weather months of calendar year 1792, or if delayed during 1793 at the latest. Moreover, the corresponding cutting dates of the cellar beams and the roof rafters demonstrate that the construction was thoroughly planned and organized, and that deliberate preparatory work for timbering of the structure as a whole was conducted during the very late autumn of 1791 or the winter of 1791/1792.[97]

Dr. Edward R. Cook and William J. Callahan, Jr. completed the dendrochronology study in September 2017. *(Appendix G)*. Samples were taken from 13 beams in the cellar *(Fig. 22)* and attic and then analyzed. The samples are now archived at the Tree Ring Research Laboratory, Lamont-Doherty Earth Observatory, Columbia University.

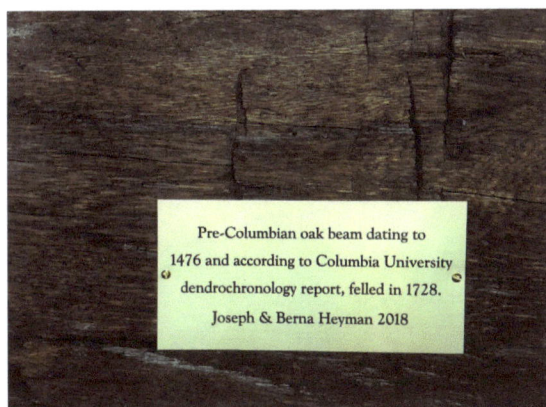

Pre-Columbian oak beam dating to 1476 and according to Columbia University dendrochronology report, felled in 1728.

Joseph & Berna Heyman 2018

Fig. 22. Oldest beam in the Peter Vroman house – oak beam in cellar, began growing in 1476 and felled in 1728.

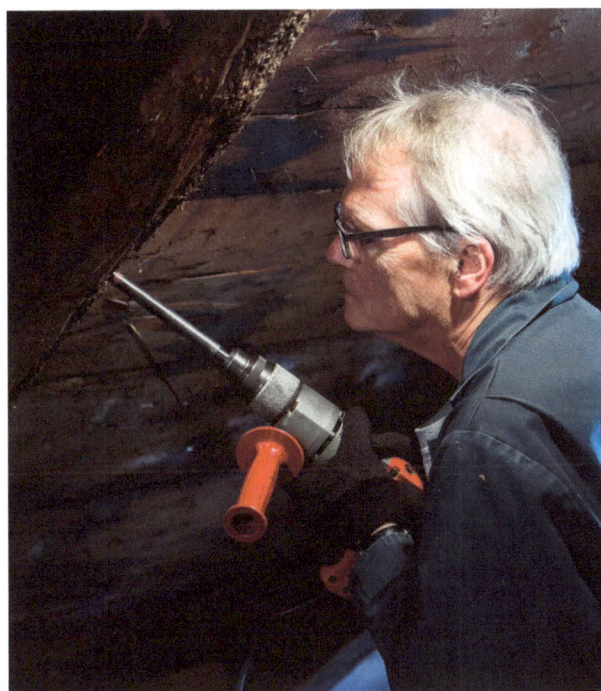

Fig. 23. William J. Callahan, Jr. drilling sample of cellar beam in Col. Peter Vroman house.

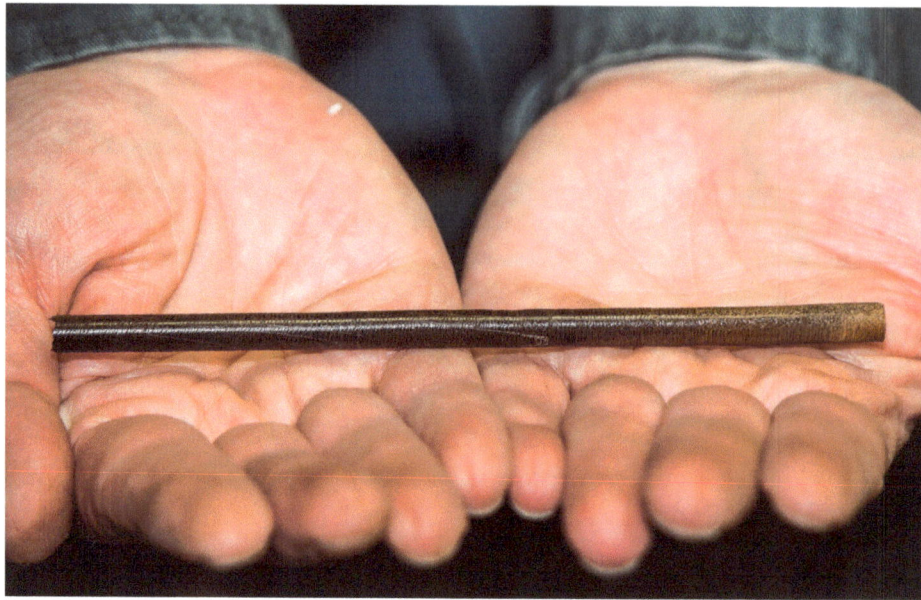

Fig. 24. Core sample drilled from one of the cellar beams of the Col. Peter Vroman house.

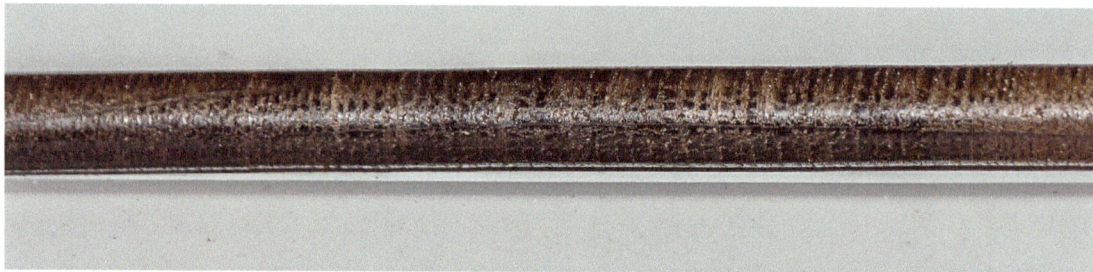

Fig. 25. Close-up of one of the dendrochronology core samples from Vroman house.

The dendrochronology data provides substantial evidence that the Col. Peter Vroman house was constructed between 1791 and 1792. Colonel Vroman's *Account Memorandum Book*[98] has an intriguing entry *(Fig. 26)* suggesting possession of the property in 1791. The entry reads: "1791 March 12th took possession of the house and lands." While this citation, written by Vroman, does not specify which house or land is referenced, the date of the transaction closely aligns with the date of construction of the Vroman house. We cannot explain the reference to "the house." Several secondary sources indicate there was a homestead on the site when Eckerson owned the property. It is an intriguing possibility that this may be the "house" referred to in Vroman's *Account Memorandum Book*.

Col. Vroman was an important figure of his time. He was acquainted with many of the leaders of New York and certainly visited substantial homes in his various official roles. The construction of his home was likely done to his specifications. The workmanship of the beams suggests that experienced craftsmen built the house. And while it is not a 'grand' house in comparison to those built in Albany or Schenectady, it is house of considerable style for a frontier home.

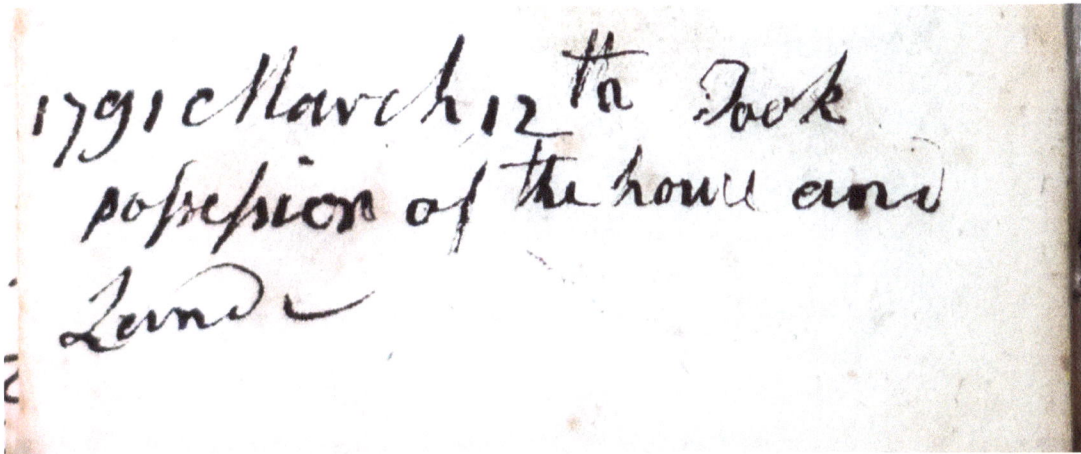

Fig. 26. 1791 notation from Peter Vroman's "Account memorandum book," 1759-1792.
Courtesy of the New York State Library, Manuscripts and Special Collections.

In a letter[99] *(Appendix F)* dated September 21, 1792, John N. Bleecker of Albany, New York writes to Col. Peter Vroman concerning wallpaper that had been purchased by Vroman. The letter lists the materials Bleecker sent for papering the walls, and gives instructions on mixing the glue and hanging the paper. The letter also indicates a cost of £6, 4 shillings (about $800) for the paper and supplies. Bleecker writes that there are separate papers for borders and for the upper and lower parts of rooms. The paper to be used in the entry has one kind of border. Vroman was undoubtedly decorating his home.

Bleecker writes that he sent Vroman three separate parcels of paper hangings, as follows:

Product	Cost	Total
5 <unknown measurement>	@ 4 shillings	£1 " 0 " 0
11 <unknown measurement>	@ 5 shillings	£2 " 15 " 0
16 yards bordering	@ 2 per 6	£2 " 0 " 0
5 yards bordering	@1 shilling	" 5 " 0
For buying & freight from New York		£ " 2 " 0
<unknown measurement> glue		£ " 2 " 0
TOTAL		£7 " 4 " 0
		7 pounds, 4 shillings, 0 pence

The unknown measurement 𝓎 might very well be a French measurement, perhaps the livre tournois. Thomas Jefferson often used the livre tournois to pay for wallpaper. Jefferson used the abbreviation ₶ to indicate livre tournois in his account books.

After the American Revolution, British colonial trading restrictions were lifted and there was a dramatic increase in the importation of French wallpapers by Americans. In 1787, the French removed export duties on wallpapers, thus decreasing the price of French wallpaper.

> The post-revolutionary popularity of French *papiers peints* was not simply the result of removal of British restrictions on non-British goods, and of the price drop on French papers when export duties were abolished. Nor was it just a byproduct of American gratitude for French assistance during the Revolution. These factors were doubtless important, but the

quality of the French papers themselves was probably their most important selling point in America during the late eighteenth century. By the 1790s, the beauty of French wallpapers had captivated American tastemakers, and they were gaining popularity among wider circles of consumers.[100]

We do not have sufficient information to determine if Colonel Vroman purchased French wallpaper for his home but it certainly is a possibility. Since Schoharie was almost wilderness at the time, purchasing wallpaper for his home might have been considered quite an extravagance.

The individual selling Vroman the wallpaper was John Bleecker, a successful businessman and landowner. He held numerous leadership positions in Albany and was also a member of the Militia. The personal information contained in the letter confirms that Bleecker and Vroman were well known to one another. Bleecker even shares information about his wife's breast cancer. Vroman used Bleecker as his conduit in 1789 for requesting his wages as a member of the New York State Constitution Convention.

Two 1787 documents *(Fig. 27-28)* certify that Peter Vroman was making amends for land quit-rent payments that had gone in arrears likely during the American Revolution. Many land grants in colonial America carried quit-rents (basically a land tax). Figures 27 and 28 are actually written on one sheet of paper but they relate to two different issues. The first document *(Fig. 27)* was for land purchased by Myndert Schuyler in 1714, then sold to Johannes Eckerson who later sold it to Peter Vroman. This document may very well include the land encompassing the Colonel Peter Vroman house. The provenance of the document lends credence to its connection to Colonel Vroman. The document was owned and displayed by Mildred Vrooman, a descendant of the Colonel. It is now in the possession of the Heymans. Vroman paid the back rent for 260 acres of land of an original 10,000 acres purchase. The Adam Vroman listed in both documents was Colonel Peter Vroman's brother. There were many land transfers between Peter Vroman and several other Vromans, including Adam Vroman, in 1763 and 1769, suggesting the family had some fluid changes in land ownership.

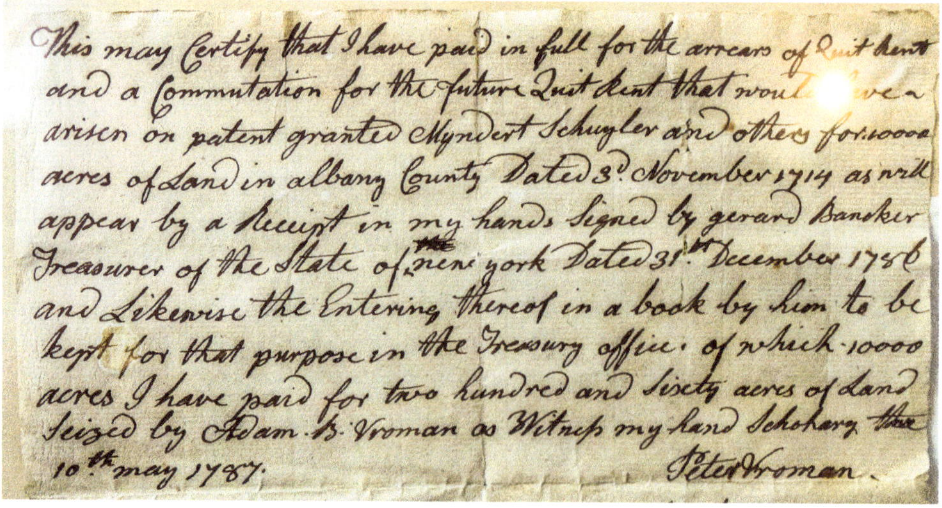

Fig. 27. Col. Peter Vroman's *certification of payment for quit rents in arrears, 1787. Original in the possession of the author.*

Transcription of Fig. 27: This may Certify that I have paid in full for the arrears of Quit rent and a Commutation for the future Quit rent that would have arisen on patent granted Myndert Schuyler and others for 10000 acres of Land in albany County Dated 3d November 1714 as will appear by a Receipt in my hand

Signed by gerard Baneker Treasurer of the State of new york Dated 31st December 1786 and Likewise the Entering thereof in a book by him to be kept for that purpose in the Treasury office of which 1000 acres I have paid for two hundred and sixty acres of Land Seized by Adam B. Vroman as Witness my hand Schohary the 10th May 1787 / Peter Vroman.

The following quick-rent document *(Fig. 28)*, also signed by Peter Vroman, refers to land sold in 1726 by Lewis Morris, a prominent landowner in colonial New York and a signer of the Declaration of Independence. Lewis Morris was one of the surveyors of the original 1714 patent to the land purchase referred to as *The Old Schoharie Patent* purchased by the Seven Partners of Schoharie. Gerard Bancker, the New York State Treasurer from 1778 to 1798, was listed as the individual who signed a receipt for these two quick-rent payments.

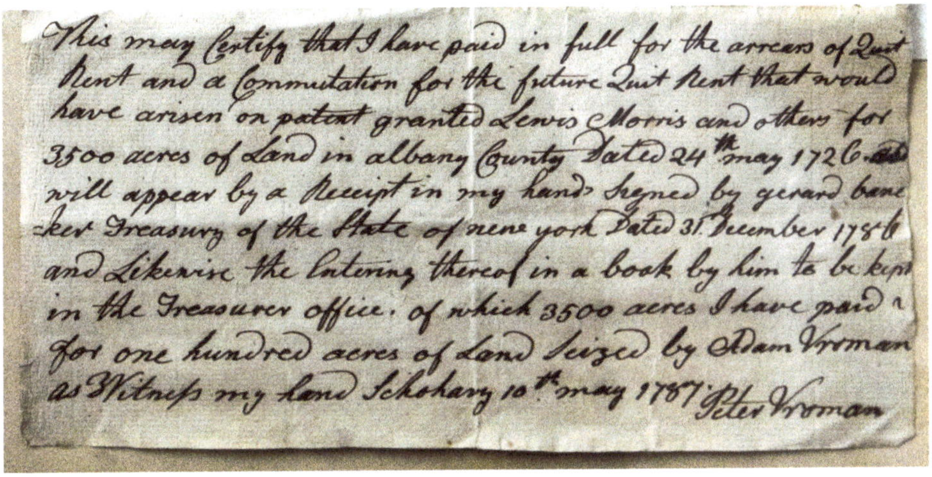
This may Certify that I have paid in full for the arrears of Quit
Rent and a Commutation for the future Quit Rent that would
have arisen on patent granted Lewis Morris and others for
3500 acres of Land in albany County Dated 24th may 1726 as
will appear by a Receipt in my hand Signed by gerard bane
-ker Treasury of the State of new york Dated 31 December 1786
and Likewise the Entering thereof in a book by him to be kept
in the Treasurer office. of which 3500 acres I have paid
for one hundred acres of Land Seized by Adam Vroman
as Witness my hand Schohary 10th may 1787 Peter Vroman

Fig. 28. Col. Peter Vroman's certification of payment for quit rents in arrears, 1787. Original in the possession of the author..

Transcription of Fig. 28: This may Certify that I have paid in full for the arrears of Quit Rent and a Commutation for the future Quit Rent that would have arisen on patent granted Lewis Morris and others for 3500 acres of Land in albany County Dated 24th may 1726 as will appear by a Receipt in my hand Signed by gerard Baneker Treasurer of the State of new york Dated 31st December 1786 and Likewise the Entering thereof in a book by him to be kept in the Treasury office of which 3500 acres I have paid for one hundred acres of Land Seized by Adam Vroman as Witness my hand Schohary the 10th may 1787 / Peter Vroman.

Colonel Peter Vroman — Death and Memorials

Colonel Vroman had very little time to enjoy his new home. He died December 29, 1793 at age fifty-seven. "At one time [he] was one of the wealthiest men in the valley, but he died comparatively poor, having given liberally to the Continental cause. His estate, which was sold after his death, brought about $4,500, some $7,000 in Continental currency, which was valueless, was also found among his effects.[101] But Vroman also left a considerable amount of land to his daughter and his descendants. Peter Vroman's original modest red sandstone headstone is in the graveyard of the Old Stone Fort Cemetery. *(Fig. 29)*.

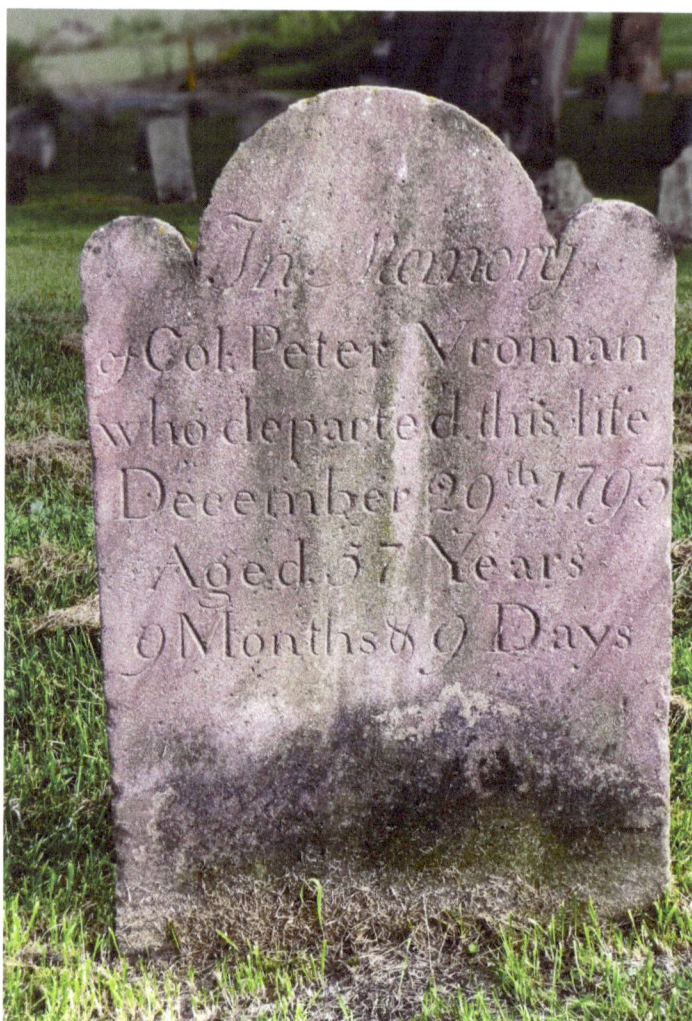

Fig. 29. Col. Peter Vroman's original gravestone, located in the Old Stone Fort Cemetery, Schoharie, New York.

The monument reads:

> In memory of Col. Peter Vroman who departed this life December 29th 1793
> Aged 57 Years 9 Months & 9 Days.

Roscoe describes Colonel Vroman's original gravestone:

> Here within the yard in which the old fort stands, lie many patriots. A small red sand stone marks the spot that contains the ashes of Colonel Peter Vroman and exhibits the 'ingratitude of Republics' in a manner too noticeable. The graves of such unflinching soldiers should be honored by more imposing looking monuments.[102]

Roscoe's comments continue earlier discussions about erecting a more substantial memorial to Col. Peter Vroman. An 1873 article in *The Canajoharie Radii* says: "we felt to urge the importance of the movement we have before suggested, to erect a respectable monument to the memory of that brave and good man."[103]

Finally, in 1912, the Schoharie Chapter of the Daughters of the American Revolution (D.A.R.) created a Memorial Fund Committee to design and fund a major monument to Colonel Peter Vroman. Members of the Committee included Mrs. George W. Snyder, Mrs. James L. Baker, Miss Kate Vrooman, Miss Ruth D. Vrooman, and Miss Anna L. Merrill. They commissioned Smith Brothers Monument Company of Cobleskill, New York to make the nine-ton monument, made of Barre granite. The monument is engraved with a draped American flag with a stars and stripes. The monument is 8 feet 2 inches tall, 4 feet 6 inches wide and 2 feet thick. It cost the D.A.R. $900.[104] The Schoharie County Board of Supervisors awarded $250 toward the monument fund. The monument *(Fig. 30)* was installed in front of the Old Stone Fort Museum and dedicated on October 17, 1913, almost 120 years after Colonel Vroman's death. That date was also the anniversary of the battle of the Middle Fort when Johnson and Brant invaded the Valley and attempted to destroy it.

The *Cobleskill Index* describes the event:

> The address of welcome by the regent of Schoharie chapter [D.A.R.] was hearty and struck a high note of patriotism, which continued in the eloquent addresses by J. D. Holden, New York State historian and Ira Mowery of East Worcester. Henry Cady, a descendant of Col. Vroman [the 'adopted son' of Col. Peter Vroman's granddaughter, Katie Vroman Hager] unveiled the large granite monument; rough, rugged, noble, strong and enduring, as were the qualities of the soldier and statesman whose memory it will perpetuate. Glorious day for sleepy old Schoharie, lying in one of the most beautiful valleys of the state. The sky was never more beautiful than on that October day, the 17th, long to be remembered not only by the proud daughters and sons of the Revolution of Schoharie, but by the great throng present from far and near.[105]

Mrs. D. J. Vrooman, also known as Louise (Stevens) Vrooman, was the Regent of the Schoharie Chapter of the D.A.R. She gave the welcoming address during the monument unveiling. Her husband, Donald J. Vrooman, was a collateral relative of Colonel Vroman. Mrs. Vrooman moved to the Col. Vrooman house in 1912 after her husband's death. Louise's family had owned the Vroman house since 1863. It was most fitting that she played a major role in bringing the monument to fruition.

An undated, unmarked newspaper article originally in the possession of Mildred Vrooman, comments:

> It is fortunate that we have an active organization for the purpose of preserving historical documents, the names of courageous men, the hallowed places in the struggle for national birth and to bring to the attention of the present generation a realization of the price paid for the privileges they now enjoy.

Fig. 30. Colonel Peter Vroman Monument erected in 1913 by the Schoharie Chapter, Daughters of the American Revolution.

Fig. 31. Detail of the bronze plate mounted on the Col. Peter Vroman monument.

Fig. 32. Photograph of the dedication of the Col. Peter Vroman monument, Oct. 17, 1913 in front of the Old Stone Fort, Schoharie, New York. Photograph from the Old Stone Fort collection.

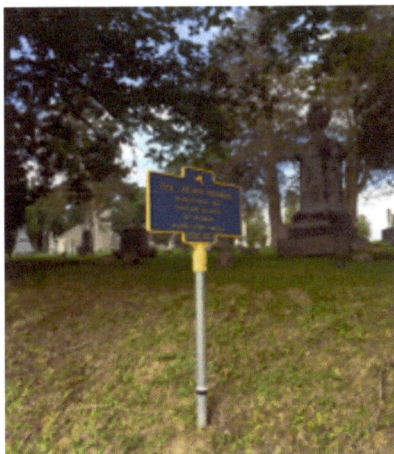

Fig. 33. Historic marker for Col. Peter Vroman.

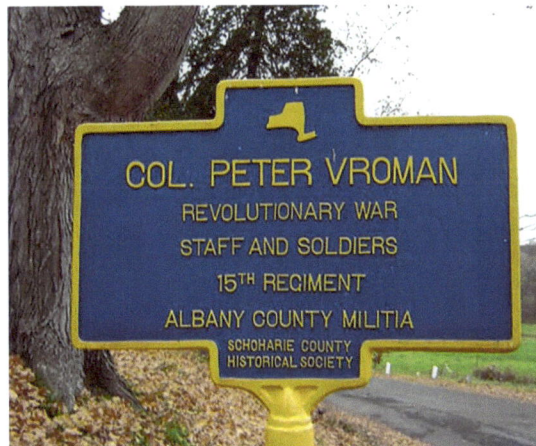

Fig. 34. Detail of the historic marker for Col. Peter Vroman. Located on Fort Road, Schoharie, New York next to the Old Stone Fort Cemetery where Peter Vroman is buried.

Following are some posthumous tributes to or descriptions of Colonel Peter Vroman:

It was the noble character, the ability of this distinguished man, his historic name, his official position, that gave to his splendid leadership, its prestige and influence. May we each offer a tribute of gratitude to this man whose high standard of honor and patriotism has a permanent memorial – a fine granite monument erected in front of the historic Old Stone Fort.[106]
— Frances B. Spencer

From the adoption of the State Constitution in 1777 to the formation of the [Schoharie] County in 1795, one member from Schoharie represented the settlements in this section. For ten years (from 1777 to 1787) the representative was that staunch patriot, gallant and fearless hero – Col. Peter Vroman who had been secretary of the local Committee of Safety, the defender of the Middle Fort in Johnson's raid in 1780, and who now lies buried in the cemetery of the Old Stone Fort at Schoharie.[107]
— Solomon Sias

Ambitious, restless, combatative, venturesome, clannish, jealous of family name and possessions, keen observer of the trend of events, physically alert, an intrepid soldier, quick to act, a wise and trusted leader in his community, a man of outstanding ability, intelligence and appearance: that is my picture of Col. Peter B. Vrooman.[108] — Arthur U. Stevenson

The old soldiers who served under him, represented him as having been a bold and determined man, and his conduct on several occasions during the war, gave good evidence of that fact. He was very much respected in the country.[109] — A. W. Clark

There are no known portraits of Col. Peter Vroman but he is depicted in a mural painted for the Poughkeepsie Post Office by Gerald Foster. The mural *(Fig. 35)* represents the New York Ratifying Convention. The original was installed in 1938 as part of a Work Projects Administration project. This is a black and white reproduction of the very large colored wall mural. The scene depicts the closing moments of the New York State ratifying convention. Colonel Peter Vroman is identified as the individual sitting, third from the left. His back is facing us, maybe because there are no known representations of Col. Vroman and, in addition, he wasn't actually present at the close of the convention.

Fig. 35. Mural painting in Poughkeepsie Post Office illustrating the New York State Ratifying Convention. Col. Peter Vroman is identified as the individual sitting, third from the left in this mural.

1735	• Peter B. Vroman birth, Vroman's Land, New York.
1759	• Appointed Lieutenant of the Militia of the Province of New York. • Fought in French and Indian War. • Began Account Book, continued using it through 1792.
1760	• Served at Fort Niagara.
1761	• Married Engeltie Swart.
1764	• Daughter Jannetie born; died one month later.
1766	• Daughter Angelica born. Only child to live until adulthood. Died in 1839.
1769	• Son Josais born; likely died very young.
1770	• Promoted to Major.
1775	• Elected Secretary of the Schoharie District Committee of Safety. • Commissioned Colonel of the 15th Regiment of Albany County Militia and served until the end of the Revolution (except when reinforcements were sent to the Valley or when the immediate command, by reason of courtesy or seniority of rank, was transferred to the visiting commandant). • Son Barent born; likely died very young.
1777-1779	• Represented Albany District in the 1st and 2nd New York State Legislatures.
1780	• Home in Vroman's Land destroyed in a raid. • Assumed command of the Middle Fort in Schoharie during a Johnson/Brant raid. • Treasurer for the Low Dutch Reformed Church.
1786-1787	• Represented Albany District in the 9th and 10th New York State Legislatures.
1788	• Represented Albany County at the New York Ratifying Convention, Poughkeepsie.
1790	• Represented Western District of Albany as an elector. • 1790 Census indicates he lived in Schoharie with a household of 11 people, including 3 slaves.
1791	• Account Book: "took possession of the house and land" (cannot verify which house and land but likely this refers to current Col. Peter Vroman home). Unknown where he lived between 1780 and 1791.
1791/2	• Col. Vroman house next to Fox Creek constructed.
1792	• Chair of the Freeholders of the Town of Schoharie. • Named Trustee of proposed college in Schenectady (to become Union College). • Purchased wallpaper for house.
1793	• Died, Schoharie, New York
1913	• Schoharie Chapter of the Daughters of the American Revolution dedicates a major monument to Colonel Peter Vroman.

1793-1832 Angelica Vroman and her husband, Peter A. Vroman
Katie Vroman and her husband, Adam D. Hager

Angelica (a.k.a. Anna, Angeletie, Engletie) Vroman (1766-1839) was the daughter of Colonel Peter Vroman and Engeltie Swart. She was their only child to live to adulthood. She inherited the Vroman house[110] and over 300 acres of land from her father. Angelica was recognized as a "woman defender" during the American Revolution for her efforts in molding bullets for Timothy Murphy in her father's tent[111] during the 1780 Raid on the Middle Fort in Schoharie. Simms writes, "Angelica Vrooman, as she informed the author, took [Timothy] Murphy's bullet mould, lead, and an iron spoon, went to her father's tent, and there moulded a quantity of bullets for that fearless ranger [Murphy], amidst the roar of cannon and musketry."-[112]Simms describes her as a "glorious example of colonial womanhood."

The Old Stone Fort Museum displays a garter *(Fig. 36)* originally owned by Angelica Vroman. Henry Cady donated the garter to the Old Stone Fort as noted in the 1899 inventory. Garters were in widespread use in the 18th century prior to the invention of elastic. Stockings were held up with garters which would typically be made of ribbon or knitted or leather strips and might tie or buckle — on, above, or below the knee. Angelica's garter appears to be made of knitted ribbon or cloth with a metal buckle closure.

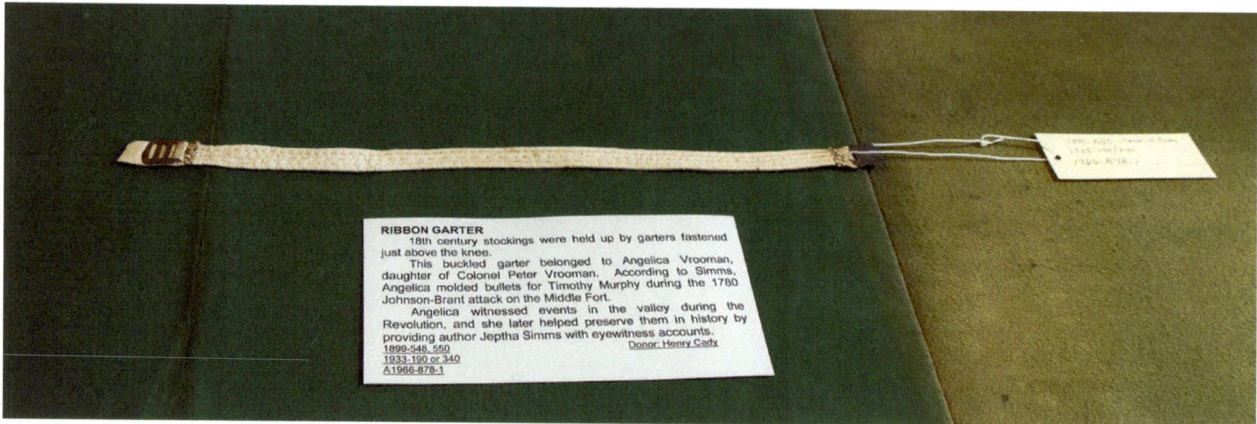

RIBBON GARTER
 18th century stockings were held up by garters fastened just above the knee.
 This buckled garter belonged to Angelica Vrooman, daughter of Colonel Peter Vrooman. According to Simms, Angelica molded bullets for Timothy Murphy during the 1780 Johnson-Brant attack on the Middle Fort.
 Angelica witnessed events in the valley during the Revolution, and she later helped preserve them in history by providing author Jeptha Simms with eyewitness accounts.
1899-548, 550   Donor: Henry Cady
1933-190 or 340
A1966-878-1

Fig. 36. Angelica Vroman's garter. Displayed in Old Stone Fort Museum.

In 1781 (or possibly 1784), Angelica married Major Peter A. Vroman (1764-1838). He was the son of Adam B. Vroman (Colonel Peter Vroman's brother as well as her first cousin). Peter A. Vroman (also known as Peter Vroman, Jr.) served for two years under Captain Chris Stubach in Colonel Peter Vroman's Regiment. He also served as a Major in the Militia after the American Revolution and was awarded a pension of $80 in 1833, which was subsequently reduced to $20 per year in 1836.

The 1800 United State Federal Census, Schoharie, New York, lists Peter A. Vroman as head of household and indicates there were 16 people in his household including four slaves:

1800 United State Federal Census, Schoharie, New York	
	'POSSIBLE' IDENTITIES
2 males 26-45	Peter A. Vroman (37 years old), head of household; Unknown
2 males 16-26	Unknown (possibly mill or farm workers)
1 male 10-16	Adam Vroman, Jr. (14 years old), son
1 female 45-	Unknown
1 female 26-45	Angelica Vroman (34 years old), wife
1 female 10-16	Sara Vroman (12 years old), daughter
4 females under 10	Jannetie Vroman (8 years old), daughter; Christiana Vroman (6 years old), daughter; Maria Vroman (4 years old), daughter; Engeltie Vroman (2 years old), daughter
4 slaves	

Angelica and Peter A. Vroman had nine children: Adam Vroman, Jr., (1786-1866), Sara (Vroman) Haginer (1788-?), Jannetje Vroman (1791-?), Christiana Vroman (1794-1885), Maria (Vroman) Quackenbush (1796-1864), Engeltie or Anna Vroman (1798-1873), Gertrude or Gitty Vroman (1800-?) who married Peter C. Vroman, Catherine (Vroman) Hager (1802-1881), and Peter Meese Vroman (1805-?).

The 1802 Machin map *(Map 7)* suggests that, indeed, Peter A. Vrooman and his wife Angelica (the daughter of Colonel Peter Vroman) were living in the house in 1802 as well as running the mill. They were supporting quite a large household. The map pictures the house and the mill. Although it is quite small, the shape of the house on the map mirrors the Col. Vroman house and it appears to also show the two chimneys on the house.

Peter A. Vroman was involved with local politics but not as actively as his father-in-law, Colonel Peter Vroman. He was appointed sheriff of Schoharie in 1801 but only held the position for a few months. In 1802, a newspaper announcement declared that Vroman, as one of the Committee of Correspondence, would not support the candidacy of George Tiffany for Senator in the Western District "because I have no confidence in his political principles."[113] In 1810, Vroman published a message that the Judges of the Schoharie Court of Common Pleas would be meeting for the inspection of cloth. It's unknown if he was one of those judges or was solely responsible for publishing announcements about the Court.

In 1921, a Mr. and Mrs. George Albert Johnston (New York State natives) donated several items to the Alabama State Department of Archives and History. Among their donations was an 1814 certificate signed by the aforementioned George Tiffany, an ancestor of the Tiffany jewelry family. The certificate was "issued to Peter Vroman giving him the authority to sell wines and spirits at his home in the town of Schoharie."[114] Roscoe also notes that Henry Cady showed him an 1811 license given to Peter Vrooman "to keep an inn as it was necessary."[115] A newspaper notice in 1814 indicates several parcels of land were to be sold at auction at the house of Peter Vroman in the town of Schoharie. And interestingly, the same George Tiffany was the lawyer involved in the case. We have not yet found other information about Vroman's career. Perhaps he turned the house into a tavern. Roscoe indicates that Vroman paid an inn or tavern keeper excise tax of $5.00 in 1805. Or, perhaps he tried numerous professions to find his right niche. The Johnston family also donated a 1713 certificate of indenture relating to the purchase of land by Adam Vroman suggesting that the Johnstons might have had some direct connection to the Vroman family. Those Alabama Archives documents could not currently be located for further examination.

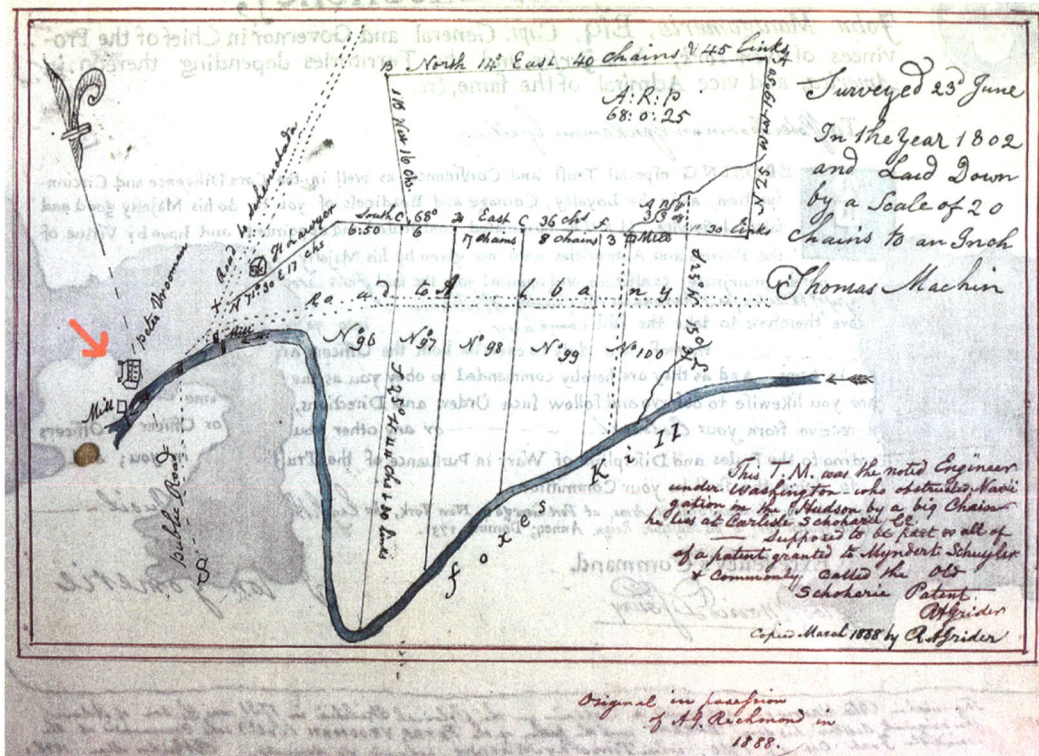

Map 7. (1802/1888) Thomas Machin's "The Old Schoharie Patent Granted to Myndert Schuyler, in the Year 1802." Copied by Rufus Alexander Grider, 1888. Grider's Albums. Courtesy of the New York State Library, Manuscripts and Special Collections. Arrow points to Peter Vroman house.

Jacob Snyder was a plaintiff in an 1813 land dispute tried in the Schoharie Circuit of the New York State Supreme Court. The case involved a partition deed which "contained an exception of all places which may be found convenient for erecting mills on a certain creek … it was held to mean only natural mill scats, or falls in the creek, and not places where mills might be erected and supplied with water by means of sluices …"[116] The case was based on a partition dead dated March 18, 1808 between Peter Vroman and Jacob Snyder and referred to lots from the Schoharie Patent that Vroman and Snyder held in common including Lot No. 117. The defendant (Lawrence) claimed he held title from Peter Vroman to 50 acres of land, including part of Lot. No. 117. The summary of the case indicated that Lawrence had erected a sawmill, an oil mill, a fulling mill, and a carding machine on the lot and that he had leased it to the sons and heirs of Jacob Snyder. And one of the witnesses testified that Lawrence "had been in quiet possession of the premises since 1789." It is unknown if the Col. Peter Vroman property was connected in any way to this claim.

In Josiah Priest's *Stories of the Revolution*, published in 1832, he writes, "the tories were in considerable strength on the road; especially at the forks where Vroman now lives, at the north end of the Schoharie flats, where the bridge crosses Foxen Creek."[117] This suggests that a 'Vroman', was living in the area in the early 1830s, perhaps Angelica and her husband Peter A. Vroman. The 'forks' noted above is also referred to as Vroman Crossing and was doubtless so named because of the various members of the Vroman family who lived nearby.

The 1810 United State Federal Census, Schoharie, New York lists Peter Vroman as head of household with 13 people in his household including two slaves:

1810 United State Federal Census, Schoharie, New York	
	'POSSIBLE' IDENTITIES
1 free white male 45 & over	Peter A. Vroman (47 years old), head of household
1 free white male under 10	Peter Meese Vroman (5 years old), son
1 free white female 26-44	Angelica Vroman (44 years old), wife
2 free white females 16-25	Jannetje (19 years old), daughter; Christiana Vroman (16 years old), daughter. *<Daughter Sara, 22, might have already been married>*
2 free white females 10-15	Marie (14 years old), daughter; Engeltie (12 years old), daughter
2 free white females under 10	Gertrude Vroman (10 years old), daughter; Catherine Vroman (8 years old), daughter
2 other free persons	Likely these were mill or farm workers
2 slaves	

The 1820 United State Federal Census, Schoharie, New York, lists Peter Vroman as head of household and indicates there were eight people in his household:

1820 United State Federal Census, Schoharie, New York	
	'POSSIBLE' IDENTITIES
1 free white male 45 & over	Peter A. Vroman (57 years old), head of household
1 free white male 10-15	Peter Meese Vroman (15 years old), son
1 free white male under 10	Unknown
1 free white female 45 & over	Angelica Vroman (54 years old), wife
3 free white females 16-25	Engeltie (22 years old), daughter; Gertrude Vroman (20 years old), daughter; Catherine Vroman (18 years old), daughter
1 free white females under 10	Unknown

The 1820 census lists one person engaged in agriculture, which was likely Peter A. Vroman. Two of the Vroman daughters, Jannetie and Christiana, were married by 1820, and Marie Vroman, who would have been about 24 years old, might not have survived childhood or perhaps she was married. The two children under 10 years old are unknown. There are no slaves listed.

Angelica and Peter A. Vroman's daughter, Catherine (known as Katie and Aunt Katy), married Adam D. Hager (1797-1873) on December 1, 1822 in her grandfather Col. Peter Vroman's, house. Katie and Adam D. Hager were 4th cousins, related through Adam H. Vroman (their common great-great-great grandfather). "On her wedding day, among other gifts, she <Katie Vroman> was presented a small negro, who later became a faithful slave."[119] It is possible Katie Vroman and her husband Adam D. Hager began their married life in the Col. Peter Vroman house. Others known to have married in the house include Mr. and Mrs. Isaac Ball and Daniel Vrooman and Louise Stevens.

Stories relating to slavery continued during the 19th century. Louise S. Vrooman wrote, in 1942, that her grandfather, Samuel B. Stevens, attached an existing slave quarter to the rear of the Vroman house. The building measured 16 ft. x 20 ft. She wrote, "It is said that once a little slave girl was pushed down these [cellar] stairs by her mistress who was undergoing a fit of temper. As the little girl fell, she hit her head and this caused the little girl's death."[120] There is no way to determine if that mistress was Katie Vroman. The same story was related in Roscoe's *History of Schoharie County*. He wrote in 1882, "The cellar stairs are still standing, down which, tradition says, a former Vrooman mistress, in anger, pushed her slave girl, thereby causing her death."[121] When Mildred Vrooman was asked if she had seen any ghosts walking the floors of the old Vroman house, she admitted, "she hears noises in the small hours of the night. But, born with a gift of humor, she adroitly parries the question of ghosts."[122]

The slave quarter was likely built prior to 1820 and attached to the west elevation of the house in the 1860s or 1870s when the Stevens were the property owners. The slave quarter was demolished in the 1950s. This building addition would not have spanned the full west elevation of the house. Map 15 provides a possible outline of that addition. The west side of the house is not symmetrical and much of the lower siding lacks beading, suggesting alterations through the centuries. The sole surviving remnant of the slave quarter is a small tilt-top table *(Fig. 37)* made of wood from the original slave quarters. The table is in the possession of the current house owners.

Fig. 37. Tilt-top table made from wood originally used in the Vroman slave quarters.

Label on bottom of table reads:
One of the early settlers in the Schoharie Valley, Secretary of the Committee of Safety, Commander of the Middle Fort during the Brant-Johnson raid of Oct 17, 1780, later Commandment of the Lower Fort, Assemblyman 1777-80, after the Declaration of Peace, Col. Vrooman came with his family to the north side of the Foxen Hill where about 1785 he built a home and mill opposite the Old Stone Fort. One of the buildings, later moved and attached to his home furnished the materials for this table. The top of virgin pine, sawed with a up and down saw, one side hand-planed covered with red "buttermilk" paint, is warped and weathered where it was exposed. The table legs are from a hand-hewn white oak timber, which once was a part of the frame of the building. It was well filled with hand cut nails. Restoration of the homestead begun in 1956 made these pieces available for combining into a replica of one of the tilt-top tables much used during the period in which the house was built. The reconstructed parts are now being returned from whence they came."

(signed) Horace M. Abrams
January 11, 1958?

The Vroman family did not list slaves after the 1810 census. In 1799, New York passed an act freeing slave children born after July 4, 1799, but those children remained indentured until they were young adults. In 1817, a new law freed slaves born before 1799 but delayed that action until 1827. Aunt Katy (Vroman) Hagar was given a young slave at her wedding in 1822 so the Vroman family were likely still slave holders into the 1820s. Indeed, in 1822, Col. Peter Vroman's brother, Adam B. Vroman deeded all of his "black men and women" to his grandsons, Alexander and Jacob.

It appears that Adam B. Vroman (Col. Peter Vroman's brother and father of Peter A. Vroman) willed *(Fig. 38)* a considerable amount of land in the town of Schoharie to his son, Peter A. Vroman as well as to various grandsons. It is difficult to distinguish the property based on the descriptions but it appears it may consist of land added to the plot owned by Col. Peter Vroman and deeded to his daughter, Angelica, the wife of Peter A. Vroman.

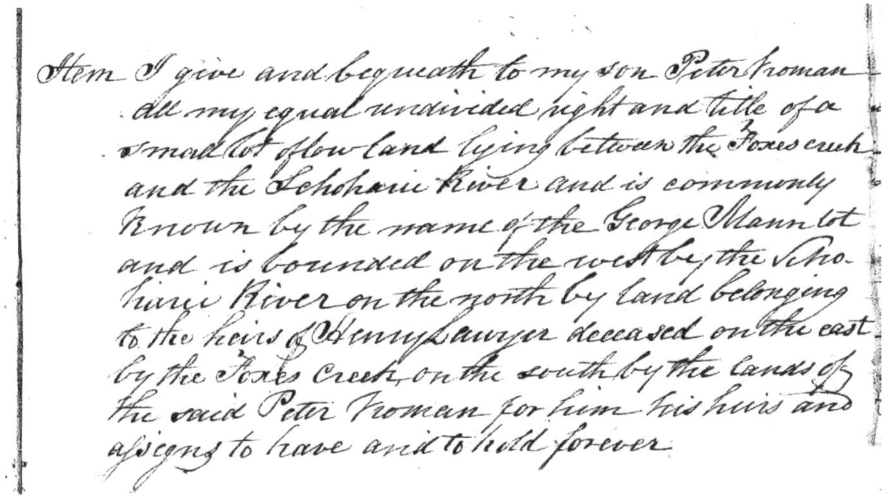
Item I give and bequeath to my son Peter Vroman
all my equal undivided right and title of a
small lot of low land lying between the Foxes creek
and the Schoharie River and is commonly
known by the name of the George Mann lot
and is bounded on the west by the Schoharie River on the north by land belonging
to the heirs of Henry Lawyer deceased on the east
by the Foxes creek, on the south by the lands of
the said Peter Vroman for him his heirs and
assigns to have and to hold forever

Fig. 38. Section of Adam B. Vroman's 1822 will deeding land to his son, Peter A. Vroman. "New York, Wills and Probate Records, 1659-1999." Accessed from Ancestry.com (March 11, 2018).

Transcription of Fig. 38: Item: I give and bequeath to my son, Peter Vroman all my equal undivided right and title of a small lot of low land lying between the Foxes creek and the Schoharie River and is commonly known by the name of the George Mann lot and is bounded on the west by the Schoharie River on the north by land belonging to the heirs of Henry Lawyer deceased on the east by the Foxes creek on the south by the lands of the said Peter Vroman for him his heirs and assigned to have and to hold forever.

It appears that starting in 1828, several pieces of the original Colonel Peter Vroman property and farm began to be sold by his heirs, Angelica Vroman and her husband Peter Vroman. In 1838, Angelica, the widow of Peter A. Vroman and daughter of Colonel Peter Vroman stated in her will:

> ...gave and bequeathed all those certain pieces and parcels of land mentioned in the will of Col. Peter Vrooman of the town of Schoharie which were bequeathed to her by said will, to her daughters, Anna and Gitty. She also mentioned all the personal estate, which was devised, to her father, Col. Peter Vrooman, in his will, dated Sept. 27, 1793. 'Should they recover land to the value of $600 I direct them to pay to granddaughter Marie Enders $700.'[123]

Gitty Vroman, Col. Vroman's granddaughter, was one of the executors of her mother's will. She married Peter C. Vroman who died in 1831, leaving Gitty (Gertie) a widow with three children under the age of five. When the three children were baptized in 1832, Gitty's parents (Major Peter A. Vroman and Angelica Vroman) were listed as "guardians of widow Vrooman's children."[124] Anna Vroman, the other daughter listed in her mother's will, apparently was a spinster. Anna and Gitty were Angelica Vroman's main beneficiaries. Angelica's husband, Peter A. Vroman, predeceased her.

1832-1844   Jacob Fisher

PROPERTY TRANSFER: Deed of Sale from Peter Vroman of Glen & his wife Angelica and others to Jacob Fisher, May 4, 1832 (recorded June 5, 1832, Schoharie, New York, Deed Book O, p. 409, County Recorder's Office, Schoharie, New York).

The Vroman family sold the house and property, after more than 50 years of ownership, for $7,500, which would translate to about $205,785 in 2017 dollars. Peter A. Vroman and Angelica Vroman (Col. Peter Vroman's daughter), then living in Glen, New York, owned the property. Other property owners were:
- Adam Vroman, Jr. & his wife Maria Lawyer – Col. Vroman's grandson; son of Angelica Vroman & Peter A. Vroman;
- Jacob Lawyer Vroman & his wife Lydia Wiley – Col. Vroman's great grandson; son of Adam Vroman, Jr. and Maria Lawyer;
- Julia Ann Vroman & her husband David Dietz – Col. Vroman's great granddaughter; daughter of Adam Vroman, Jr. and Maria Lawyer.

The property is described as the "patent granted to Myndert Schuyler and others commonly called the Old Schoharie Patent between the Schoharie Creek and Foxes Creek and bounded north by lands of Cornelius P. Vroman; the one half of which was devised to the said Peter Vroman by his father Adam B. Vroman deceased and containing in the whole thirty acres of land … including the buildings where the said Col. Peter Vroman formerly lived."[125] There are several separate parcels of land in the grant. The grant seems to combine lands of Col. Peter Vroman (the father of Angelica Vroman) and his brother Adam B. Vroman (the father of Major Peter A. Vroman, Angelica's husband).

Peter Snyder, who owned land contiguous to the Vroman property, also sold land to Jacob Fisher in 1832. Jacob Fisher (1805-1889) was a farmer and miller born in New York. His parents were Christine Lawyer and Peter Fisher. Roscoe in his *History of Schoharie County* writes, "The old mill [first known as the Eckerson mill] stood for many long years, and was replaced by the present one, by Jacob Fisher.[126] The mill was replaced about 1835.

The 1840 United State Federal Census, Schoharie, New York, lists Jacob Fisher as head of household and indicates there were nine people in his household and one was employed in agriculture. Agriculture has always been one of the mainstays of livelihood in the Schoharie Valley.

1840 United State Federal Census, Schoharie, New York	
	'POSSIBLE' IDENTITIES
1 free white male 30-39	Jacob Fisher (35 years old), head of household
1 free white male 15-19	Unknown – perhaps a worker
1 free male 10-14	Peter Fisher (10 years old), son
1 free male under 5	Albert Fisher (2 years old), son
1 free white female 70-79	Possibly Christina (Lawyer) Fisher, mother of Jacob Fisher
1 free white female 30-39	Sophia (Schell) Fisher (36 years old), wife
2 free white females 10-14	Nancy L. Fisher (12 years old), daughter; Unknown
1 free white female 5-9	Amanda Fisher (5 years old), daughter; Maria (1 year old), daughter

In 1842 and again in 1843, Jacob Fisher advertised for the sale of:

> A valuable farm, grist mill, saw mill, and other out buildings, pleasantly situated in the town and county of Schoharie, one mile north of Schoharie court house, and thirty miles from Albany, containing 250 acres of choice land, of which about 90 acres is interval land of the best quality. On the premises are about 400 bearing apple trees and other fruit. The grist mill will be sold separate or with the farm. The farm will be sold all together or in parcels to suit purchasers. A man wishing to buy about 50 or 100 acres cannot suit himself better elsewhere. Separate lots may be purchased, and payments made easy.... The subscriber likewise offers for sale the one half of the farm formerly owned by Jacob Lawyer, Jr., deceased containing 600 acres of land, lying one mile north of the court house, in the town and county of Scho-harie.[127]

The advertisement does not include mention of the house but it does include the mills and a sizeable amount of land. The Fisher family kept the property for about twelve years. By 1850, Jacob Fisher and his family were living in Esperance, Schoharie, New York.

PROPERTY TRANSFER:
- Deed of Sale from Jacob Fisher & his wife Sophia to Lorenzo Huff, July 16, 1845 (recorded July 2, 1845), Schoharie, New York, Deed Book 10, p.260, County Recorder's Office, Schoharie, New York $1,510.
- Deed of Sale from Lorenzo Huff & Jerusha Huff to Paul Haverly, March 28, 1848 (recorded March 30, 1848), Schoharie, New York, Deed Book 15, p. 159, County Recorder's Office, Schoharie, New York $1,850.
- Deed of Sale from Jacob Fisher & his wife Sophia to Smith Youngs, May 10, 1845, Schoharie, New York, Deed Book 10, p. 165. $2,266.
- Deed of Sale from Jacob Fisher & his wife Sophia to Cornelius P. Vroman, April 4, 1847 (recorded April 24, 1847). $200.

Schoharie experienced considerable expansion and growth after the American Revolution because the land was abundant and fertile. Census data showed steady increases in the population through the first half of the 19th century followed by a steady population decline. Much of the land was cleared for agriculture. This clearing provided an alternative source of income through lumbering. The mills at Foxes Creek supported both the lumbering industry and agriculture. Flax and hops were major crops grown in Schoharie. Flax was a household necessity used to make linen and hops was the key ingredient for beer production. By the mid 19th century, agricultural activities changed and the New York hops and flax industries began declining. The land suffered from over-cultivation, production shifted to the Midwest and the northwest coast, diseases attacked crops, and the mechanization of farm equipment all contributed to the late 19th century decline of agriculture and lumbering in Schoharie County. Gristmills were no longer essential for agriculture and sawmills were no longer essential for lumbering. The area's agriculture switched to other products such as dairy, potato, and alfalfa farming.

It appears that Fisher likely experienced some of the agricultural decline of Schoharie. He sold off parts of the considerable acreage he had purchased from the Vroman and Snyder families. The deed to Lorenzo Huff reads "land situate … on the north side of Foxes Creek and bounded on the north by lands of Cornelius P. Vroman, east by lands of Jacob M. Swart, and south and west by lands of John P. Griggs and the Foxes Creek, containing 23 acres and 24/100th of an acre … subject to a lease for one year to Jacob M. Snyder, and to a lease of the dwelling house for one year."

Lorenzo Huff (a.k.a. Lanzo) was listed in Louise Vrooman's account of residents of the Colonel Peter Vroman house but the deed description might not be sufficient to identify that he lived in the Vroman house, he might have lived next door. By 1848, Huff had sold the property to Paul and Maria Haverly, who owned property between 1848 and 1852. According to the 1850 United State Census, Huff was a hotel keeper. He and his wife, Jerusha, might have died shortly thereafter (between 1850 and 1861) because his two oldest sons moved to Michigan and the two youngest children ended up in St. Catharine's, Canada at what might have been an orphanage or some other type of institution.

1844-1860   John P. Griggs; Benjamin Griggs

PROPERTY TRANSFER
- Deed of Sale from Jacob Fisher & his wife Sophia to John P. Griggs, July 30, 1844 (recorded Aug. 6, 1844), Schoharie, New York, Deed Book 9, p. 206, County Recorder's Office, Schoharie, New York. $4,000.
- Deed of Sale from Jacob Fisher & his wife Sophia to John P. Griggs, May 10, 1845 (executed 20, 1845), Schoharie, New York, Deed Book 10, p. 164, County Recorder's Office, Schoharie, New York.

John Peter Griggs/Grigs (1797-1869) was christened at the High and Low Dutch Reformed Congregation of Schoharie. In 1823, John Griggs, Robert Knox and Schuyler Briggs were authorized to set up, keep, and maintain a ferry across the Schoharie River, near the fording place of John Enders. Prior to 1840, Griggs lived in Carlisle, Schoharie, New York. He and his family are listed in the 1840 Federal United State Census as living in Schoharie.

The 1844 deed from Fisher to Griggs for $4,000, has interesting descriptions of the property.

> … patent granted to Myndert Schuyler and other … called the Old Schoharie Patent, being the premises upon which the saw mill and grist mill erected by [Fisher] … shed … saw mill … mill dam… to the bulk head at the bridge above the mill; together with the privilege of the water for the use of the mill on said premises and the right to maintain the dam across said Foxes Creek at its present height. Also the right to a good road to and from said Mill. Also the right to the stone in the bottom of the creek for the use of said premises.

Griggs was actively involved in operating the mill. In 1844, he received an award at the Schoharie Fair for 50 pounds of superior manufactured buckwheat flour.[128] He was a leader in the community and was named as the Supervisor for the Town of Schoharie in 1846.[129] He was also the President of the Schoharie County Agricultural Society when it held a fair in Middleburgh, one year prior to either the Schoharie or Cobleskill fairs.

The 1845 deed from Fisher to Griggs includes another piece of land described as starting at the corner of the garden occupied by William Shay and including 43/100th of an acre upon which is situation the house occupied by Griggs. A note is made that the land doesn't include a small piece of land south of Foxes Creek previously sold to Cornelius Vroman.

The 1847 deed from Jacob Fisher to Cornelius P. Vroman included three acres south of Foxes Creek that had been fenced and occupied by Fisher. The deed "assigns the privilege [to Griggs] of going on and over the said premises for the purpose of repairing or rebuilding his Mill-Dam and cross the same [with] horses & … drawing timber and stone."[130]

Unfortunately, tragedy struck the Griggs family in 1849 *(Fig. 39)*. Jerome Griggs (1831-1849), a son of John P. Griggs, the owner of the Schoharie Mills near Fox's Creek Bridge, was killed on his way to Albany with a wagon filled with flour, almost certainly from his father's mill. Griggs and his friend, Francis Ross, were descending a hill near Gallupville when something disturbed his team of horses. Ross reined in the team and the wagon suddenly overturned. Rescuers were able to extract both Griggs and Ross and they were taken to a nearby home. John P. Griggs was notified and quickly came to his son's side. It is reported that they conversed with one another and there was hope that young Griggs would recover. But doctors discovered that Jerome's spine had been very gravely injured and he could not feel his limbs. Jerome died the next day. His companion, Ross, who had been trapped beneath the wagon was not severely injured and survived the accident. Jerome Griggs was only 18 years old when he died. He was buried at the Old Stone Church.

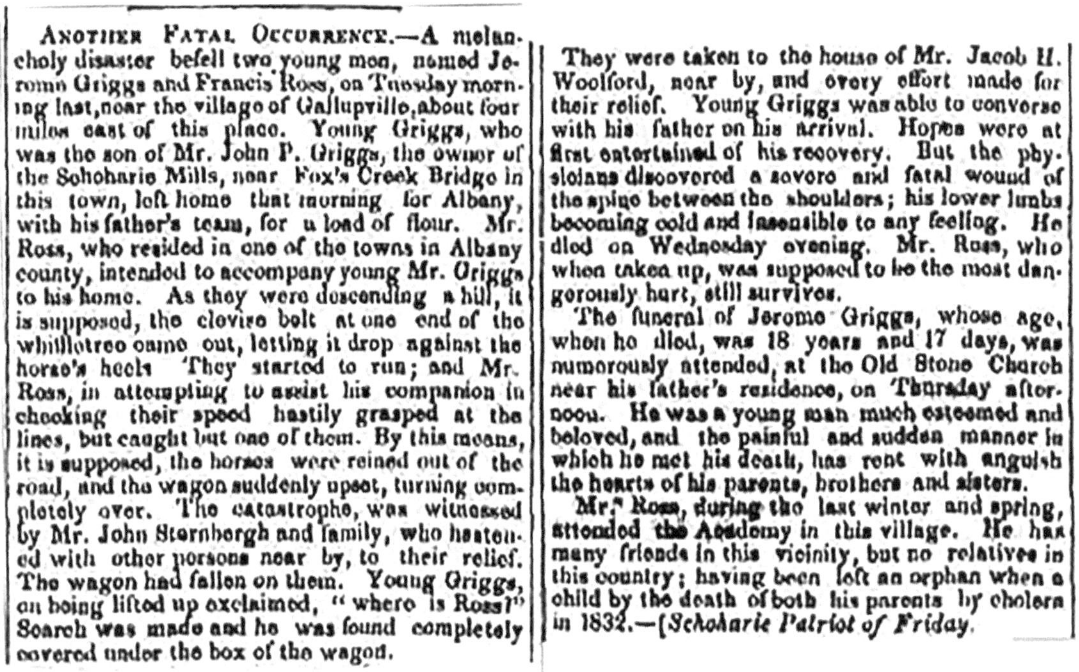

ANOTHER FATAL OCCURRENCE.—A melancholy disaster befell two young men, named Jerome Griggs and Francis Ross, on Tuesday morning last, near the village of Gallupville, about four miles east of this place. Young Griggs, who was the son of Mr. John P. Griggs, the owner of the Schoharie Mills, near Fox's Creek Bridge in this town, left home that morning for Albany, with his father's team, for a load of flour. Mr. Ross, who resided in one of the towns in Albany county, intended to accompany young Mr. Griggs to his home. As they were descending a hill, it is supposed, the clevis bolt at one end of the whiffletree came out, letting it drop against the horse's heels. They started to run; and Mr. Ross, in attempting to assist his companion in checking their speed hastily grasped at the lines, but caught but one of them. By this means, it is supposed, the horses were reined out of the road, and the wagon suddenly upset, turning completely over. The catastrophe was witnessed by Mr. John Sternbergh and family, who hastened with other persons near by, to their relief. The wagon had fallen on them. Young Griggs, on being lifted up exclaimed, "where is Ross?" Search was made and he was found completely covered under the box of the wagon.

They were taken to the house of Mr. Jacob H. Woolford, near by, and every effort made for their relief. Young Griggs was able to converse with his father on his arrival. Hopes were at first entertained of his recovery. But the physicians discovered a severe and fatal wound of the spine between the shoulders; his lower limbs becoming cold and insensible to any feeling. He died on Wednesday evening. Mr. Ross, who when taken up, was supposed to be the most dangerously hurt, still survives.

The funeral of Jerome Griggs, whose age, when he died, was 18 years and 17 days, was numerously attended, at the Old Stone Church near his father's residence, on Thursday afternoon. He was a young man much esteemed and beloved, and the painful and sudden manner in which he met his death, has rent with anguish the hearts of his parents, brothers and sisters.

Mr. Ross, during the last winter and spring, attended the Academy in this village. He has many friends in this vicinity, but no relatives in this country; having been left an orphan when a child by the death of both his parents by cholera in 1832.—[Schoharie Patriot of Friday.

Fig. 39. Newspaper article about Jerome Griggs fatal accident. Albany New York Argus, June 27, 1849.

Jerome was described as a "young man much esteemed and beloved, and the painful and sudden manner in which he met his death, has rent with anguish the hearts of his parents, brothers and sister."[131]

The 1850 United State Federal Census, Schoharie, New York, lists John P. Griggs as head of household and indicates there are eight people in his household and three members of the household were millers. Griggs' real estate was listed as being worth $2,000. The household consisted of:

1850 United State Federal Census, Schoharie, New York			
Name	Age	Relationship	Profession
John P. Griggs	52	Head of household	miller
Margaret Griggs	45	Wife	
Benjamin Griggs	23	Son	miller
Mary Griggs	21	Daughter	
Hiram Griggs	14	Son	
Gideon Griggs	12	Son	
Mary Griggs	82	Mother of John P. Griggs	
Attwood Quackenbush	21		miller

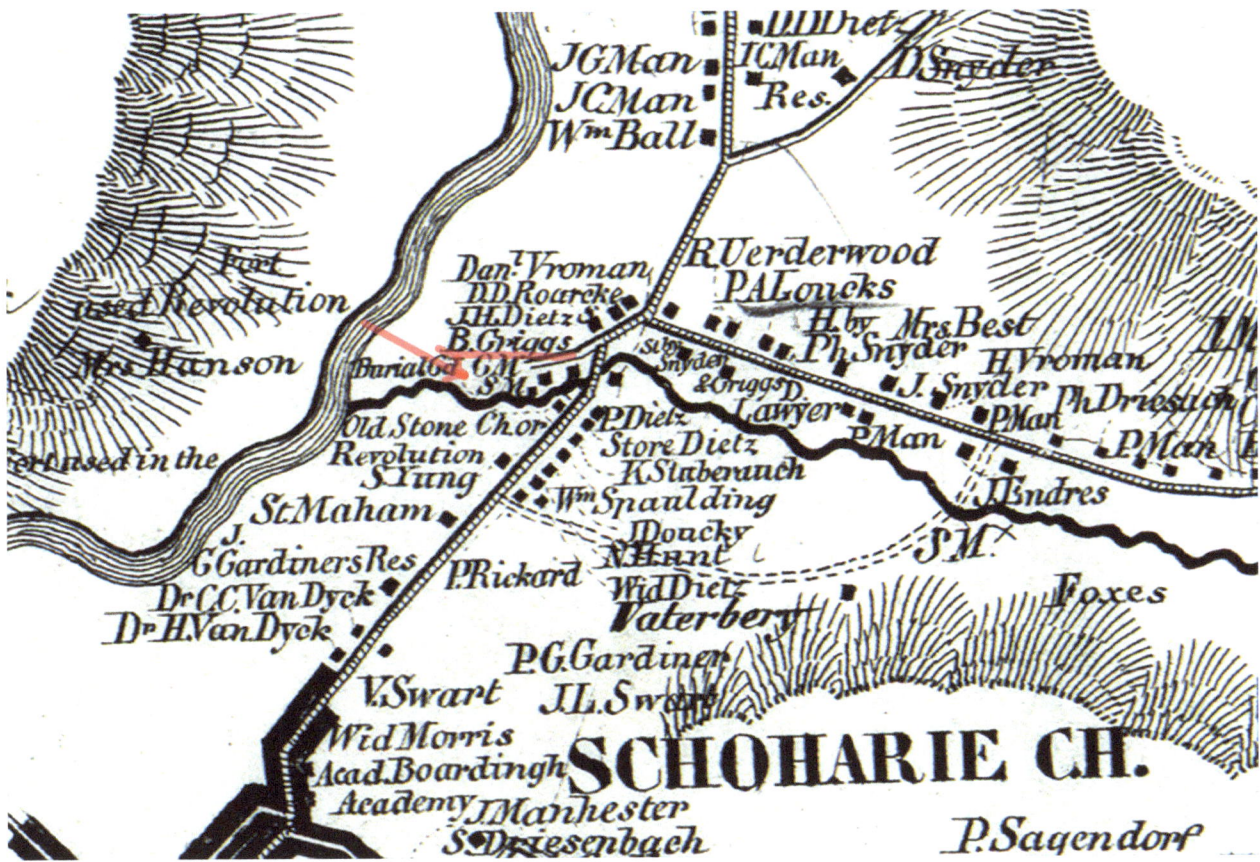

Map 8. Detail from E. Wenig, Wm. Lorey and Robert Pearsall Smith's "Map of Schoharie County, New York." Retrieved from the Library of Congress. Note: B. Griggs (underlined in red); G.M. and S.M. grist mill and saw mill (red arrow).

According to the 1855 New York State Census, it appears that there are three families living in the Col. Peter Vroman house: the John P. Griggs family, the John J. Dietz family, and the Benjamin Griggs family. The house is listed as a frame house worth about $800. Two of the male adult occupants are millers (John Griggs and his son Benjamin Griggs) and one is a mason (John Dietz). The household of fourteen people consisted of:

1855 New York Census, Schoharie, New York			
Name	**Age**	**Relationship**	**Profession**
John P. Griggs	57	Head of Household	miller
Margaret Griggs	54	Wife	
Mary E. Griggs	26	Daughter	teacher
Hiram Griggs	19	Son	
Gideon V. Griggs	16	Son	
John J. Dietz	40	Head of Household	mason
Cynthia Dietz	29	Wife	
Catharine L. Dietz	7	Daughter	
Edwin Dietz	6	Son	
Charles Dietz	1	Son	
Benjamin Griggs	28	Head of Household	miller
Catharine Griggs	29	Wife	
Mary E. Griggs	2	Daughter	
Nancy Keyser	58	Mother-in-law	widowed

In 1856, the property was sold to John P. Griggs's eldest son, Benjamin Griggs and to Hiram Hunt. Hiram Hunt was a mason and Benjamin Griggs was a miller. It is unknown how their businesses might have intersected.

[Deed of Sale from John P. Griggs & his wife Margaret to Benjamin Griggs and Hiram Hunt, March 31, 1856, Schoharie, New York, Deed Book 30, p. 545, County Recorder's Office, Schoharie, New York $4,000].

The property is described as the "mills and premises, now and lately occupied by the said John P. Griggs on the west side of Foxes Creek, bounded north by lands of Jacob H. Deitz, east and south by Foxes Creek and west by Foxes Creek and the lands of the said Jacob H. Deitz. Containing 7 acres of land, more or less." Hiram Griggs, a son of John P. Griggs, assisted his father at the mills for a few years after 1856. Hiram later became a lawyer, was elected to the State Legislature,[132] and became the first mayor of Altamont, New York

An 1856 map of New York *(Map 8)* includes the names of many residents including B. Griggs (Benjamin Griggs) and J. H. Dietz (Jacob H. Dietz). The bridge over Fox Creek is in the same location as the present covered bridge.

The Griggs family had financial problems during this time. The property was mortgaged and in 1858 it appears that John P. Griggs was unable to pay his considerable debt. His property and effects were to be sold with the proceeds going to his creditors.[133] The inventory to be sold to pay Griggs debts is quite extensive and gives us a sense of the type of animals, vehicles, and materials he owned.

- 1 black mare; 1 bay gelder; 1 lumber two-horse wagon; 1 truck wagon; 1 lumber one-horse wagon; 1 buggy 1 set double harness; 1 set one-horse harness; 1 lumber two-horse sleigh; one-horse sleigh; 1 saddle; 1 lock sleigh; a lot of fowls
- quantity of hay in the barn; quantity of straw in the barn
- 136 butter firkins at Seeleys; 71 butter firkins at Jacob Matties (sp.?); 72 butter firkins at J. Chamberlaine; 15 butter firkins in cellar
- 4,500 staves at home; 2,000 staves at D. Smithens (sp.?)
- timber sawed on Shafer's land to make about 2,000 staves at the halves; 2,000 hoop poles in cellar; 142 saw logs at the mill; 42 saw logs on mill yard, drawn, from Shafers to be sawed for one half; 100 saw logs cut in Shafers woods to be drawn and sawed, for one half; 2,800 feet of pine lumber at the mill

The inventory specifies that some items, such as butter firkins and hoop poles,[134] were stored in the cellar, probably of the house. In addition, staves[135] were stored "at home," perhaps in an outbuilding or maybe even the cellar.

The bankruptcy document also includes the individuals to whom Griggs was indebted. A dollar in 1858 would be equivalent to $29.41 in 2015. His debt of $12,431 owed in 1858 would be equivalent to the sizeable sum of $365,595 in 2015 money. Some of the individuals Griggs owed money to include:

•	Hiram Hunt $50	•	Peter S. Swart $62
•	John Deitz $4	•	Jacob Becker $20
•	William Dietz Jr. $250	•	Weidman Dominick $12.24
•	Heirs of Margaret Vroman $50	•	Caty Dietz $25
•	Peter Dominick $150	•	Stephen Badgley $20
•	Schoharie County Bank $50	•	Benjamin Griggs $500
•	Schenectady Bank $200	•	Abram Hunt $462
•	George B. Badgley $30	•	Gideon V. Griggs $100
•	George Manning $34	•	Hiram Griggs $100
•	Josiah Mann $18	•	B. Potter Lake $3

Many of the names are familiar Schoharie families. In addition, there were unsettled accounts from people including Smith Youngs, Jacob Vroman, David B. Vroman, Adam Vroman, John Stryker, and Benjamin Griggs among others. By 1860, Griggs was able to sell the property.

John P. Griggs is listed as living in Schoharie in the 1859 *New York State Business Directory*. By 1860, John P. Griggs, his wife Margaret, and two members of their family are living in Guilderland, Albany, New York where John is listed as a farmer with a personal worth of $200. His son, Gideon, was listed as a farm laborer and daughter, Mary, was a teacher.

1860-1863 Simeon Fairlee

Property Transfer: Deed of Sale from Hiram Griggs and Benjamin P. Lake, assignees of John P. Griggs and Margaret Griggs to Simeon Fairlee of Knox, Albany County, April 2, 1860 (recorded April 6, 1860), Schoharie, New York, Deed Book 37, p. 315, County Recorder's Office, Schoharie, New York. $6,500. The mortgage on the property and the interest were to be paid from this sale.

Simeon Fairlee (1816-1908) was a miller. The 1860 United State Federal Census, Schoharie, New York, lists Simeon Fairlee as head of household and indicates there were two families, nine people in his household. The household consisted of:

1860 United State Federal Census, Schoharie, New York			
Name	**Age**	**Relationship**	**Profession**
Simeon Fairlee	40	Head of Household	miller
Susan Fairlee	30	Wife	
Anne E. Fairlee	6	Daughter	
Charles W. Fairlee	4	Son	
Milton Fairlee	1	Son	
Ephraim Mann	43	Head of Household	mechanic
Sophia Mann	34	Wife	
Ida Mann	14	Daughter	
Edward v. Mann	5	Son	

The Fairlee Family did not live in the house for very long. An advertisement *(Fig. 40)* appeared in the *Schoharie New York Patriot* in October 1860, only six months after Fairlee purchased the property. In the advertisement, Fairlee indicates he wants to move west. He was a resident of Knox, Albany County in 1860 when he purchased the house and by 1865, Fairlee was back in Knox. The advertisement lists the property at seven acres including mills and a "good house and outbuildings." The house is described as "large and suitable for three families."

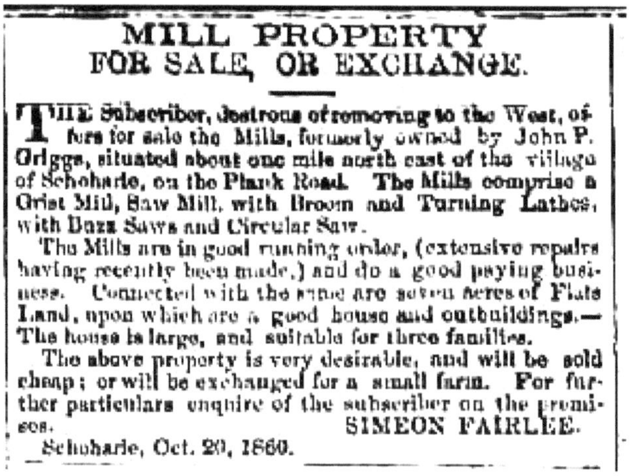
MILL PROPERTY
FOR SALE, OR EXCHANGE.

THE Subscriber, desirous of removing to the West, offers for sale the Mills, formerly owned by John P. Griggs, situated about one mile north east of the village of Schoharie, on the Plank Road. The Mills comprise a Grist Mill, Saw Mill, with Broom and Turning Lathes, with Buzz Saws and Circular Saw.

The Mills are in good running order, (extensive repairs having recently been made,) and do a good paying business. Connected with the same are seven acres of Flats Land, upon which are a good house and outbuildings.—The house is large, and suitable for three families.

The above property is very desirable, and will be sold cheap; or will be exchanged for a small farm. For further particulars enquire of the subscriber on the premises.
SIMEON FAIRLEE.
Schoharie, Oct. 20, 1860.

Fig. 40. Mill property advertisement, "Schoharie New York Patriot," October 1860.

1863-1879   Samuel B. Stevens (Stephens)
1879-1912   Charles B. Stevens

PROPERTY TRANSFERS:
- Deed of Sale from Smith Youngs to Samuel B. Stevens, March 20, 1863, Schoharie, New York, Deed Book 42, p. 91, County Recorder's Office, Schoharie, New York.[136]
- Deed of Sale from Samuel B. Stevens and Pamelia Stevens to Charles B. Stevens, April 10, 1877 (recorded March 4, 1879), Schoharie, New York, Deed Book 83, p. 415, County Recorder's Office, Schoharie, New York.
  - o   Samuel Stevens transferred his property to his son, Charles B. Stevens.
- Deed of Sale from Mary M. Handy, Pamelia Stevens, Martha H. Cady and Giles Stevens to Charles B. Stevens, Feb. 11, 1884, Schoharie, New York, Deed Book 95, p. 609, County Recorder's Office, Schoharie, New York.
  - o   This deed appears to provide greater clarity and description to the 1877 deed. Mary M. Handy (daughter of Samuel B. Stevens); Pamelia Stevens (wife of Samuel B. Stevens); Martha H. Cady (daughter of Samuel B. Stevens); Giles Stevens (son of Samuel B. Stevens).

Samuel Burlingame Stevens (1803-1884) was a farmer in Schoharie prior to purchasing the Colonel Peter Vroman home and mill in 1863. Stevens is listed in several Tax Assessment Lists. In 1864, his income exceeded $600 and he had a carriage and harness valued at $75. In 1865, he had a carriage and pianoforte and paid a $3 tax.

Samuel Stevens, along with his son, Charles Stevens (1838-1915), operated the grist and saw mills on the property for a considerable amount of time. Mary (or Mercy) Handy, the daughter of Samuel Stevens, moved into her parents' home along with her four young children when her husband, Marvin Handy, died in 1859. The Stevens family was quite large and at times, there were up to 14 people living in the house. Louise Vrooman wrote that her grandfather, Samuel Stevens, some time in the 1860s or 1870s, moved the former freestanding slave quarters and attached it to the house with long iron rods. The addition increased the capacity of the house.

During one of their renovations, the Stevens family might have hidden a shoe above the door lintel between the ceiling of the second floor and the attic floor. The shoe *(Fig. 41, 42)* was found during a 2013 restoration. Al Saguto, the Colonial Williamsburg master shoemaker, indicated it is probably a woman's shoe from about 1870. It couldn't be much earlier because the top part of the shoe has machine stitching and sewing machines were not introduced until 1861. Parts of the shoe are hand-sewn. This 'country' shoe is made of kid leather with a diagonal weave cotton twill lining. The sole of the shoe retains some field dirt and there's even some evidence that mice have nibbled on the shoe.

The practice of *concealed shoes* appears to have originated about 1500. People sometimes hid old boots and shoes in chimneys and walls to bring good luck to their houses and to ward off evil spirits. The shoes are always worn out and very often there is only one shoe. Most concealed shoes have been found in Britain but occasional cases have been reported in the United States. The discovery of the shoe was reported to the Northampton Museums and Art Gallery, Northampton, England to be included in their international Concealed Shoe Index. The Stevens concealed shoe has been replaced with a ca. 2010 Heyman shoe along with several mementos of Schoharie and events occurring in 2014.

Fig. 41. Concealed shoe shown in its original location, between the ceiling of the 2d floor bathroom and the attic floor.

Fig. 42. Concealed shoe found in Vroman house.

In 1864, Charles B. Stevens married Ida Mann, who spent part of her youth in the Vroman house when Simon Fairlee was the homeowner. The 1865 New York State Census, Schoharie, New York, lists eight people in the house including Samuel B. Stevens and Charles B Stevens but not yet Ida (Mann) Stevens. The household consisted of:

1865 New York State Census, Schoharie, New York				
Name	Age	Relationship	Profession	Other Information
Samuel B. Stevens	62	Head of Household	miller	Living in a frame house
Permelia Stevens	57	Wife		
Mercy Handy	35	Widowed daughter		
Charles B. Stevens	26	Son		
Martha Stevens	21	Daughter		
Benjamin Handy	15	Grandson		
Ellen Handy	10	Granddaughter		
Mary Pamelia Handy	8	Granddaughter		

Marian S. Lynes reported that a "Mr. Dings and Mr. Silas Baker lived in the [Vroman] house."[137] In 1850, Dings operated the Bramanville Grist Mill (near Howes Cave, Schoharie, New York) and in 1866, he operated the Huntersland Grist Mill (Huntersland, Schoharie, New York). In 1863, David Dings of Schoharie registered for the United State Civil War draft as a 30-year-old married miller from Schoharie. He enlisted on September 3, 1864 and mustered out on June 10, 1865. Paul Mattice in his book on grist mills reported that Dings was considered an expert millwright and a mechanical genius and was often called upon to repair mills. Louise Vrooman wrote that:

> Mr. Dings was lost one day, so the story goes, and a search was started as his family was greatly concerned lest he might have fallen in the creek and drowned. As it turned out, Mr. Dings had imbibed too freely and had put himself away to sleep it off. As night was coming on and the searchers were becoming discouraged, who should appear apparently from nowhere but Mr. Dings. The din and calling of the searchers had aroused him. Being scolded by Grandmother Cady,[138] he winked and blinked and finally stuttered, 'Are you sorry I was not drowned?'[139]

An 1866 Beers map *(Map 9)* of Schoharie County displays the Stevens property on Fox's Creek as well as the G[rist] Mill and S[aw] Mill. The small rectangle at the crossroads of the Fox Creek and two roads likely represents the Col. Vroman house even though the name "Stevens" is shown on the other side of the road. It has been suggested that this map is somewhat difficult to read, "as a result of the placement of the Old State Highway, Structures … [Colonel Peter Vroman house] appear on different sides of the street."[140] There wasn't sufficient room to show full resident surnames in the correct places. The railroad tracks shown in the 1866 map were for the Schoharie Valley Railway built in 1866 and founded by Jacob Vroman, a great nephew of Col. Peter Vroman.

In 1866, Charles B. Stevens sold his interest in the Stevens & Barton flour and feed business[141] to his partner, Alonzo W. Barton. Barton was a miller and had served in the Civil War. The business was located in a building then called the Gates building in Schoharie.

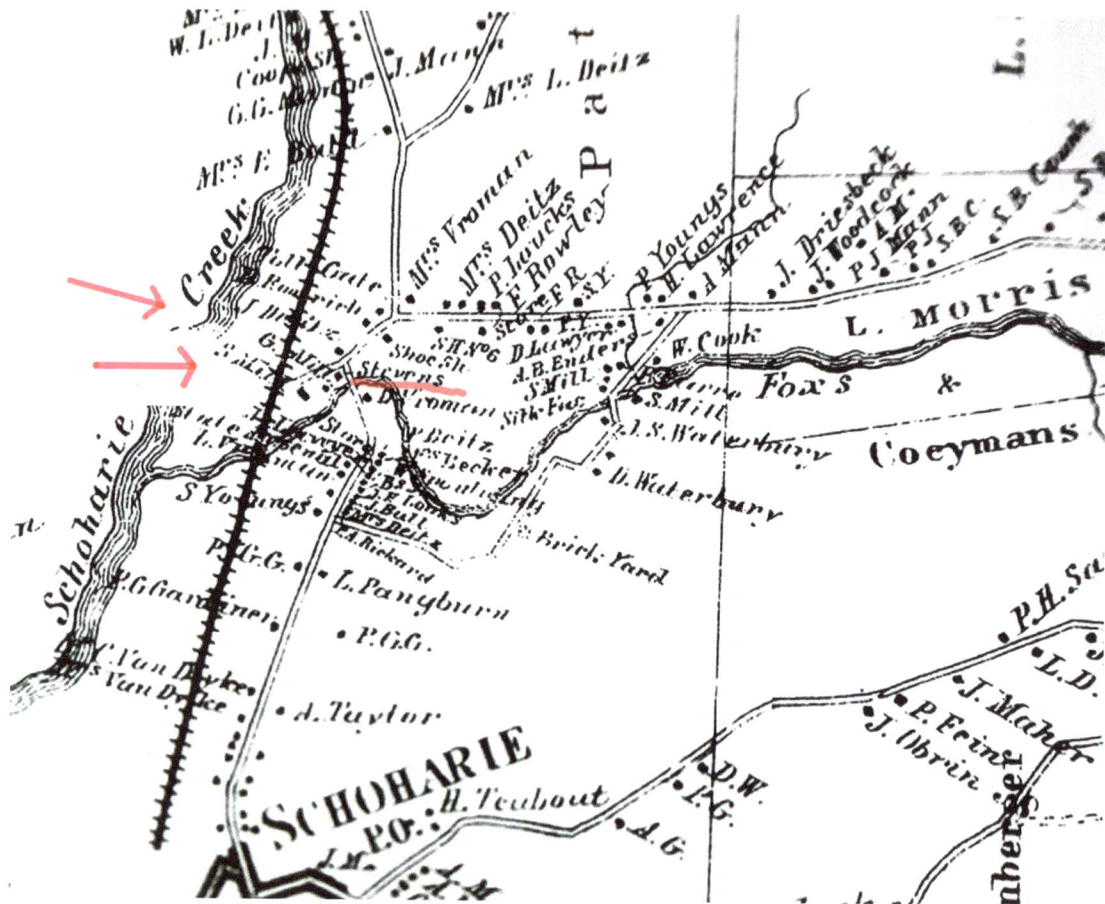

Map 9. (1866) Detail from S.N. Beers & D.G. Beers' New Topographical Atlas of Schoharie Co., New York.
Note: Stevens (underlined in red), arrows point to G[rist] Mill, S[aw] Mill along Foxes Creek and a square
representing Stevens house.

The 1870 United State Federal Census, Schoharie, New York, lists Samuel B. Stephens, a miller, as head of household and indicates there were 14 people in his household. The household consisted of:

1870 United State Federal Census, Schoharie, New York				
Name	**Age**	**Relationship**	**Profession**	**Other Information**
Samuel B. Stephens	67	Head of household	Miller	Real estate $12,000 Personal estate $3,000
Permelia Stephens	62	Wife	Housekeeper	
Mary M. Handy	40	Widowed daughter of Samuel Stephens	Dressmaker	Personal estate $1,000
Ellen Handy	15	Mary Handy's daughter		
Permelia Handy	13	Mary Handy's daughter		
Charles R. Stephens	32	Samuel Stephens' son	Miller	Personal estate $400
Ida Stephens	25	Charles R. Stephens wife	Housekeeper	
Frances Stephens	3	Charles R. Stephens' daughter		
Mary L. Stephens	4 mnths	Charles R. Stephens' daughter		
Jacob H. Rosekrans	39	Head of household	Miller	Personal estate $500
Alidale Rosekrans	32	Jacob Rosekrans' wife	Housekeeper	
Charles Rosekrans	7	Jacob Rosekrans' son		
Josiah M. Rosekrans	5	Jacob Rosekrans' son		
Arthur Rosekrans	3	Jacob Rosekrans' son		

Jacob Rosekrans was most likely helping Samuel B. Stevens and his son, Charles B. Stevens, with the mill operation. Rosekrans was one of the "last of the Schoharie mill wrights who had the know-how of dressing millstones for the grinding of wheat for bread."[142]

Samuel B. Stevens is listed in the 1872/3 *Gazetteer and Business Directory of Schoharie County, New York*, as the proprietor of grist, saw, and turning mills. The 1875 New York State Census, Schoharie, lists Samuel B. Stevens as head of household and indicates there were 11 people in his household. The household consisted of:

1875 New York State Census, Schoharie, New York				
Name	**Age**	**Relationship**	**Profession**	**Other Information**
Samuel B. Stevens	72	Head of household	Farmer	Frame house worth $1,500
Pamelia Stevens	61	Wife		
Maria Handy	43	Widowed daughter		
Benjamin Handy	25	Maria Handy's son	Law student	
Ella Handy	20	Maria Handy's daughter		
Permlia Handy	18	Maria Handy's daughter		
Charles Stevens	37	Son	Farmer	
Ida Stevens	28	Wife of Charles Stevens		

Francis Stevens	7	Charles Stevens' daughter		
Louisa Stevens	5	Charles Stevens' daughter		
Samuel B. Stevens	2	Charles Stevens' son		

Louise Stevens Vrooman, in her article in *The Schoharie County Historical Society Quarterly Review* states that a Silas Baker also lived in the Col. Vroman house. Silas Baker was born in 1840 in Middleburgh, New York. He and his wife had a daughter who was born in Wisconsin in 1867 and he continued to reside in Wisconsin where he is working in a gristmill, according to the 1870 United State Federal Census. By 1875, the New York State Census lists Baker, along with his wife and young daughter, but not as part of the Stevens household. So, we do not know exactly when he might have lived and likely worked on the Stevens property but it was likely at the beginning or end of the 1870s. By 1880 Silas Baker and his family were living in Esperance, Schoharie, New York and by 1900 he was a baker, rather than a miller, living in Broome, New York.

The Stevens' mill business appeared successful. In 1879, Charles Stevens announced he would install a steam engine in his Fox's Creek mills.[143] Stevens & Son indicated they were going to build a stone dam across Fox's Creek.[144] The Stevens were waiting until the weather warmed up before making those improvements.

In the late 1870s, Samuel and Pamelia Stevens transferred the property to their son, Charles B. Stevens. Samuel likely thought it time to pass along responsibility for the mills since he was in his 70s. The deed states Charles "agrees to take charge and operate said mills in a good and faithful manner and to work said land in a good and husband like manner." Yet in the 1880 U.S. Federal Census, Samuel is still listed as a miller and his son, Charles, is listed as working in a mill.

The 1880 United State Federal Census, Schoharie, New York, lists Samuel B. Stevens as head of household and indicates there were only two people in his household. His son, Charles Stevens is listed below him in the schedule but he is living in a separate residence. The household consisted of:

1880 U. S. Federal Census, Schoharie, New York			
Name	**Age**	**Relationship**	**Profession**
Samuel B. Stephens	77	Head of household	Miller
Pamelia Stephens	72	wife	Keeping house

Charles Stephens has a separate listing in the 1880 census:

1880 U. S. Federal Census, Schoharie, New York			
Name	**Age**	**Relationship**	**Profession**
Charles Stephens	42	Head of household	Works in mill
Ida Stephens	28	Wife	Keeping house
Francis E. Stephens	13	Daughter	Attending school
Mary L. V. Stephens	10	Daughter	Attending school
Samuel B. Stephens	8	Son	Attending school

Fig. 43. Rufus Alexander Grider's drawing of the Lower Fort area, 1887. Grider's Albums. Courtesy of the New York State Library, Manuscripts and Special Collections. The Vroman house is barely visible in the lower right corner. The view is from the north bank of Fox Creek with the Old Stone Fort in the background.

In 1887, Rufus Alexander Grider drew a watercolor scene looking towards the Lower Fort from the north bank of Fox Creek *(Fig. 43)*. The house shown in the lower right corner is probably the Colonel Peter Vroman house. The drawing includes Fox Creek, the Old Stone Fort, and the mountains surrounding the area. Grider was an historic preservationist. Many of his drawings are the only existing record of buildings long gone. Unfortunately, in this case, Grider did not draw details of the house. But he certainly provided a glimpse of its idyllic setting along the creek. The earliest known views of the Vroman house and the existent photographs of the mill and dam are from the late 19th century or early 20th century. *(Figs. 47-53)*

The 1895 New York State Census, Schoharie, New York, records Charles Stevens and a total of six people in his household. Charles B. Stevens continues to be a miller. The household consisted of:

1895 New York State Census, Schoharie, New York			
Name	**Age**	**Profession**	**[Assumed relationship]**
Charles B. Stevens	56	Miller	Head of household
Pamelia Stevens	84		Charles' mother
Ida Stevens	46		Charles' wife
Francis E. Stevens	25	Music teacher	Charles' daughter
Louise V. Stevens	22	Attending school	Charles' daughter
Burne? Stevens	20	School teacher	Charles' daughter

There were at least three known mill fires. The first was in 1780 during the Johnson/Brant Raid on Eckerson's mill. Then, on May 22, 1886, a fire broke out at the Stevens gristmill. The loss was listed at $5,000 with Stevens' insurance paying $2,200.[145] Unfortunately, in 1898 "the grist mill at Fox's Creek, just below Schoharie, owned by Mr. Stevens, was destroyed by fire on Thursday. He was running the mill at the time of the fire was discovered, and it is supposed that the heating of the journal caused the conflagration. The mill was built some fifteen years ago. There was $1,500 worth of insurance on the property.[146] Evidently, the second Stevens fire was just too much and almost 140 years of milling on the Vroman property came to an end. The 1899 *Directory and Reference Book of Schoharie County* lists Charles B. Stevens but he is no longer listed as a miller, indeed he is not listed with a profession.

According to local lore, there continued to be some remnants of the mill until about 1989.[147] The land around the mill was disturbed by the 1954 relocation of Route 30 and the realignment of Fox Creek. There is no above ground evidence of the mill location although there continues to be one physical feature that might give hints of the old mill site *(Fig. 44)*.

Fig. 44. Stone wall or fence on Vroman property. It is believed that this stone wall or fence might originally have been associated with the mill. It is located west of the Col. Peter Vroman house.

Fig. 45. Grinding wheel fragments, likely from the mill originally on the Vroman property.

Fig. 46. Hand-wrought iron bolts found near stone wall.

Fig. 47. Photograph of Stevens mill. Note partial view of house in upper right corner. Unknown date but likely ca.1900. The original photograph is in the Old Stone Fort Museum.

Fig. 48. Blow-up of Fig. 47 showing the west elevation of the Col. Peter Vroman house. It might show part of the slave attachment added to the house in the 1860s/1870s.

75

Fig. 49. Col. Vroman house, later owned by Samuel & Charles Stevens. Photograph from "Souvenir Book of Schoharie," 1904.

Fig. 50. Another view of the Col. Peter Vroman house showing part of the mill works.
Original photograph in the Old Stone Fort Museum. This was likely around the same time as Fig. 49.

Fig. 51. View of the Stevens mill dam and the south elevation of the Col. Peter Vroman house. The Dietz house is also partially visible to the right as is the Tory Tavern to the east. The iron bridge, built in 1872, served as the main road going south into the Village of Schoharie. A concrete bridge replaced the iron one in 1917. This photo can thus be dated no earlier than 1872 and no later than 1917.

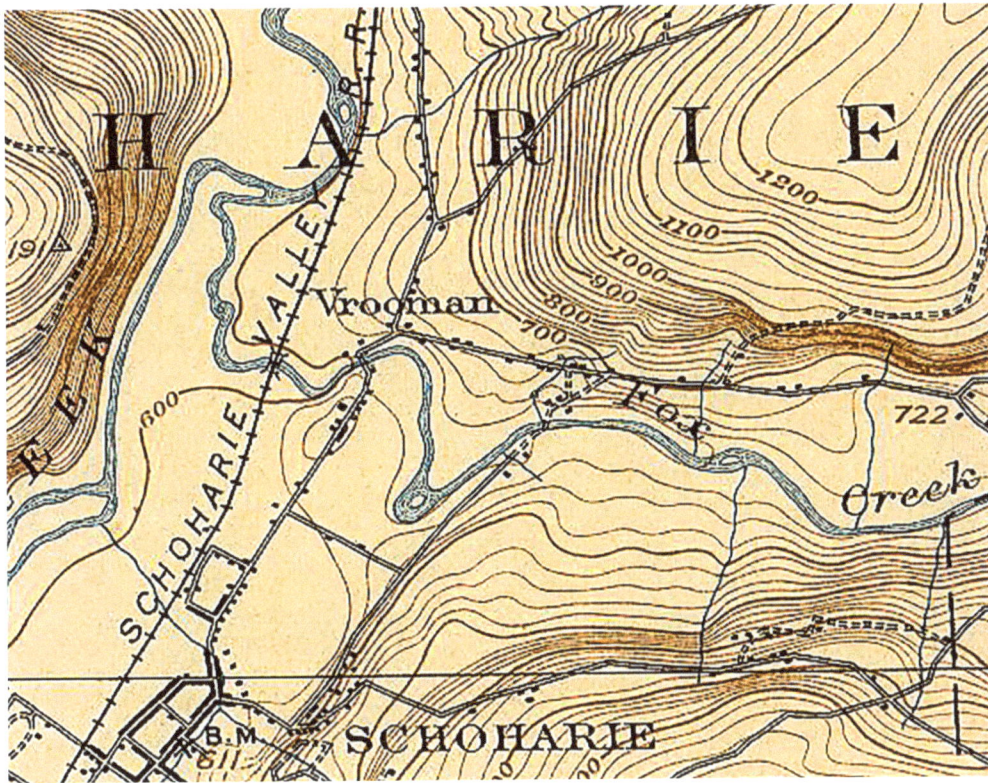

Map 10. (1900) Map showing homes (designated by dots) along Fox Creek. 'Vrooman' likely refers to the area, close to the house, called Vroman Corners. This map also shows the railroad that was close-by. USGS Maps of New England & New York, Schoharie, New York

Fig. 52. Remnants of the mill dam, looking west towards the Schoharie Creek.
Photograph from "Souvenir Book of Schoharie," 1904.

Fig. 53. View looking west on the Schoharie Creek. Note: men fishing in the Creek. Photograph from
"Souvenir Book of Schoharie," 1904.

Several fragments of grinding wheels have been found on the property *(Fig. 45)*. A large iron bolt *(Fig. 46)* was also found near the stone wall. It is thought to possibly be a remnant of the mill. The long bolt is hand wrought and varies in thickness. It might be some type of fastener, for example to connect a beam. Fire might have caused its bend. The bolt was made in the late 18th or early 19th century. The lower bolt was found nearby.

In 1900, an article reported that D. B. Vroman[148] was driving a spirited team of John H. Warner's horses. When the team got near the Fox Creek Bridge, the team spooked. Warner jumped out but Vroman stayed in the carriage and struck his head when the carriage hit a ditch. One of the horses ran across the bridge, hit a tree at Charles Stevens' home, and was killed. Vroman was knocked unconscious and suffered amnesia for about two hours and then "he finally came to his senses."[149] This newspaper story confirms that the Charles Stevens family was living in the house in 1900.

Charles B. Stevens and his wife, Ida, are living alone, and he is recorded as a farmer in the 1910 United States Federal Census. It is likely they are still living in the Col. Vroman house. Ida Stevens died in 1912 and Charles left Schoharie to live with his daughter, Francis E. (Stevens) West, in Geddes, Onondaga, New York. Charles died in 1915. His obituary states, "For many years Mr. Stevens conducted a prosperous milling business known as the Stevens mills, grist and sawing in Schoharie."[150] It reported that he made frequent visits to his old house, the home of his daughter Mrs. Daniel J. Vroman and it was "his desire that his funeral be held from the old home, and that wish was complied with."[151] Charles B. Stevens was buried in the family plot in the Old Stone Fort Cemetery.

1912-1945 Louise (Stevens) Vrooman

PROPERTY TRANSFER: Deed of Sale from Charles B. Stevens to Louise S. Vrooman, March 6, 1912 (recorded Jan. 14, 1913), Schoharie, New York, Deed Book 161, p. 161, County Recorder's Office, Schoharie, New York.

After Ida Stevens died in 1912, her husband Charles B. Stevens deeded the property to their daughter, Louise (Stevens) Vrooman (1870-1949). The 1892 marriage of Louise Stevens to Daniel Jacob Vrooman took place in the Colonel Peter Vroman house. Daniel J. Vrooman was a son of Charles Vroman, one of the Directors of the Schoharie Valley Railroad. He was also a great-great grandnephew of Colonel Peter Vroman. With Daniel J. and Louise (Stevens) Vrooman's possession of the house, it once again, after almost a century, returned to Vroman family ownership.

Louise S. Vrooman was the administrator of her husband's estate upon his death in 1918 and she arranged an auction of their farm in November 1918. The farm was located about two miles from Schoharie towards Central Bridge. The auction included "a lot of household furniture, including a piano, and a quantity of farming implements, hay, straw, oats and several head of horses, cows, and young stock."[152]

Louise (Stevens) Vrooman was an active member of her community. According to contemporary newspapers, she was a leader in the local suffragette movement. She frequently hosted Fortnightly Club meetings in her home. The fortnightly clubs were founded in the 19th century as a place for women to have intellectual discourse. Louise served on committees of the local library, becoming perhaps the first of a long line of library supporters living in the Colonel Vroman home. Mrs. Vrooman was particularly active in the Schoharie Chapter of the Daughters of the American Revolution. She served in numerous positions and frequently presented papers. She was the Regent of the Schoharie Chapter of the Daughters of the American Revolution and helped bring the Col. Peter Vroman monument at the Old Stone Fort to completion.

Louise (Stevens) Vrooman was quite an enterprising and intriguing individual. After she moved to the Vroman home, she established an antique business in the house and called it a "Mecca for dealers and collectors."[153] In the 1925 New York State Census, she is living in Schoharie with her son, Charles S. Vrooman. She is an antique dealer and her son is a farmer. A notice in a 1925 issue of a local newspaper told of an "Orson Wilsey [who] took a load of antique furniture to Glen, New York, this week for Mrs. Louise S. Vroman and brought back another load. He reports high snow banks on the way despite the spring weather."[154] A 1926 advertisement for a two-day auction *(Fig. 54)* emphasizes that the auction is at "her Ancestral Home." It was likely a rather high-end auction with good quality merchandise including Chippendale, Sheraton, and early American furniture.

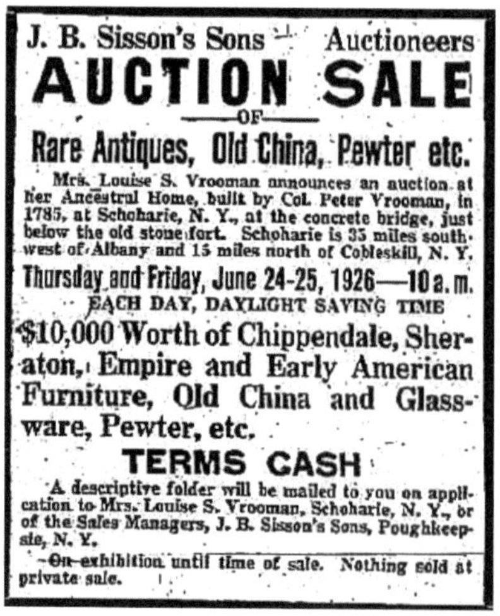
J. B. Sisson's Sons Auctioneers

AUCTION SALE

OF

Rare Antiques, Old China, Pewter etc.

Mrs. Louise S. Vrooman announces an auction at her Ancestral Home, built by Col. Peter Vrooman, in 1785, at Schoharie, N. Y., at the concrete bridge, just below the old stone fort. Schoharie is 35 miles southwest of Albany and 15 miles north of Cobleskill, N. Y.

Thursday and Friday, June 24-25, 1926—10 a. m.

EACH DAY, DAYLIGHT SAVING TIME

$10,000 Worth of Chippendale, Sheraton, Empire and Early American Furniture, Old China and Glassware, Pewter, etc.

TERMS CASH

A descriptive folder will be mailed to you on application to Mrs. Louise S. Vrooman, Schoharie, N. Y., or of the Sales Managers, J. B. Sisson's Sons, Poughkeepsie, N. Y.

On exhibition until time of sale. Nothing sold at private sale.

Fig. 54. Newspaper advertisement for auction to be held by Louise S. Vrooman in the Col. Peter Vroman house. "Amsterdam New York Daily Democrat & Recorder," p.2 (June 2, 1926).

According to the 1930 United State Federal Census, Louise S. Vrooman is living alone in the Vroman house and she reports no occupation. In the 1940 United State Federal Census, Louise S. Vrooman reports she owns the house and it is worth $5,000. She is listed as an antiques dealer and likely continued to run her antique business from the home even at the age of 70.

A 1928 article reported that Mrs. Vrooman was confined to home with an infection caused by a bite from her pet cat and that Dr. Herbert J. Wright was taking care of her.[155] Louise led quite a life of danger and intrigue. In 1938, a newspaper article reported that she narrowly escaped being hit by a rifle bullet. She was working in her kitchen when a bullet whizzed past her head. The bullet landed in a wall in an adjoining room. The sheriff believed they found the shell from the bullet about an eighth of a mile away near the rail-road bridge.[156] We did not find any bullet holes while renovating the house.

Louise S. Vrooman had been a widow for more than ten years when she was involved in quite the scandal *(Fig. 55)*. In 1930, she brought a breach of promise suit against Wellington D. Becker, the President of the Farmers and Merchants Bank of Cobleskill, New York. Mrs. Vrooman, 60 years old at the time, claimed that Becker, 66 years old, promised to wed her at the same time he promised another woman, Margaret Hevenor, to marry her. Hevenor also sued Becker for breach of promise. Interestingly, Becker actually married a third woman likely precipitating the suits by Vrooman and Hevenor. Vrooman's suit brought in a verdict of no cause of action. And, in 1934, Margaret Hevenor's suit was discontinued prior to going to trial.

Newspaper Caption: "These were the principals in Schoharie county's $50,000 breach of promise case that ended in a verdict of no cause of action last night. Left, Mrs. Wellington S. Becker, formerly Mrs. Jennie Levingston of Altamont and Albany, whose marriage to the millionaire Cobleskill banker precipitated the suit by Mrs. Louise S. Vrooman of Schoharie (center), against the wealthy defendant (right).[157]

Fig. 55. Headlines of Albany Evening News article from 1930 about Louise S. Vrooman's breach of contract suit.

Mrs. Vrooman posted a notice in the local newspaper in 1938. She wrote: "NOTICE – No more swimmers will be allowed to go down through my drive from now on. Parents please see to it, that this warning is heeded, or other means will be used to stop this nuisance." [158] The Vroman property provides easy access to Fox Creek and so was frequently used as an access point to Fox Creek.

It is believed that Louise S. Vrooman renovated the house into colonial revival style. A photograph of the house taken ca. 1930s *(Fig. 56)* shows the addition of three dormer windows, a portico with columns, a small rectangular window on the first floor, and an oval wheel window. Slave quarters, attached to the house by Samuel B. Stevens, were still in place, according to Mrs. Vrooman. This photograph was taken for the Historic American Buildings Survey (HABS). The HABS began during the Great Depression in December 1933 with the intent to document 'America's antique buildings.' HABS became a permanent program of the National Park Service in July 1935 and was formally authorized by Congress as part of the Historic Sites Act of 1935.

Fig. 56. East elevation of the Col. Peter Vroman house. Historic American Buildings Survey, Creator. Colonel Peter Van Vrooman House, Schoharie, Schoharie County, New York. ca.1930s
[Note: identified as Colonel Peter Van Vrooman house rather than the Colonel Peter Vroman house]

In 1942, Louise S. Vroman authored an article on "The Home of Colonel Peter Vrooman"[159] in the *Quarterly Bulletin – Schoharie County Historical Society*. The cover of the issue *(Fig.57)* is a photograph, which appears to have been taken about the same time as *Fig. 56*. The vegetation looks similar but not identical; the furniture on the porch is different. The journal cover photographer was Edward Scribner, who owned an appliance and electronics store in the Village of Schoharie. Scribner was the projectionist for the first talking pictures ever shown outdoors which took place in 1931 on Schoharie's Main Street.

The Vroman house can easily be identified in several 20th century maps *(Map 11, Map 12)*. These maps were created as the roads surrounding the house underwent changes. The original roads followed closely the early Native American routes.

The Quarterly Bulletin

PUBLISHED BY

Schoharie County Historical Society

VOLUME VI	JULY, 1942	NUMBER 3

Photo Courtesy Edward Scribner

HOME OF
COLONEL PETER VROOMAN

on Foxes Creek near the Old Stone Fort,

Schoharie

For Description See Page Four

Fig. 57. Col. Peter Vroman house featured on the cover of July 1942 issue of The Quarterly Bulletin – Schoharie County Historical Society.

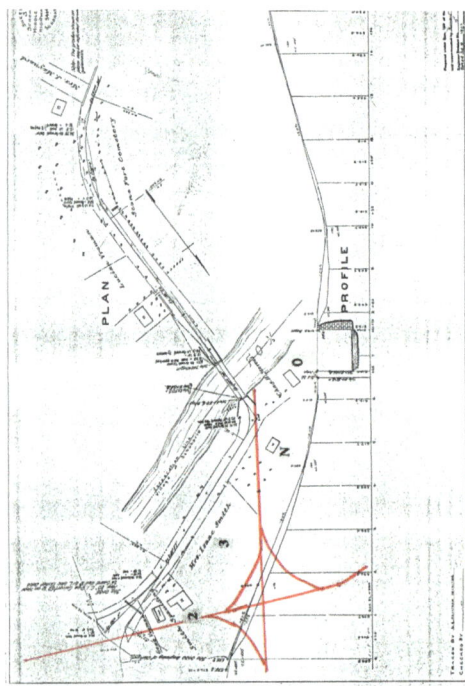

Map 11. (1914) Plans for Improving the Schoharie-Middleburg State Highway (NYSDOT). The Fox Creek Bridge is in the same location as the current covered bridge. The Old State Highway is shown in its old location, in close proximity to Fox Creek. Structure N is the Dietz house (now demolished). Arrow points to Structure O, the Chas. B. Stevens house (e.g. Colonel Peter Vroman house).

Map 6: 1914 *Plans for Improving the Schoharie-Middleburg State Highway.* (NYSDOT)
s map also depicts just a part of the Vrooman Corners Section. The bridge is located on the same location
he current covered bridge. The Old State Highway is shown in its old location, in close proximity to Fox
eek. Structures N (untitled) and O (Stevens) are located at the corner of the Old State Highway, and MDS

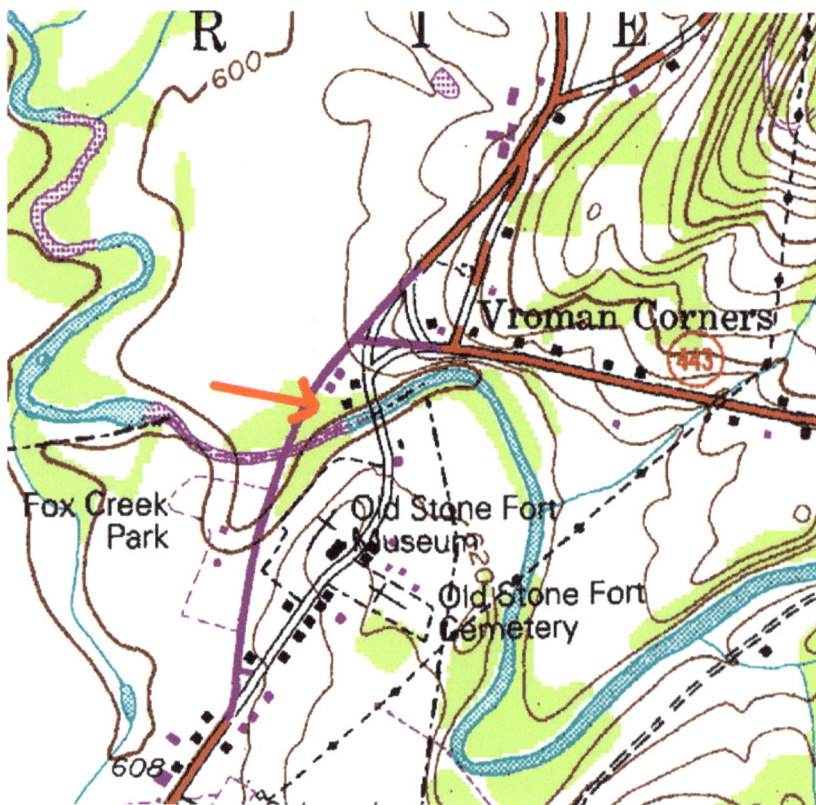

Map 12. (1943. Rev. 1994). Detail from USGS 7.5 min Schoharie Quadrangle. (USGS). The bridge and the Old State Highway have been replaced since the 1914 map (Map 12). The Old State Highway is no longer the main avenue for north bound traffic. Instead, Route 30 runs north from the bridge, directly in front of the Dietz house and curves to rejoin [old] Route 30. East/West traffic joins Route 30 in a Y-shaped intersection directly north of the bridge. This Y-shaped intersection was to be replaced in 1954. Because of the realignment, the Dietz house and the Stevens/Vroman house are adjacent to one another. Arrow points to area of Peter Vroman house.

1945-1956?   Charles S. Vrooman

- Deed of Sale from Louise S. Vrooman to Charles S. Vrooman, March 19, 1945, Schoharie, New York, Deed Book 238, p. 545, County Recorder's Office, Schoharie, New York.
- Mortgage to Charles Vrooman, Jan. 19, 1948, Schoharie, New York, Book 128, p.419, Commission of Public Welfare. Mortgage satisfied Nov. 12, 1948.
- Deed of Sale from Charles S. Vrooman to Augustus Von Linden & Helen Von Linden, filed Nov. 29, 1949, Schoharie, New York, Deed Book 257, p. 287, County Recorder's Office, Schoharie, New York.
- Deed of Sale from Augustus Von Linden and Helen M. Von Linden, Dec. 21, 1950, Schoharie, New York, Deed Book 261, p. 83, County Recorder's Office, Schoharie, New York.

Louise S. Vrooman conveyed the house and property to her son, Charles S. Vrooman (1901-1972) in 1945. Charles S. Vrooman was married to Beatrice Gagan. It is believed that they had no children.

At various times, the house was divided into apartments. Jerry K. Jaqueway, a Schoharie resident, recalls that in the 1940s Charles Vrooman rented at least three apartments in the house. Robert and Elmina (Jaqueway) Bender, Jerry Jaqueway's aunt and uncle, along with Robert Bender's widowed father Frank rented one of the apartments. Their apartment might have consisted of the two rooms on the north side of the upper floor. Jerry Jaqueway recalls that they used a small hot plate for meals. Robert E. Bender, his wife Elmina, and his father Frank are listed in the 1940 Federal Census, one family away from Louise S. Vrooman and he is a renter who lived in the same place in 1935. Robert is mechanic with an income of $650. Another local Schoharie resident recalled that the room now used as the dining room was once part of an apartment. They thought the individuals renting that apartment added the small rectangular window. The window was removed probably in the 1950s.

A newspaper announcement from 1950 states that Dr. and Mrs. Griff L. Jones moved into the upper apartment in the Charles Vrooman home. The Jones' had come from Camden, New Jersey. Dr. Jones was a graduate of Temple University, Philadelphia and the Kansas City University of Physicians and Surgeons. He was doing graduate work at Albany State Teachers College to prepare for a career in medical librarianship. Mrs. Jones was a music education graduate of the Westchester Pennsylvania State Teachers College.[160]

Local residents remember that Charles S. Vrooman sold horseradish from his home. He evidently also made some of his money by selling eggs and poultry. At one time, the Vrooman porch was supposedly so overgrown with vegetation that local children were afraid to go near the house. Charles appears to have had financial problems and the property was sold to Augustus Von Linden and Helen Von Linden in 1949 and eventually to Cora W. Vroman and her daughter, Mildred Vroman.

Through the years there were several changes in the roads surrounding the Colonel Peter Vroman property. The following maps (Map 13, Map 14) depict the final construction phase of a confusing 20th century intersection in the Vroman Corners Section. Route 30 was realigned to the west of the Vroman house (Structure O) and the adjoining Dietz house (Structure N) and access roads to this new route were constructed. In addition, to the southwest the bed of the Fox Creek was realigned. This map might show the configuration of the Colonel Vroman house before the slave quarters were removed.

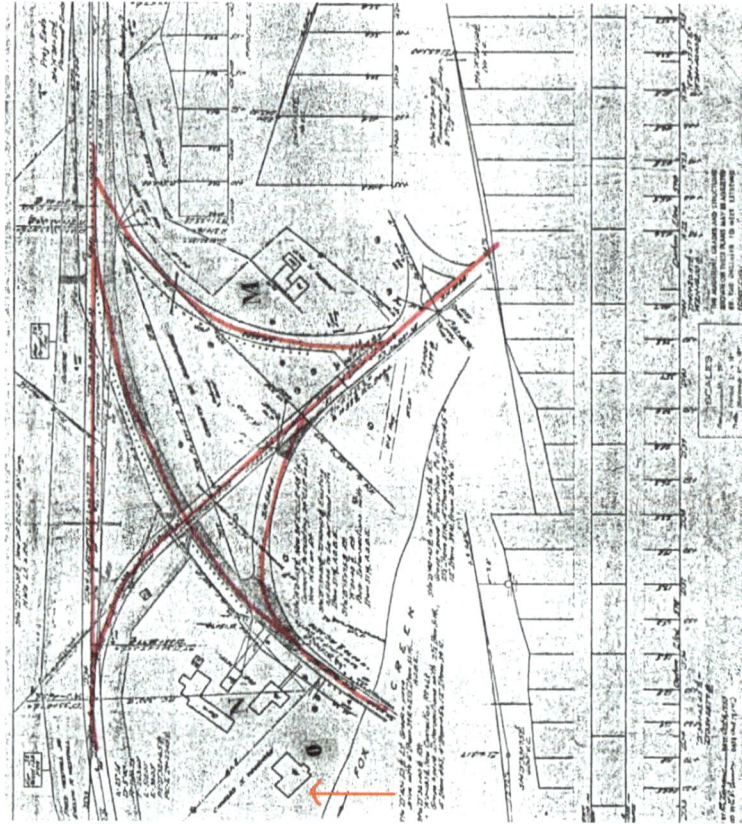

Map 13. (1954) Plans for Reconstructing a Portion of the Schoharie-Middleburg Highway and a Portion of the Gallupville-Vrooman Highway. (NYSDOT). Arrow points to Structure "O" the Colonel Peter Vroman house.

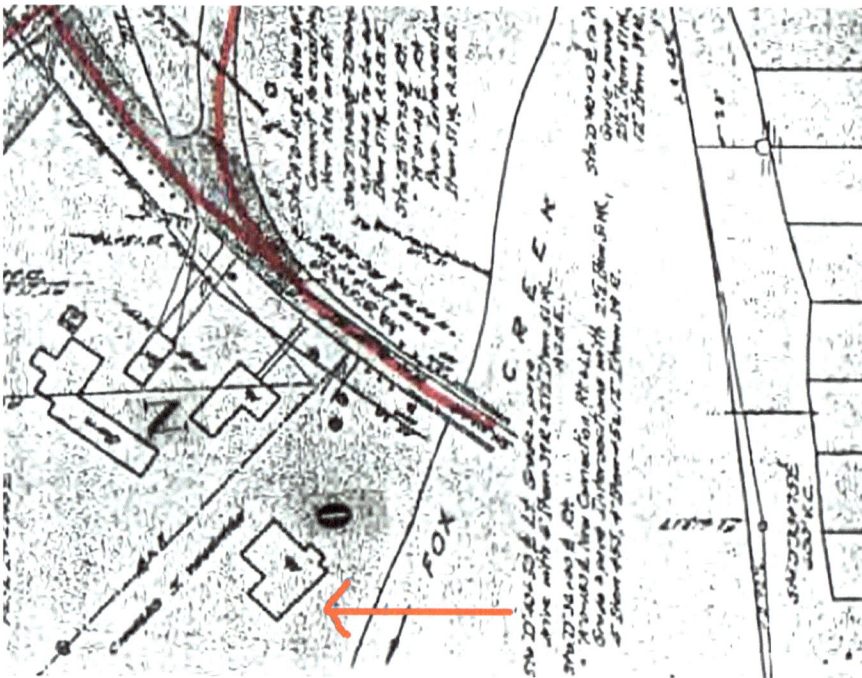

Map 14. (1954) Detail of Map 13 - Plans for Reconstructing a Portion of the Schoharie-Middleburg Highway and a Portion of the Gallupville-Vrooman Highway. (NYSDOT). Arrow points to Structure "O" the Colonel Peter Vroman house, possibly showing outline of slave quarters attached to the west side of the house.

1956-2013 Cora W. Vrooman and Mildred Vrooman

PROPERTY TRANSFERS:
- Deed of Sale from Charles Vroman, foreclosure sale to Cora W. Vroman and Mildred G. Vroman, May 31, 1956 (recorded June 1, 1956), Schoharie, New York, Deed Book 275, p. 136, County Recorder's Office, Schoharie, New York Foreclosure of mortgage on Charles S. Vrooman, Dec. 21, 1950 Book 136 of Mortgages p. 26. Conveyed from Harry J. Donaghuy, referee, to highest bid.
- Deed of Sale from Cora W. Vroman to Mildred G. Vroman, March 22, 1972, County Recorder's Office, Schoharie, New York, Deed Book 953, p.218.

Cora Ward (1886-1983) married Hoyt S. Vrooman (1878-1948), a great-great grandnephew of Colonel Peter Vroman in 1906. They had one daughter, Mildred Vrooman (1909-2012). Mildred was a great-great-great grandniece of Colonel Peter Vroman. Hoyt S. Vrooman was a poultry farmer and the family lived together on Main Street in the Village of Schoharie, New York until the early 1920s. Cora and Hoyt separated and divorced in 1926. After 1925, records indicate that Mildred and her mother lived together, first in Schoharie Village and then in the Town of Schoharie at the Col. Vroman house. Hoyt S. Vrooman moved to Schenectady.

Fig. 58. Col. Peter Vroman house ca. 2010.

Cora and Mildred Vrooman had a close relationship and were often involved in similar activities. Both were members of the Order of the Eastern Star (O.E.S), Mildred serving as its flag marshal and later the O.E.S. historian for Schoharie Valley. Cora and Mildred were enthusiastic supporters of the Schoharie Chapter of the Daughters of the American Revolution (D.A.R.). Their interest in the Vroman house and its history were a natural compliment to their D.A.R. activities. Cora served as both the President and a Trustee of the Schoharie Library while Mildred was appointed Librarian of the Schoharie Free Library in 1944 and served in that capacity for many years until her retirement. The Schoharie Business and Professional Women's Club awarded Miss Vrooman and her mother, Cora, the 1955 Women of the Year award for their public library work. The Schoharie Rotary Club named her Citizen of the Year in 1975. In 1987, Mildred G. Vrooman was inducted into the Schoharie High School Hall of Fame.

In 1956, Cora and Mildred Vrooman moved to the Peter Vroman house. They expended great effort in restoring the house to its original glories. They made changes to both the exterior and interior of the house: the three dormer windows were removed; a small window on the first floor was eliminated; the slave quarter extension was removed. They likely replaced almost all of the windows. The current exterior of the house has not changed since that time. The following photograph *(Fig. 58)* shows dark accents around the windows. When the house was repainted in 2013, the windows were painted with white rather than dark accents but the overall yellow color was retained.

Cora Vrooman and her daughter Mildred took great pride in furnishing their house with antiques and creating beautiful outdoor gardens. A later part of this work includes a section, the *Peter Vroman House During Mildred Vrooman's Occupancy*, with photographs of the house as it looked before Mildred Vrooman's death.

Fig. 59. Mildred Vrooman and some of her hand-painted Easter eggs.

Fig. 60. Mildred Vrooman (left) and Elizabeth Warren in front of one of the egg scenes they created.

Mildred Vrooman began her lifelong love of decorating eggs *(Fig. 59)* with her very good friend Elizabeth Warner *(Fig.60)*. Upon reading the 1953 Caldecott children's award winning book, *The Egg Tree* by Katherine Milhouse, they decided to create the first Schoharie Easter Egg tree on the lawn of the D.A.R. Lasell Hall. Each year the exhibit expanded in both size and complexity. The exhibit started with simple colored eggs along with eggs hand-painted in the Pennsylvania Dutch tradition. Later they created fanciful and elaborate egg scenes with backdrops along with accessories using costume jewelry, fur, shells, ribbons, lace, etc. Miss Vrooman spent endless hours working in the cellar of the Vroman house painting eggs. She used all types of eggs — pea hen to ostrich. The painted faces of the egg people demonstrate artistic talent and often a whimsical sense of humor. It took between four to six hours for her to paint and decorate each egg. She took great pride in making each egg face unique. One of her favorite scenes was the Old Stone Fort complete with a stone façade and the local hero Timothy Murphy. It is a shame that Colonel Vroman was at the Middle Fort rather than the Lower Stone Fort, otherwise perhaps he too would have been depicted in the scene.

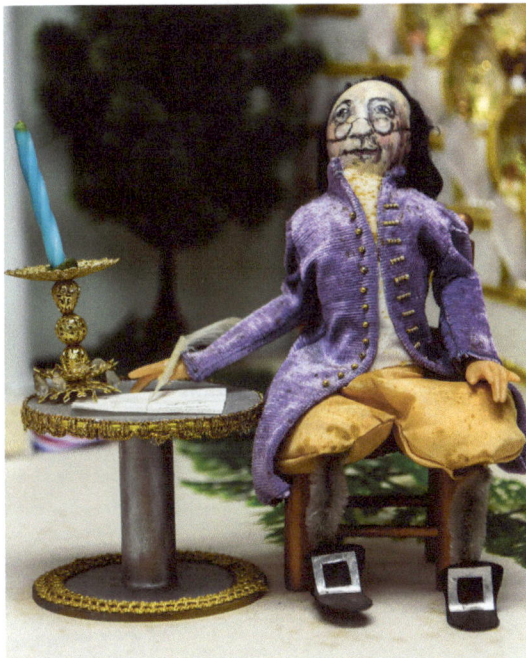

Fig. 61. Examples of Mildred Vrooman's egg folk art.

Through the years, the collection was moved to various sites around Schoharie. In 1997, Mildred Vrooman purchased the property adjacent to the Colonel Vroman house, known as the Dietz house. She demolished the Dietz home and built the Easter Egg Museum on the property. She was about 90 years old when she opened the Museum displaying her lifelong work creating a totally unique Easter egg collection. Her last major project was a tableaux she called 'Saturday Afternoon in the Park.' She worked on it for several years but never completed it. Its half-finished state is a pungent tribute to her tenacity. The egg exhibit was only open a few years before Miss Vrooman could no longer manage all the upkeep. Mildred Vrooman died December 9, 2012, at almost 103 years old. She is buried in the cemetery at the Old Stone Fort, not far from her beloved Easter Egg Museum.

The Easter Egg Exhibit attracted thousands of visitors to this unique and 'eggs-traordinary' folk art collection of decorated eggs. Miss Vrooman rejoiced in sharing her vision of a peaceful and simple time with others. She transformed a labor of love into a treasure to be shared. She and Elizabeth Warner were credited with helping to raise over $30,000 for Schoharie's Mary Beatrice Cushing Memorial Library from visitors to the Museum. The Museum is still, in 2019, exactly as Miss Vrooman left it. It is a unique monument to a different time.

Map 15 depicts the Vroman Corners area in 1977. Fox Creek is on a new alignment but the confusing intersection of Rt. 30 and Rt. 443 will not be realigned until later. The dot on the map north of Fox Creek and the Old Stone Fort is the Col. Vroman house. Map 16 is the configuration from 2012 to date.

After Ms. Vrooman died, most of the contents of her house were sold at auction *(Fig. 62)*. The auction was held at the home and included numerous antiques. The following is an advertisement for that auction:

"OLD FASHION"

ON SITE ESTATE AUCTION

Saturday April 27th

Schoharie, New York

10:30 a.m. - Preview from 9:00 a.m.

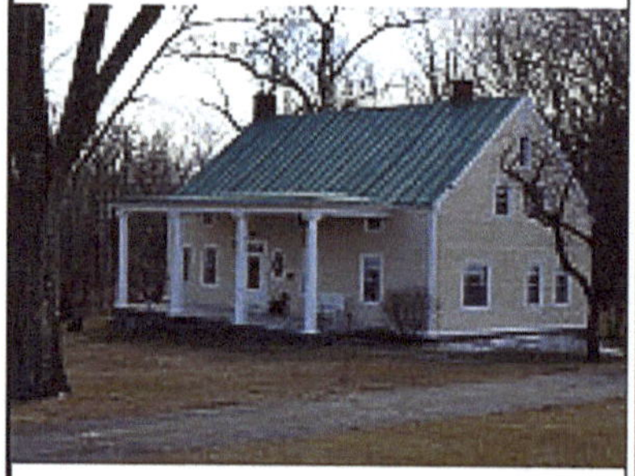

We will be selling the contents of the period home (1785) of the late Mildred Vrooman located at the junction of rte. 30 and rte. 443 (Covered Bridge Lane), Schoharie NY. Most of the home contents are composed of 19th c. furniture, collectables and decorator items. The public auction will be held under tent, rain or shine.

We accept MC/Visa and there is a 15% buyer's premium. Please bring a chair and a box for your purchases. Over 500 lots throughout the day, everything must be sold by days end.

Photos and listing are at **Auctionzip.com**, auctioneer #14163.

Photos and listing are at **Auctionzip.com**, auctioneer #14163.

Partial listing: Cherry, mahogany and walnut furniture*four poster beds*Victorian parlor furniture*Empire period sofa, chest of drawers and stands*desks*framed chandler prints*group of tole ware*spider leg candle stand*tapered leg cherry stand*center pedestal writing desk*wing back chairs*claw foot drum tables*bear skin comforter/rug*quilts and textiles*ladies drop front desk*Pr. Staffordshire dogs 16 in. h.*electric organ and bench*two room size Kazan rugs*oriental scatter rugs*rag rugs*spinet desk*majolica jardinière and other majolica*turned leg drop side table*NY leg drop side table*set of six tiger maple mid 19th c. dining chairs*an amount of flow blue and transfer china*pewter charger*step back china hutch with two drawers*stenciled blanket chest bracket feet*spinet piano*Victorian side chairs with needle point seats*West Troy jug and other crocks with cobalt blue*single shot shotgun*single shot .22* early mini baseball pennants with pix, Cubs, Jim Vaughn, Giants Charles Dooin, Phillies Gabby Garvath, Pirates, Hans Wagner, decorated sheet music cabinet* ginger bread clock*pillar and scroll shelf clock*Wainscot one door 40" h. cupboard*ironstone china*nine pcs. Coffee/tea plated serving set with figurative rams head*cranberry glass epergne*small folio Currier and Ives framed prints*group of pattern glass, "Blue flower" *banquet lamps* Wedgewood "tyrol" serving china*sterling silver hollowware*collection of local and regional reference and history books*and much more.

Directions: from the south, NYS Thruway to exit 21, follow rte. 23 to rte 145 to Middleburg, right on rte 30 to Covered Bridge Lane and the auction site. From the north, travel NYS Thruway to exit 25A, rte. 88 to rte. 30A to slight right on rte 30 to Covered Bridge Rd and the auction site.

Carlsen Gallery
info@carlsengallery.com
Info: 518-634-2466

Lincoln Auctions
Linkonauction@aol.com
info: 518-258-3108

Fig. 62. Advertisement for auction of the Mildred Vrooman estate, 2013.

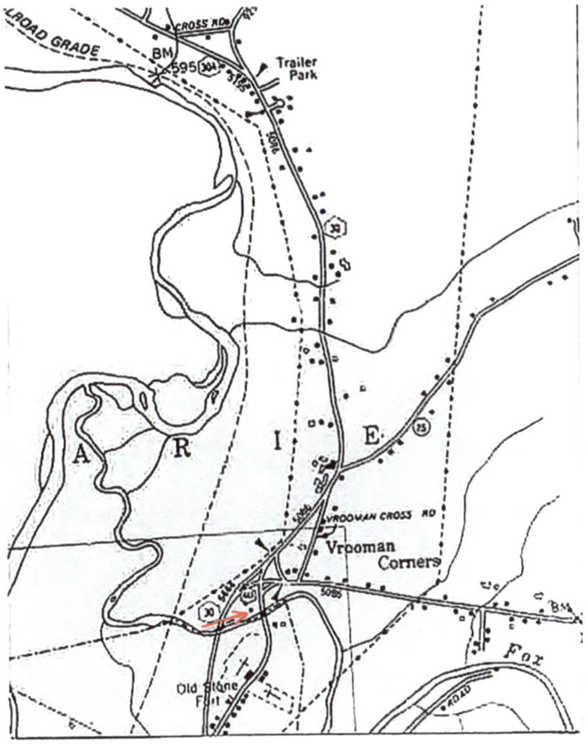

Map 15. (1977) New York State Department of Transportation 7.5 min Schoharie Quadrangle. New York State Department of Transportation. Note: arrow points to Colonel Peter Vroman house.

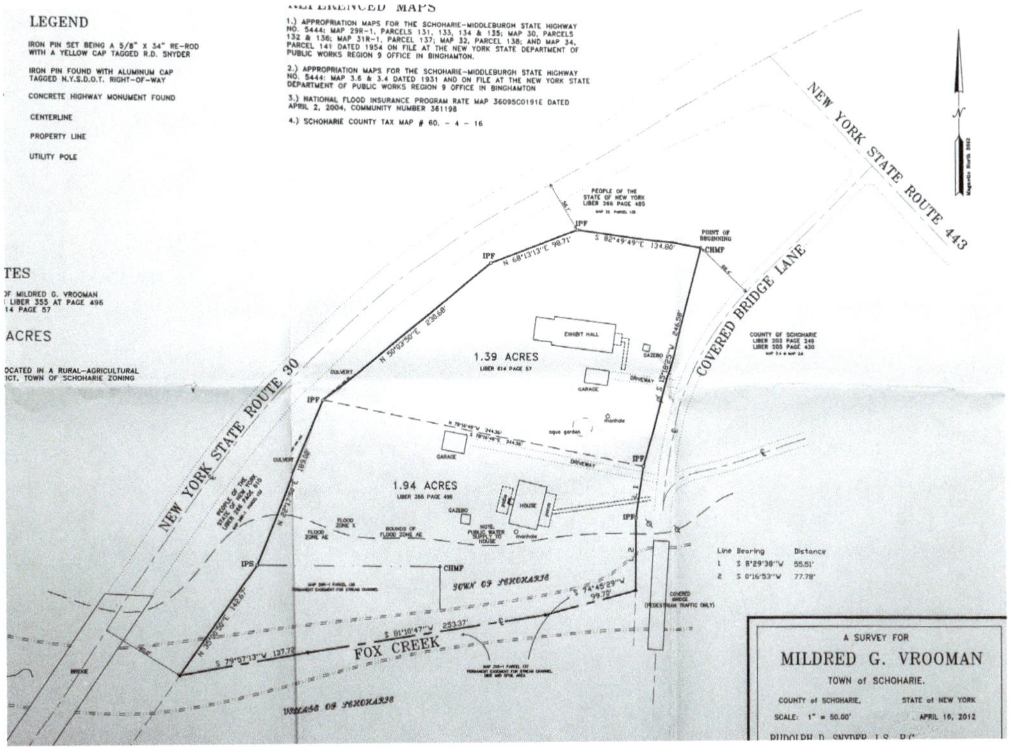

Map 16. (2012) Plat of the Col. Peter Vroman property. Surveyed for Mildred G. Vrooman, April 16, 2012.

2013-   Joseph and Berna Heyman

PROPERTY TRANSFER:

- Deed of Sale from Mildred G. Vrooman, deceased, executor Hawley Zwahlen to Joseph S. Heyman and Berna L Heyman, June 3, 2013, Deed Book 953, p.218, Document no. 646733, County Recorder's Office, Schoharie, New York.

Fig. 63. Berna and Joseph Heyman.

The Heymans purchased the Col. Vroman house in 2013 shortly after Miss Vrooman passed away. They have enjoyed joining the Schoharie community and particularly being close to their daughter, Laura Rosenthal and grandson Max Rosenthal, who live on the other side of the covered bridge crossing the Fox Creek.

Joseph Heyman was born in New Bedford, Massachusetts. He earned his undergraduate degree with honors from Northeastern University, Boston. His PhD in Physics was from Washington University in St. Louis. Joe retired from NASA Langley Research Center as its Chief Technologist in 2001 after a 37-year career with the National Aeronautics and Space Administration. Dr. Heyman conducted groundbreaking research and development in many areas of diagnostic measurement science for NASA and was the founding Branch Head of the Nondestructive Sciences Branch. After his retirement, Joe joined Luna Innovations Inc. and served as their Chief Scientific Officer. Joe currently teaches photography courses for the Christopher Wren Association of the College of William and Mary. He was the chief photographer for this work.

Berna (Levine) Heyman was born in Chicago, Illinois She received her undergraduate degree in American History and Literature from Washington University in St. Louis, Missouri and her graduate degree in Library Science from Simmons College, Boston, Massachusetts. She worked at Massachusetts Institute of Technology and the University of Missouri–St. Louis. Most of her library career was spent at the College of William and Mary in Williamsburg, Virginia where she was a pivotal leader shaping the national movement for digital libraries. She retired from her position as Associate Dean of University Libraries, College of William and Mary, in 2007. Since retirement, she has been actively engaged as a Board member of the Williamsburg Regional Library Foundation and the Board of the Christopher Wren Association of the College of William and Mary, a lifelong learning organization. She also does genealogic research on her family. She spent more than three years researching and writing about the Vroman property and all the people who lived there.

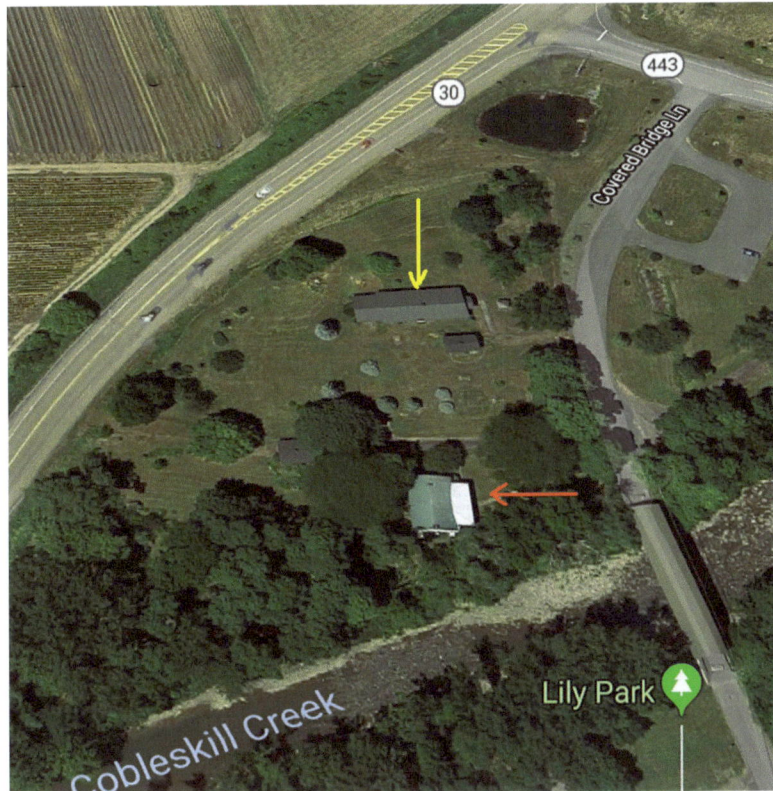

Fig. 64.. Overhead Google view of Col. Peter Vroman property, 2018.
Note: red arrow points to the Vroman house; yellow arrow points to the Mildred Vrooman Easter Egg Museum.

When the Heymans purchased the Vroman property, they also 'inherited' the Mildred Vrooman Easter Egg Museum. In April 2014 and again in April 2019, the Heymans reopened the Museum so the Schoharie community and others could enjoy it. The openings served as fundraisers for the Schoharie Free Library and encouraged increased recognition of the marvels available in the beautiful community of Schoharie.

The Heymans interest in having the Colonel Peter Vroman property recognized for its wonderful history and extraordinary construction helped lead to its nomination for the State and National Register of Historic Places in December 2018.[161] Anne Hendrix, the Village of Schoharie Historian, said, "the Vroman house is a beautiful, well-preserved, post-Revolutionary home. It's a gem, and the colonel was quite active in the local militia during the Revolution. They were a very important family in Schoharie and still are a prominent family in the area."[162] Daniel Beams, Acting Director/Museum Curator of the Old Stone Fort Museum said, "the owner of the house across Fox Creek [Vroman] played a significant role in the early days of the American experiment. He was in charge of the 15th Albany Regiment of the militia, because Schoharie was part of Albany County back then … He was an important individual."[163] The research for this book was largely the basis for the nomination document.

Adjacent Property (Dietz House)

The house is referred to as the Dietz house likely because the 1856 Wenig map *(Map 8)* and the 1866 Beers map *(Map 9)* both include the location for J. H. Dietz or J. Dietz (a.k.a. Deitz)

<Note: the deeds for the Dietz house are listed in the bibliography>

The earliest deeds for the adjacent property are likely those between Peter M. Vroman and Adam Vroman dated March 22, 1828 (Schoharie County Recorder's Office. Book J, p.131). And another deed between Peter M. Vroman and Maria Vroman, the wife of Adam Vroman Junior, also dated March 22, 1828. Peter M. Vroman and Adam Vroman, Junior were brothers and both were grandsons of Col. Peter Vroman. Maria (Lawyer) Vroman, was the wife of Adam Vroman, Jr. So the property was staying within the family. The deed describes the property as part of the farm formerly owned by Colonel Vroman, in a patent granted to Myndert Schuyler and others. There are indications that at least some of the adjacent land was sold by John Eckerson to Captain Jacob Snyder, who bequeathed the property to his eldest son, Peter M. Snyder. It is unclear if or where Snyder built a small residence on that property. It may or may not have been the house referred to as the Dietz house, which was adjacent to the Col. Vroman house.

In 1832, the property was deeded from several Vroman family members to Jacob Fisher. The sellers included Peter Vroman of Glenn and his wife Angelica (Col. Vroman's daughter and her husband); Adam Vroman, Junior and his wife Nancy (Col. Vroman's grandson and his wife); Jacob L. Vroman and his wife Lydia (Col. Vroman's great grandson and his wife); David Dietz and his wife Julia Ann (Col. Vroman's great grand-daughter and her husband). This deed, (Schoharie County Recorder's Office. Book O, p.409) was for several parcels of land and included both parcels of the Col. Vroman property.

Jacob Fisher began selling off parts of the property in 1844. The mill and Col. Vroman home were sold to John P. Griggs. The adjacent property was sold to Lorenzo Huff in 1845; Huff sold it to Paul Haverly in 1848. It next passed to Jacob H. Dietz and his wife Sarah in 1853 for $2,600. Jacob Dietz owned the property from 1853 to 1866. Dietz, a farmer, sometimes used the spelling 'Deitz.' It is unclear if there is a connection between Jacob H. Dietz and David Dietz (the husband of Julia Ann Vrooman), prior owners of the property and part of the Vroman family. The property consisted of about 23.24 acres at the time.

Prior to purchasing the property, the 1850 United State Federal Census lists Jacob Deitz as single and living with Charles Rich (a painter) and his wife Sophina Rich. Charles Rich was Sarah (Rich) Dietz's brother. From later census, it appears that Jacob and Sarah Dietz helped to raise several of her siblings.

In the 1855 New York State Census, the Dietz household consisted of six people living in the house:

1855 New York State Census, Schoharie, New York			
Name	**Age**	**Relationship**	**Profession**
Jacob H. Deitz	32	Head of household	Farmer
Sarah E. Deitz	22	Wife	
Marshall Rich	11	Brother-in-law	Born in Michigan
George Rich	9	Brother-in-law	Born in Michigan
Amelia Rich	3	Sister-in-law	Born in Michigan
Mary Westfall	14	Domestic	

In the 1860 United States Federal Census, the Deitz household consisted of:

1860 United States Federal Census, Schoharie, New York			
Name	Age	Relationship	Profession
Jacob H. Deitz	38	Head of household	Farmer
Sarah E. Deitz	28	Wife	
Marshall Rich	16	Brother-in-law	Born in Michigan
George Rich	14	Brother-in-law	Born in Michigan
Amelia Rich	9	Sister-in-law	Born in Michigan
Elizabeth Deitz	4	Daughter	

By 1865, Marshall and George Rich had moved out of the house; Marshall was working as a servant for Peter Osterhoutsen in Schoharie and George was married and living in Ulster, New York. Jacob H. Dietz and Sarah Dietz had three children:

1865 New York State Census, Schoharie, New York			
Name	Age	Relationship	Profession
Jacob H. Deitz	42	Head of household	Farmer
Sarah E. Deitz	22	Wife	
Libbie Dietz	9	Daughter	
Laura Dietz	3	Daughter	
Erwin Dietz	2	Son	
Amelia Rich	3	Boarder [Sister-in-law]	

In 1866, the home and 23 acres of land were sold to Adam D. Hager and his wife, Catherine Vrooman, the granddaughter of Col. Peter Vroman. Louise Vrooman wrote that Katie Vrooman married Adam Hager in the old Col Peter Vroman house. And Katie was the individual reported to have received a "very black slave boy"[164] as a wedding present. Adam and Katie Hager never had children but they adopted Henry Cady and he was their beneficiary. Henry Cady is the major link to many Vroman-related documents and artifacts.

The Hagers lived in Schoharie County throughout their lives. In 1840, they were living in Fulton, Schoharie, New York. By 1860, they were residing in Middleburgh along with John Van Pharick (a 14-year-old mulatto), Henry Cady (a 12-year-old boy), Wealthy A. Borst (a 13-year-old girl), and William Pratt (a 23-year-old farm laborer). According to the 1865 New York State Census, Adam and Catherine Hagar were still living in Middleburgh with Henry Cady, who is listed as their "adopted child," along with Rhoda Bishop (a 13-year-old servant).

The Hagers and Henry Cady were living in the Dietz house in 1870 according to the United State Federal Census. Both Adam Hager and young Henry Cady are farming. The house is valued at $4,000. Henry Cady married Kate Spaulding in 1871. They had one son, Harry Cady, who was quite young when he died in an automobile accident, and a daughter Celia, who married Alva Loucks.

Adam D. Hager died in 1873. In the 1880 United State Federal Census, Catherine (Vrooman) Hager is living with Henry Cady and is listed as "great aunt" in his household. Aunt Katie died just a year later, in 1881, at age 78. A stone slab *(Fig.65)* with the name "Henry" is still located on the Col. Peter Vroman property and likely relates to Henry Cady. The purpose of this stone is unknown. Henry Cady's substantial monument is in the Old Stone Fort Cemetery where he is buried.

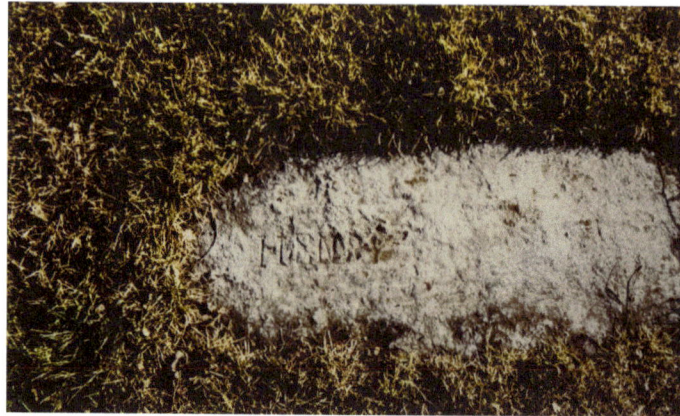

Fig. 65. Stone slab inscribed 'Henry,' likely refers to Henry Cady, a descendant of the Vroman family.

Henry Cady was born in Auriesville, Montgomery County, New York. In 1860 he moved to Schoharie where he lived with Catherine (Vrooman) Hager and her husband, Adam. Henry's 1919 obituary indicates for many years he had a store near the Old Stone Fort. Upon closing the store, he became the postmaster. "He took a lively interest in local history, was a charter member of the County Historical Society and one of its officers He was probably one of the best posted men on local history in the county."[165] He served as the Old Stone Fort's first curator and actively collected information on the genealogy of Schoharie County families. He created hand-written notes from numerous sources such as cemeteries, family bibles, church records, land patents, and family recollections. Unfortunately, he did not provide the sources for these records but they are still considered an important resource housed in the Library of the Old Stone Fort Museum.

A *New York Genealogical and Biographical Record* obituary states, "On his mother's side, Mr. Cady was descended from the Vrooman family."[166] This likely refers to his 'adopted' mother Katie (Vrooman) Hager. The article further states that as a young man, Cady was given many valuable historical documents from his maternal grandfather – which would have been Col. Peter Vroman. An 1899 inventory of the Old Stone Fort listed several items relating to Vromans that were donated to the Old Stone Fort by Henry Cady. Some of those documents and artifacts continue to be available and even displayed in the Old Stone Fort Museum.

Henry Cady sold the Dietz property to Charles B. Stevens in 1883 for $4,000. Charles B. Stevens was the son of Samuel B. Stevens, who bought the Col. Peter Vroman property in 1863. Samuel Stevens had transferred the Col. Vroman part of the property to his son Charles in 1877, so this sale brought the two properties back together.

The Stevens family sold the Dietz/Hager property to Nancy C. Smith (1908), it was then sold to the following individuals: John C. Wilber (1916), Lloyd S. Guernsey (1923), Carey Mattice (1926), Fred Westfall, Jr. (1938), Arthur E. Jenner (1959), Paul Westheimer (1977), and Mildred Vrooman (1997). All of these transactions are listed in the Bibliography under 'Deeds to the Adjacent Property.' With Mildred Vrooman's purchase in 1997, the property returned to its original, though reduced, 18th century configuration.

The house was commonly referred to as the "Dietz" house and was likely built some time between 1820 and 1850. The property was used as a small farmstead. The house was a one and a half story building. It had a cut field stone foundation, aluminum siding, metal roof with open overhanging eaves and an exterior brick chimney. There were three outbuildings, one of which still stands. The existing one-and-a-half story barn, built between 1920-1950 is currently a garage. In 1997, Mildred G. Vrooman demolished the Dietz residence.

There is some archaeological significance to the site based on a test dig done in 1995, which revealed prehistoric artifacts. In addition, historic artifacts consisting of brick fragments, nails, ceramic fragments, and pieces of glass bottles were also identified. Several of the nails pre-dated 1820, while the majority of them dated after 1835. Ceramics consisted of redwares, creamwares, pearlwares, and whitewares. The pearlwares date to between 1780 and 1830 and the whitewares were mid-eighteenth century.[167]

There are a few remaining photographs of the now demolished Dietz residence *(Fig. 66-68):*

Fig. 66. Dietz house. Photograph from: "Plans for Reconstructing a Portion of the Schoharie-Middleburg Highway and a Portion of the Gallupville-Vrooman Highway." FARC 54-33. New York State Department of Transportation, 1954. Note: the garage to the right of the house still exists.

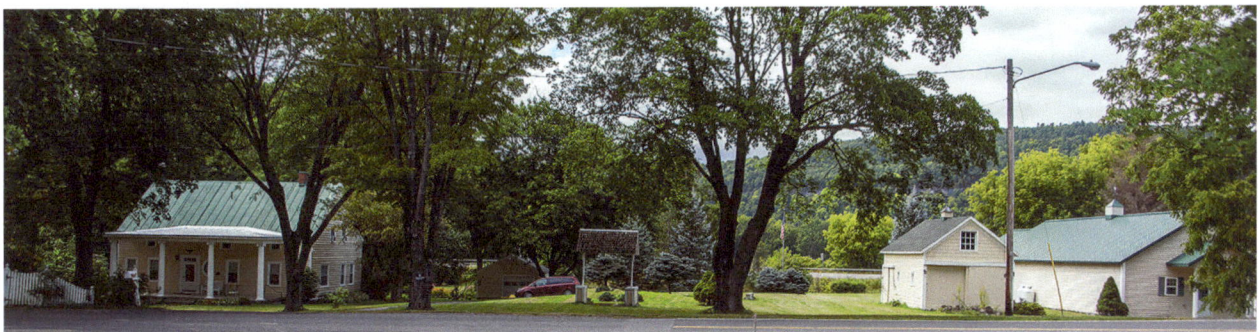

Fig. 67. Photograph of the one and a half story small Dietz homestead barn (right). Photograph 2016. The Colonel Vroman house is on the left.

Fig. 68. Dietz house, view from the Fox Creek Covered bridge looking north. Photograph from: "Plans for Reconstructing a Portion of the Schoharie-Middleburg Highway and a Portion of the Gallupville-Vrooman Highway." FARC 54-33. New York State Department of Transportation, 1954.

Fig. 69. Photograph of Dietz and Vroman houses, 1954. Vroman house on the left; Dietz house on the right. Photograph from: "Plans for Reconstructing a Portion of the Schoharie-Middleburg Highway and a Portion of the Gallupville-Vrooman Highway." FARC 54-33. New York State Department of Transportation, 1954.

Vroman House Description and Features

Note: Much of the detailed description of the house was taken from the National Register of Historic Places nomination documents for the Colonel Peter Vroman House written by William Krattinger in 2018. The author has only a layman's understanding of the structure of the house. Mr. Krattinger provided the expertise. The photographs in this section provide supplemental documentation about the Vroman house.

Exterior Description

The Colonel Peter Vroman House is a story-and-a-half eyebrow New World Dutch-framed structure with a full basement and full walk-up attic. It is an example of a later 18th century vernacular house with a New World Dutch timber frame and first-period and subsequent historic-period features. The gable-roofed house's frame was constructed, in part, with hand-hewn oak timbers about 11 inches in diameter. The house measures 48 feet long and 30 feet wide. Original hand-hewn oak beams are exposed in the cellar and first floor. The foundation was laid up in mortared limestone with roughly dressed stones laid in regular courses. The foundation wall is 20 inches thick and there is a partition wall in the cellar that is also 20 inches thick.

A flat-roofed Colonial Revival-style portico spanning most, but not all, of that elevation, front the principal roadside/east elevation. Fluted Ionic-order wood columns support the portico. Large rectangular cut stone steps provide an approach to the portico. The present standing-seam metal roof covers an older wood shingle roof and previous owners of the house indicated there are four layers of roofing underneath. The house has two brick chimneys both of which rise above the ridge. Some portions of the walls are brick-lined with nogging behind the clapboard. A brochure written in 1975 indicates that the inside hall is also brick-lined.[168]

Much of the native yellow pine clapboard siding covering the house is beaded and presumably early in date, and likely original. The non-beaded clapboards, particularly on the west elevation and near window openings, provide visual evidence of alterations made through the years.

The house's fenestration is asymmetric on the longer east and west elevations but more symmetric on the north and south gable ends. The east elevation is five-bays wide with an offset entrance flanked on both sides by two windows at first-story level. An elliptical-shaped window, added in the early 20th century, is located to one side of the door. Three small square-shaped "eyebrow" windows bring natural light to the upper story. All of the windows are replacements.

The north gable elevation is three-bays wide with three windows (one larger than the other two) on the first-story level, two windows on the second story, and one window on the attic level. The west or rear elevation is four-bays wide with a central door. There are three windows (one larger than the other two) on the first-story level and one small casement eyebrow window on the half-story level. The south gable elevation is two-bays wide and has two windows at first-story level (one larger than the other); two smaller windows are at the half-story level and also at the attic level, these are 'stacked' in the vertical plane. Centered between the two first-story windows is a brick fireback. Small wood-louvered vents are present in the gable end, below the roof apex on the south elevation. All of the windows have simple casings with drip caps. There are windows in the cellar as well as evidence of additional cellar windows that have been closed off.

Fig. 70. Earliest known view of the Colonel Peter Vroman house ca.1900. Photograph from the Old Stone Fort.

Fig. 71. Colonel Peter Vroman property, looking north, 2018. One of the two garages and the
Easter Egg Museum are shown on the right.

Fig. 73. Colonel Vroman House looking east, 2018.

Fig. 74. Colonel Vroman House looking south, 2018.

Fig. 75. Colonel Vroman House looking north.

Fig. 76. Col. Peter Vroman property, looking towards west and south elevations, 2018.

102

Interior Description

The internal walls of the house are a mix of plaster with old and new lathe and sheetrock. Some of the studs are very large and retain bark on the outside. The studs were installed during a wide range of time periods.

Cellar: The fully excavated basement is divided into two rooms by a 20-inch thick stone partition wall going east/west. The partition consists of mortared limestone, as does the foundation wall. The stone work in the partition is integrated with the outer wall but it is not battered out suggesting it might not have been intended as an outside wall. The walls are plastered and there are remnants of whitewash in sections of the cellar. A large rectangular-shaped mortared stone chimney base is in the north section of the cellar. This is also the section of the cellar with some markings that are described in a later section. The north section has a dirt floor and was supposedly the kitchen and later served as a root cellar until the 2011 flood. There has been speculation that the north part of the cellar might have been part of the foundation of a previous house located on the site, given that documentation suggests a dwelling existed on the property ca. 1760-1780, however no definitive evidence to that effect has been found.

The south section of the cellar has a brick chimney support positioned against the south wall, which corresponds with the fireplace above, and the fireback on the south elevation. It is largely blocked from view by a cistern and may have originally served as the base for paired corner fireplaces. The south section has at-grade access by means of stairs sheltered by a Bilco-type hatch. Simple wood steps in the south room provide vertical access between the basement and first floor hallway. These stairs are not original; they were likely built in the 1950s. Several beams were cut to accommodate the stairs. There are two doors next to one another on the first floor hall. The second door was likely added when the 'new' staircase was built to minimize the steepness of the steps. The original steep steps might have been those mentioned in the story about a young slave girl who was pushed down stairs and subsequently died. This south section of the basement was later used as Mildred Vrooman's workplace where she painted all the eggs and egg scenes now in the Easter Egg Museum.

Fig. 77. Stairs leading from 1st floor to cellar.

Fig. 78. Southwest section of cellar, showing bottom of stairs. Log beam on left was added 20th century when beams cut for replacement stairway.

103

Fig. 79. Southwest section of cellar with entry stairs.

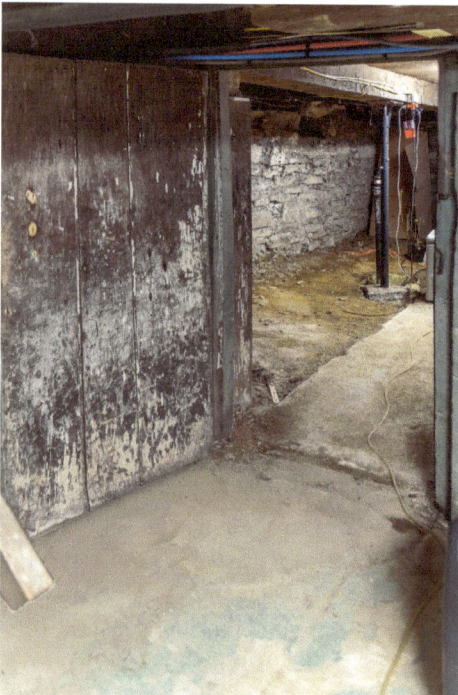

Fig. 81. Northeast section of cellar.

Fig. 80. Entry door from south
to north part of cellar.

Fig. 82. Southeast section of cellar.

Fig. 83. Chimney base north section of cellar.

Fig. 84. Close-up of chimney base.
Lighter color mortar is 21st century repair.

First Story: The first floor has a center hall with original Dutch divided doors offset on each end. The wood mouldings in the hallway are more ornate than anywhere else in the house. There is also paneled wainscoting and a moulded chair rail in the hall. The ceiling beams are cased. The staircase leading to the half-story is aligned with the front door on the east elevation. It is of an open-stinger type with handrail, rounded balusters and a turned newel post of distinctive Greek Revival characteristics and likely a ca. 1840 modification.

Fig. 85. Staircase showing newel post, balusters, and handrail.

Fig. 86. Hall 1st floor looking east.

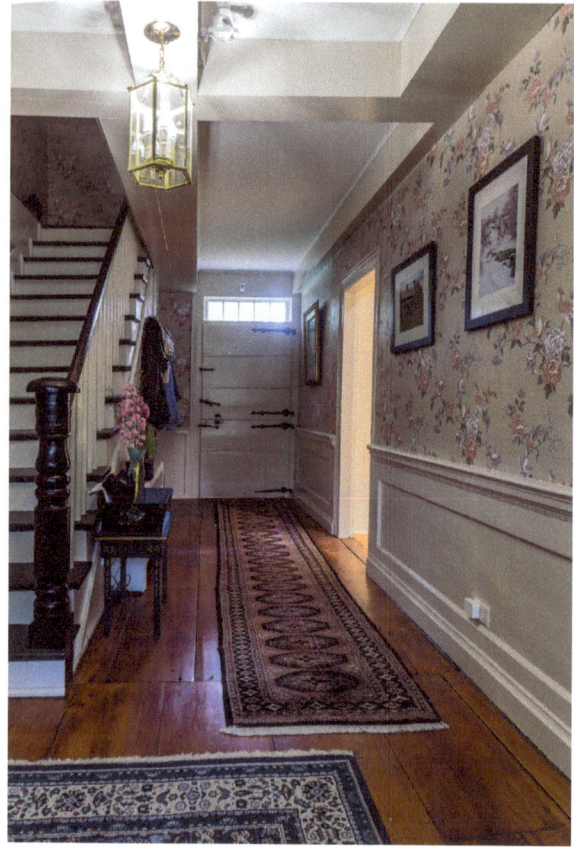

Fig. 87. Hall 1st floor looking west.

Fig. 88. Dining room, northeast, 1st floor.

The northeast side off the hallway consists of a dining room with a fireplace. Five beams spanning the ceiling of the dining room are all cased and some of them have been cut. The kitchen, a small pantry, a bathroom, and a small closet are on the northwest side off the hallway. The kitchen and bathroom were stripped back to the studding and fully renovated in 2013. The beams in the kitchen are cased and had been cut.

Fig. 89. Kitchen, northwest, 1st floor.

Fig. 90. Kitchen, northwest, 1st floor.

Fig. 91. Pantry, 1st floor, mid–20th century cabinet.

Fig. 92. Bathroom, 1st floor, all new drywall.

Fig. 93. Living room, looking southwest, 1st floor.

The south side of the first floor consists of a living room running the full length of the house, from east to west. Four hand-planed and beaded 29.1 feet oak ceiling beams span this room. They exhibit lime staining from a plaster ceiling that was added sometime subsequent to the original building but later removed. The smoothly finished nature and beading of the beams indicates that the original intent was to expose these beams. The flooring provides evidence that the room was divided at least into two rooms at some time. Corner fireplaces might have served it as evidence by the hearth support in the basement and the side curves of the fireplace walls. The current fireplace is centered against the south wall and has a projecting chimney breast and rebuilt firebox. The wood mantel is unusual. Its five-part frieze and moulding are suggestive of a conventional Federal-style mantel of the early 19th century; however, it features applied decoration in the form of roundels and foliate motifs that might have been added at a later time.

Fig. 94. Living room, looking southeast, 1st floor.

Fig. 95. Living room, southeast, 1st floor, fireplace.

109

Fig. 96. Living room, southeast, 1st floor, exposed beams.

There are variations in ceiling height throughout the house and only the newest construction is plumb. The height from floor to ceiling on the first floor ranges from 8.3 to 8.5 feet.

Half-story: The half-story has a wide center hall with a fully modernized bathroom occupying a portion of this space. The half-story has low ceilings throughout, ranging from 6.6 to 6.7 feet high. All of the floor-boards are oriented north to south. The north elevation of the half-story has 2 bedrooms. In each of these rooms the rake of the roof is expressed and there are small eyebrow windows positioned at the floor level. Closets have been added to these bedrooms. The northeast bedroom also has a half bath added in 2013. On the south elevation of the half-story, there is a library and another bedroom separated by a full staircase leading upwards to the unfinished attic. The staircase was likely added in the 20th century. The library has an eyebrow window. Windows corresponding with the north and south gable ends have window sills, which are aligned the full length of the room.

Fig. 97. Hall, half-story.

Fig. 98. Bedroom northwest, half-story.

Fig. 99. Bedroom northeast, half-story.

Fig. 100. Half-bath off northeast bedroom, half-story.

Fig. 101. Bathroom off hall, half-story.

Fig. 102. Library southeast, half-story.

Fig. 103. Bedroom southwest, half-story.

Attic: The enclosed staircase on the south side of the half-story provides access to the attic, where the upper portion of the house's pine rafter pairs, above the collar ties, are visible. The rafters bear carpenter marks indicating that the frame was built using scribe-rule framing methods. Visible in the attic is evidence of three gable-roofed dormers that were added to the principal elevation in association with Colonial Revival modifications that also included the addition of the portico and the elliptical window next to the entry east door. The dormers were removed in the mid-twentieth century. The attic flooring is not original.

Fig. 104. Stairs leading to attic.

Fig. 105. Attic beams.

113

Fig, 106. Attic view.

Fig. 107. Attic beams and roofing.

House Features

Beams and Construction of the House: The wood used in the cellar and attic beams are from old-growth forests that were probably located in Schoharie. It is possible that Colonel Vroman even owned the property where the stand of trees was located. The trees were likely chosen very deliberately and the construction was careful and professional. They would have been recognized as fairly remarkable timbers even at the time they were felled. They were likely felled at the same time, suggesting careful planning for the building of the house. The construction of the house was consistent with some of the finest construction done at the time.

Most of the dendrochronology-tested beams were felled during the dormant period of 1791/1792 (e.g. about November/December 1791 to January/February 1792). The beams would then have been prepared for construction while still green, making it easier to work. And it is likely that they began building the house some time between April and September 1792. There may have been some work done on the house after that period. It is possible that the house would have been occupied as early as the fall of 1792.

The cellar beams are white oak. The earliest growth was from about 1476 while the latest was 1606. The pre-Columbian ca.1476 beam is an example of one of the earliest trees identified from the region. That tree was about 320 to 340 years old when it was felled. The attic beams are white pine. Their beginning date of growth ranges from 1677 to 1701 and they were felled when 88 to 115 years old.

At some time there was speculation that the house might have been built in stages. But the dendrochronology results clearly suggest that the house was built at one time. One of the tested cellar beams was the lintel connecting the north and south sections of the cellar. The dendrochronology results from that beam were consistent with all the other beams tested in the cellar.

Doors: The Peter Vroman house has several intriguing doors. The front and back doors in the wide center hall are very old divided Dutch doors of heavy planking with upper and a lower leafs and fielded panels. The top leaf has three panels and the lower leaf has two panels. The doors are offset rather than parallel. The front door (east elevation) has ball and dart wrought iron hardware. The back door (west elevation) has double ball and dart wrought iron hardware with a rattail lock. Five-pane transoms span the front and back doors. Horizontally divided doors allowed light and fresh air in the upper half while keeping livestock or small critters out with the closed lower half. These doors are often called 'Dutch doors' likely because they were common in the Netherlands in the 17th century. This style of door was also typically found in the Dutch areas of New York before the American Revolution.

The doors were sufficiently significant to be photographed as part of the *Historic American Building Survey* (HABS) (*Fig. 108. 109*). The HABS was established in 1933 during the Great Depression to create a public archive of America's architectural heritage. It was the first significant boon to historic preservation at the national level. HABS was part of a groundswell of interest in collecting and preserving information, artifacts, and buildings, related to our early history. The permanent collection of the HABS documents is housed at the Library of Congress

Fig. 108. Outside view of front Dutch door (east elevation) from Library of Congress. Historic American Buildings Survey. ca. 1940. Louise S. Vrooman occupied the home at that time.

Fig. 109. Inside view of front divided Dutch door (east elevation), from Library of Congress; Historic American Buildings Survey. ca. 1940. Notes: door is dark, ceiling appears to be dropped, and wainscoting is dark. Louise Vrooman lived in the house when this photograph was taken.

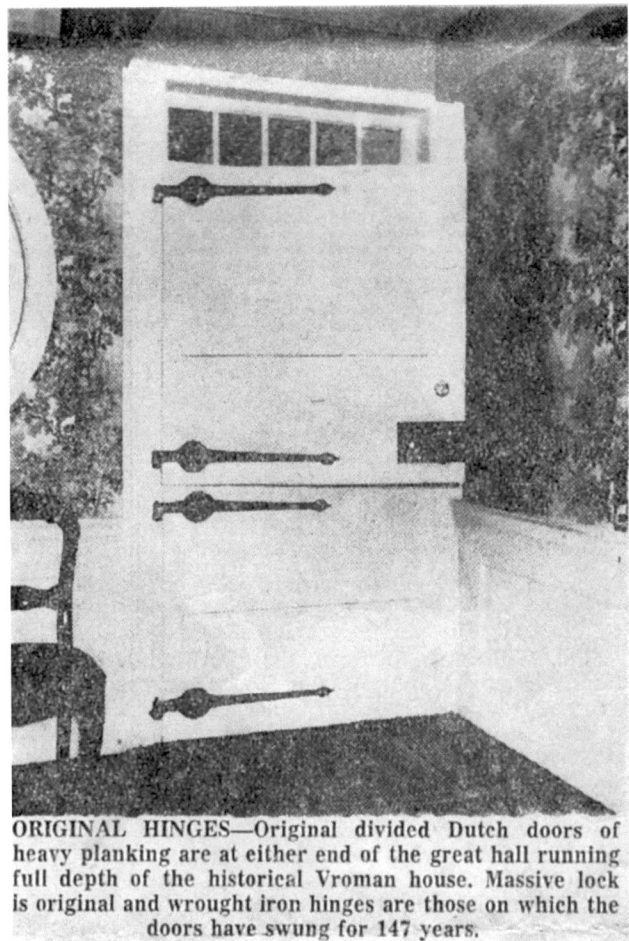

ORIGINAL HINGES—Original divided Dutch doors of heavy planking are at either end of the great hall running full depth of the historical Vroman house. Massive lock is original and wrought iron hinges are those on which the doors have swung for 147 years.

Fig. 110. Inside view of front divided Dutch door (east elevation), 1959. Notes: door is painted white, ceiling is exposed and beam appears to be natural wood, wainscoting is painted white, wallpaper is different from the paper in ca. 1940 photograph. Cora and Mildred Vrooman were the occupants when this photograph was taken.

Fig. 111. View of front divided Dutch door (east elevation), 2017. Notes: door is painted white, beams are cased and painted, wainscoting is painted white, Cora and Mildred Vrooman installed wallpaper some time around the 1950s. The current owners retained that wallpaper.

Fig. 112. View of back divided Dutch door (west elevation), 2017. Notes: door is painted white, beams are cased and painted, wainscoting is painted white, Cora and Mildred Vrooman installed wallpaper some time around the 1950s. The current owners retained that wallpaper. The short door on the left is the entry to the cellar. It is not believed to be the original cellar entry door.

118

Two doors, next to one another, in the first floor hallway lead to the cellar. The door currently used was added later in order to make the cellar steps less steep and required cutting some basement beams. The following photographs are of the supposedly older and now unused door.

Fig. 113. Old door from 1st floor to cellar.

Fig. 114. Back of old door from 1st floor to cellar.

119

The cellar door separating the north and south sections of the cellar is very distinctive and it is thought to be quite old, perhaps 1750 or earlier. Dendrochronology on the house demonstrates that both cellar sections were built at the same time ca. 1792. The door might have been repurposed from elsewhere. It was likely originally used as a front door. It is intriguing to consider why a door would have been placed between the two sections of the cellar. The door is a two-panel type hung on surface mounted hinges with 'pancake' nailing plates. Faintly discernable on this door, with correct lighting, are a variety of lightly etched markings such as crosses, circles, straight lines and perhaps a daisy wheel and compass rose. The compass rose supposedly was a symbol for protecting women.

Fig. 115. Old door in cellar separating north and south sections.

Fig. 116. Another view of the old cellar door.

Fig. 117. Close-up of cellar door hardware.

Fig. 118. Close-up of cellar door hardware and some markings.

Fig. 119. Close-up of some of the cellar door markings.

Floors: The house has original hardwood floors throughout. The wide plank pine floors range in width from 15 to 18 inches. Today it would be almost impossible to find such large floorboards. The boards are laid east to west on the first floor, and north to south on the upper floor. The floorboards were milled on four sides. Several layers covered the original kitchen pine floor, including linoleum and a narrow plank grooved wood floor. Floor patches visible in several rooms indicate spaces at one time used for different purposes. The well-worn area in the kitchen may well indicate the original location of a stairway to the upstairs half-story.

Fig. 120. Example of pine wood floor on half-story of house.
Note floor patch on right bottom, likely result of chimney use at some time.

Linoleum was removed from several locations in the house during the 2013 renovation. The kitchen, pantry and bathroom on the first floor had linoleum covering the original wide-plank floors. It is likely that linoleum was added in the 1950s or 1960s. The kitchen floor retains the original wide-planks. It, perhaps, had a floor cover because the wood is not as fine in quality as the rest of the house and wood bark can be seen on some of the flooring planks. In addition, there are numerous small nail marks suggesting a floor covering. The original kitchen floor was covered by a narrow tongue-in-groove wooden floor, which in turn was covered by two layers of linoleum. Carpeting covered the upstairs bathroom floor and the two upstairs closets were covered with linoleum.

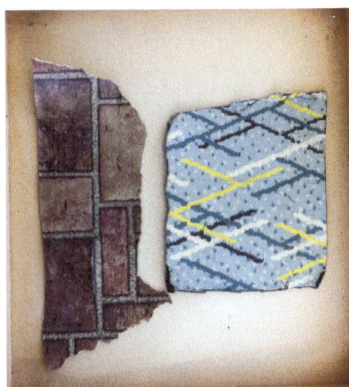

Fig. 121. Left: kitchen linoleum removed in 2013. Right: linoleum removed from upstairs closets in 2013.

Markings in the Colonel Peter Vroman House: There are several fascinating carvings in the white-washed plastered walls in the north section of the cellar. It is unknown when these carvings were made or for what purpose. They remain one of the wonderful mysteries of the house.

Some of the markings are a stylized 'PV' and others have the date '1780' as well as the stylized 'PV'. It is unknown who carved these marks. Some signature examples suggest that Peter Vroman had a few different ways of signing his name. Writing in a book would likely be different than carving letters into a wall. The significance of 1780 is unknown although that was the year Peter Vroman's home in Vroman's Land was destroyed and the mill on this property was attacked during the Johnson/Brant Raid. We also do not know if the "PV" stands for Peter Vroman or something else. We do know from dendrochronology that the house was built ca. 1792 not 1780. But we do not know if part of the cellar structure was from an earlier home built on the same foundation. This is another of the great secrets the house continues to harbor.

Fig. 122. Initials 'PV' carved in cellar wall.

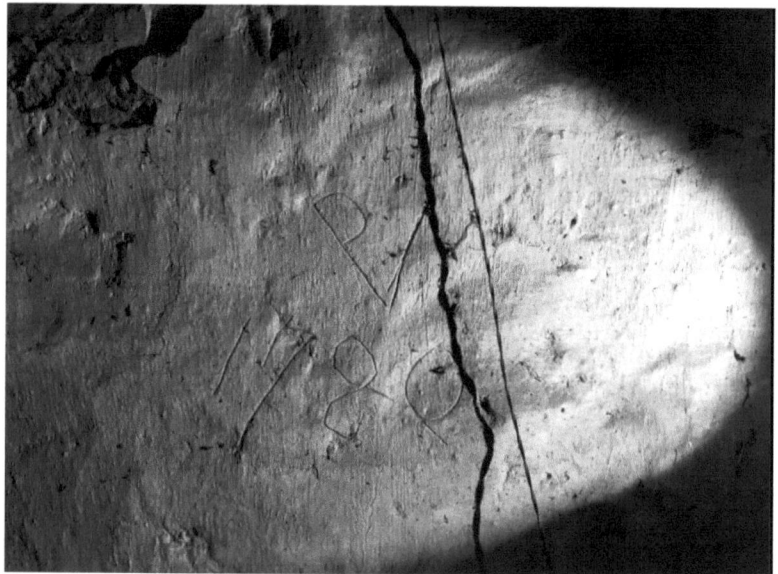

Fig. 123. Initials 'PV' and '1780' date carved in cellar wall.

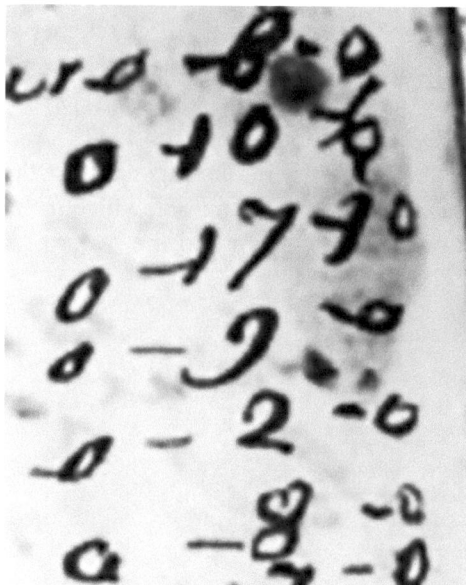

Fig. 124. Examples of some numbers from Vroman's "Account Book."

Fig. 125. Examples of some Peter Vroman signatures.

There are other really interesting carving marks in the cellar. The northwest wall of the cellar has a series of red hash marks. They appear to be made in red chalk and perhaps were used for some type of tally. It is unknown when these marks were made, who made them, or what they might signify. Were these made when this part of the cellar was used as a kitchen? Who made the marks? What were they counting? When were the marks made? Why did they use red? Why are there lines through some of the hash marks and lines above and below other hash marks? So many questions!

Fig. 126. Red hatch marks on cellar wall.

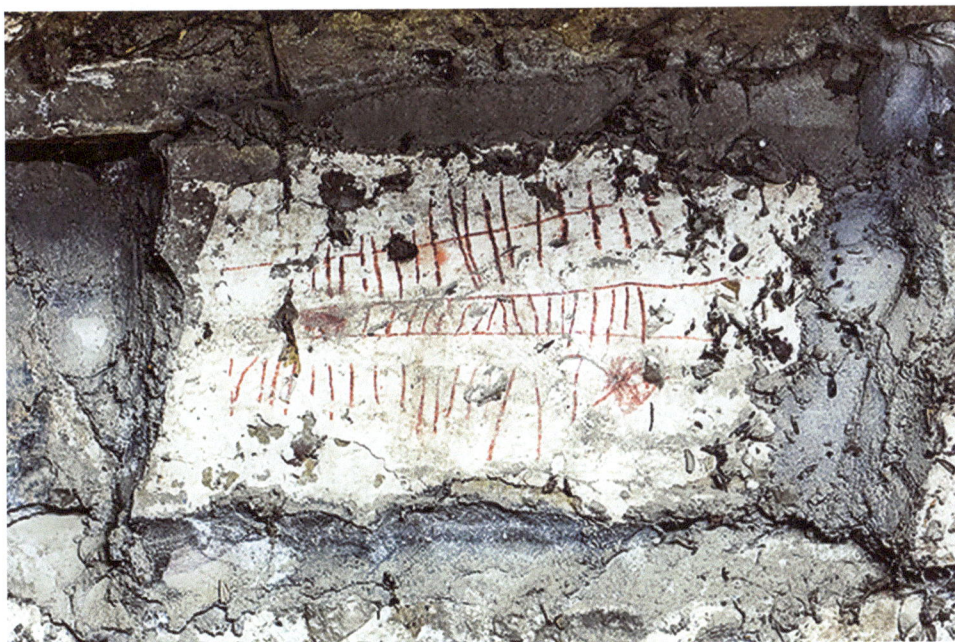

Fig. 127. Close-up of red hatch marks on cellar wall.

Chimneys and Fireplaces: There are two large chimney structures in the house – one in the north side of the cellar and the other near the wall on the south side of the cellar. The chimney in the center of the north side of the cellar is a very large structure. Some char is identifiable near the top of the chimney. This is believed to be the original chimney. It has inside and outside bricks. The chimney in the south section of the basement appears to be a semi-circle with a point. Surrounding construction on the first floor, suggest this might have been a back-to-back fireplace. There are two fireplaces on the first floor of the house with traces of fireplaces upstairs. The living room fireplace (south) mantle face appears to be late 18th or early 19th century but it likely was 'updated' in the 1860s or 1870s with additional embellishments. The dining room fireplace (north) mantle is likely from the first quarter of the 19th century with a Delft tile surround, added at an unknown time.

Fig. 128. Large basement chimney, north side of cellar.

Fig. 129. First floor fireplace mantle in living room.

Fig. 130. First floor fireplace mantle in dining room.

Wallpaper: Colonel Peter Vroman received wallpaper for his house in September 1792 *(Appendix F)*. His colleague and friend, John N. Bleeker, sent the wallpaper along with a letter itemizing the costs, providing directions on preparing and using the glue, and giving instructions for hanging the wallpaper. The letter indicates Vroman was sent three separate parcels of paper hangings. Bleeker writes that the entry room paper had only one border suggesting that other rooms had multiple borders. Bleeker writes that he cut slits in the borders and provided directions to hang the upper, sides, and lower parts of the wallpaper. The use of wallpaper borders was very popular in America from the mid-18th century, largely because sophisticated architectural detailing was expensive to produce and wallpaper borders could provide a similar decorative touch. Unfortunately, we have no hints of the appearance of Vroman's wallpaper. We do know he wallpapered the entry hall but we do not know the other wallpapered areas.

Fig. 131. In ca. 1940, the entry hall has scenic wallpaper with trees, two-tiered fountains, classical stairways and porticos.

Fig. 132. In ca. 1959, the entry hall had a different wallpaper. It is difficult to discern the pattern but it appears to be a floral and it is darker and more dense than the wallpaper used in ca. 1940.

The same entry hall had a different wallpaper when the Heymans purchased the home in 2013. They retained this wallpaper in the downstairs entry and upstairs halls.

Fig. 133. Hall wallpaper 1950s.

Following are photographs of some of the wallpaper installed by Mildred Vroman, likely ca. 1950s/1960s. These wallpapers were on the walls when the Heymans purchased the Col. Peter Vroman house in 2013. All were painted over during the 2013 renovation. The wallpapered ceilings in most of the rooms on the upper floor were also painted in 2013. The narrow wood lathe on the ceilings can be discerned through the paint.

Fig. 134. Living room floral pattern wallpaper 1950s

Fig. 135. Dining room floral pattern wallpaper 1950s.

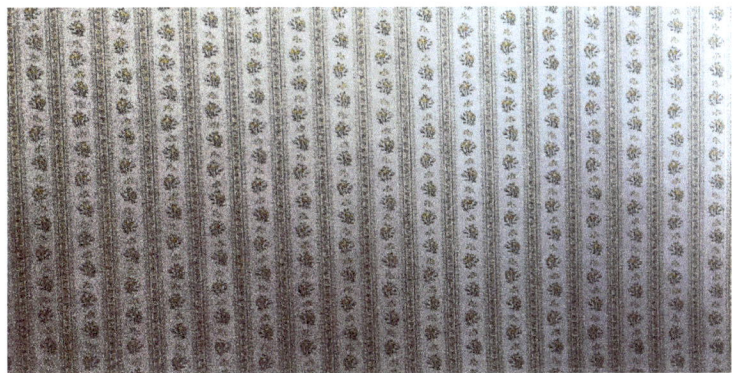

Fig. 136. Northeast bedroom wallpaper 1950s.

Fig. 137. Northwest bedroom wallpaper 1950s.

Fig. 138. Wallpaper fragment used in attic stairway.

Miss Mildred Vrooman's Artistry in the House: Miss Vrooman was quite a talented artist, as her hand-painted egg collection demonstrates. She also applied her talents to the Colonel Peter Vroman house. She painted stencils in the kitchen, the pantry, the first floor bathroom, and an upstairs bedroom. All of the first floor stencil work was lost in the 2013 renovation since walls had to be straightened and leveled. Following are examples of some of Mildred Vrooman's stencil work.

Fig. 139. Mildred Vrooman 1st floor bathroom.

Fig. 140. Mildred Vrooman stencil work in pantry.
Note: Mildred Vrooman painted the tole platter hung between the windows.

Fig. 142. Mildred Vrooman kichen stencil.

Fig. 141. Fragment of Mildred Vrooman stencil from pantry

131

Fig. 143. Upstairs bedroom with Mildred Vrooman stencil work. This stencil remains in the house.

Known House Alterations

The fireplace mantels located on the first-story level in the living room and dining room likely date from the 1820s to the 1850s. The living room mantel, as noted, appears to be of traditional Federal-style design but is embellished with applied decorations, presumable added later. The dining room fireplace has a surround of Delft tiles that are not original to the house The principal staircase appears to date to ca. 1840 and does not appear to be located in its original position, given the manner in which the basement stair required cutting through existing framing. There is a mantel in the half-story northwest bedroom that lacks a corresponding firebox. It likely dates to ca. 1870 and has an Italianate-style design motif.

There was a major renovation in the 1860s-1870s when the owner, Charles B. Stevens, added an existing 16-foot by 20-foot slave quarter to the west elevation of the house. The addition was attached using long iron rods. The slave quarters were removed in the 1950s. Much of the lower clapboard on the west elevation is not beaded and probably was replaced when the slave quarter was removed. A "concealed shoe" suggests other renovations were done during this period.

During the Colonial Revival period (likely 1910s to 1940s), then owner Louise Stevens Vrooman added an elliptical wheel window and a small rectangular window to the east facade. The rectangular window was later removed. Three dormers, the central one being larger than those flanking it and embellished with a Palladian window, were added to the roofline on the east elevation at this time, as was the flat-roofed Ionic order portico. These features appear in HABS photographic documentation dating to ca. 1940, which includes a perspective view of the east and north elevations, along with interior and exterior views of the main door.[169] Early 20th century photographs of the house do not depict the portico or these other features, which probably date to ca. 1910-20. Cora W. Vrooman and her daughter, Mildred Vrooman, removed the dormers and small rectangular window in the 1950s or 1960s as they aimed to return the house to something more in keeping with its original appearance.

The current owners of the Colonel Vroman House, Berna and Joseph Heyman, renovated the bathrooms and kitchen of the house in 2013. In some instances this required stripping the house down to the original studs, exposing lath and brick nogging. Sheetrock replaced the plaster-on-lath walls in those rooms. The closet in the northeast upstairs bedroom became a half-bath and small linen closet. Additional space was used in that bedroom to create new closet space. The infrastructure of the house, including heating, plumbing, and electrical connections, was also replaced and updated at the same time.

There are several changes that were made during unknown time periods. "An upstairs fireplace is gone as is the one at which the first Vromans cooked and baked in the cellar kitchen."[170]

None of the original windows survive, as these were replaced over time. A photograph dating to the later 19th century indicates that the first-story windows were a 12-over-12 pane configuration; they are now all hung with more recent six-over-six sash.

Following are photographs documenting some of the various stages of construction and renovation of the house during the 2013 modernization.

Fig. 144. Upstairs bathroom mortared brickwork east elevation of house, over front door.

Fig. 145. Upstairs bathroom inner wall showing: lathe, studs with bark and knot.

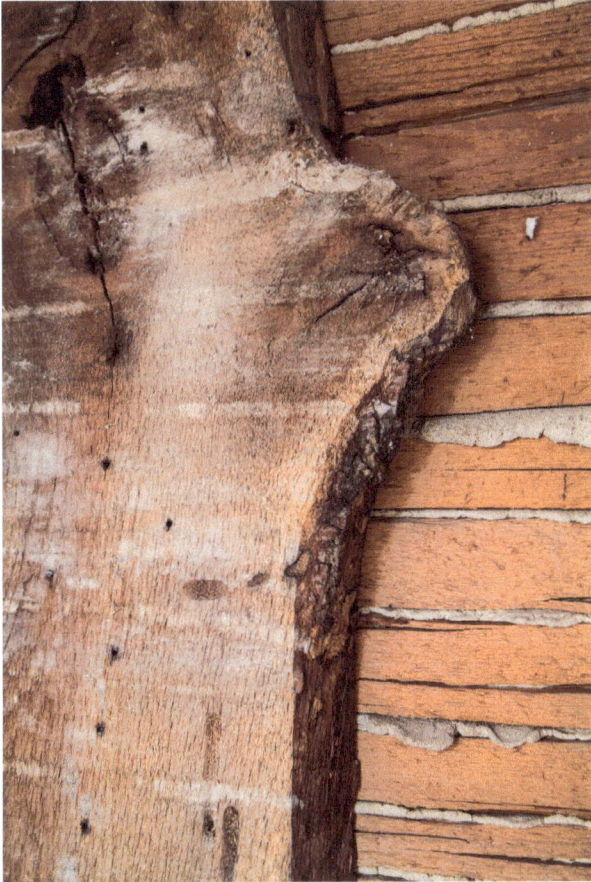

Fig. 146. Close up of stud with bark and knot exposed during 2013 renovation.

Fig. 147. Close-up of cased beam exposed during 2013 renovation.

Fig. 148. Mortared brick over front door.

135

Peter Vroman House During Mildred Vrooman's Occupancy

These photographs were taken in 2012 when Mildred Vrooman owned the home and before Joseph and Berna Heyman purchased it.

Fig. 149. Dining room.

Fig. 150. Dining room.

Fig. 151. First floor hall.

Fig. 152. Living room.

Fig. 153. Living room floor.

Fig. 154. Kitchen.

Fig. 155. First floor bathroom.

Fig. 156. First floor pantry.

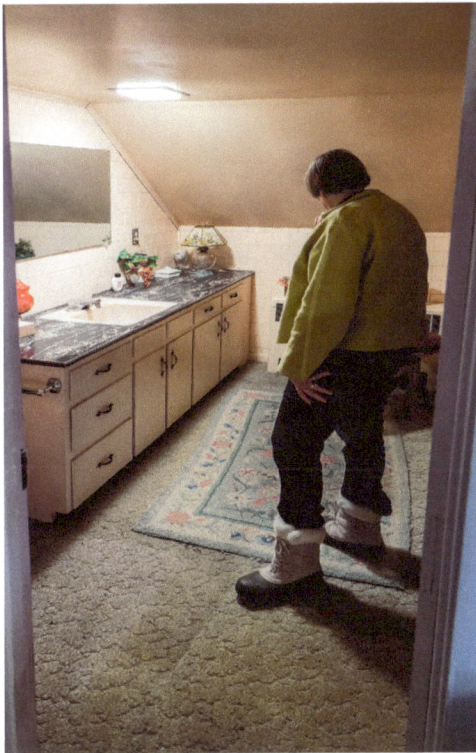

Fig. 157. Upstairs bathroom.

*Fig. 158. Upstairs northeast
bedroom closet*

Fig. 159. Upstairs hall.

Fig. 160. Upstairs hall.

Fig. 161. Upstairs library.

Fig. 160. Upstairs northwest bedroom.

Fig. 159. Upstairs northeast bedroom.

Fig. 161. Upstairs southwest bedroom.

139

Appendices

Appendix A: *A Deed from Myndert Schuyler to John Eckerson for Lands att Schoharie, 1752.*
Transcribed by H. Cady. Printed from http://ancestry.com [Accessed June 29, 2018]
https://tinyurl.com/y97h5kpx and https://tinyurl.com/yaep782h
Original document was in the Old Stone Fort, currently not available.

A^deed from Myndert Schuyler
to John Eckerson for Lands
att Schoharie 1752

VR

is Indenture made the Seventh day of March anno Dom. one thousand Seven
hundred and Fifty Two.. Between Myndert Schuyler of the Citty of Albany
merch^t of the one part And John Eckerson of Schohary in the County of
albany Black Smith of the other part, Witnesseth that the Said myndert
Schuyler for and in Consideration of the Sum of Sixty five pounds------
Currant money of the province of new york to him in hand paid by the Said
John Eckerson att and before- the Ensealing and delivery of these presents
the Receipt whereof he doth hereby acknowledge And him Self to be there With
fully Satisfied & Contented Hath granted Bargained-Sold Alleinated And
Confirmed And by these presents doth grant Bargain-Sell Alliene Enfeoffe
and Confirme unto the Said John Eckerson and to his heirs & assigns for Ever
All that one Equall third part of a Certain Lott of Land att Schohary afores^d
in the Creepelbush behind Wysers flatt. being known & Distinguished and
marked in the Generall draft or Chart of the land Lately devided by the
owners of the Said land att Schoharie No.51. Beginning att the north West
Corner of Lott No 50 And Runs thence north Eaighty Degrees-East Six Chains
& fifty links then north Eighty five degrees East twenty Chains, then South
Sixteen degrees East Six Chains and fifty Links, then South Eighty five degrees
west to. the place where it first begun Containing in the whole Thirteen
Acres, AS Also, one Small Lott of Land att Schohary afors^d Lying to the south
of foxes Creek nigh the Church Beginning by a pitch pine Tree Standing about
three Chains Southerly from the Church And Runs from the Said Tree North
forty Seven degrees west Three Chains & 50 Links then north Thirty two degrees
East five Chains & fifty Links, then north twinty one degrees East five Chains
to foxes Creek down the Said Creek one Chain & forty Links, then South
three Chains to the fott of the sd. hill, then South fifty Six degrees Westerly
along the foot of Said hill Nine Chains to a Stake then South fifty degrees
East eaight Chains, then With a Straight Line to the place where it first
begon, Containing Three acres, As Also. two Equall Seaventh part of four
Acres of-Land Lying a Lidle blow the bridge on foxes Creek, to the north
of Said Creek, Which was Reserved by the owners of Schoharie for a mill
place, together With the two Seventh part of the Stream-of water in foxes
Creek from the bridge to Schohary River, Together With all the profitts-
binofitts Liberties priveledges hereditainents And appurtenances to the afores^d
one Equale third part of Lott No 51. & the Said Lott of three ackers of Land
Lying to the South of the Church & to the two Equall Seaventh parts of
the afores^d four Acres of Land for a mill & of the two Seventh part of
the Streem of water in foxes Creek from the bridge to the Schohary River,
And the Reversion and Reversion Remainder and Remainders Rents Issues &
profitts of all and Singular the Said premisses and Every part & parcell
thereof, And also all the Estate Right title Interest property possession
Claim & Demand whatsoever of him the Said Myndert Schuyler of in or to the
afors^d Severall & Respective. parts of And in all and Every the Afores^d
Severall Lotts or parcell of land & premises afores^d With the appurtenances
To Have and to Hold the afores^d one Equale third part of Sd. Lott No 51.. &
the Said Lott of three acres, & the two Equall Seventh parts of the afores^d
four Acres of Land, And the two Seventh part of the Strem of foxes Creek
Afores^d mentioned and meant or Intended to be hereby granted Released and
Confirmed With these and Every of these Appurtenances unto the Said John
Eckerson his heirs and assigns for Ever, to the only proper use and behoof
of him the Said John Eckerson his heirs and assigns for Ever. Yeelding
and paying therefore yearly and Every year for Ever, hereafter unto the
Said Myndert Schuyler his heirs and assigns the yearly rent of Nine pence
-----Currant money of new york on the twenty fifth of March yearly
the first payment thereof to begin And to Comade on the 25 day of March
one thousand Seven hundred and Fifty Three, which Said yearly Rent of Nine
pence +++ the Said John Eckerson for him soly his heirs and assigns

and for Every of them doth Covenant grant promiss and agree to And with
the Said Myndert Schuyler his heirs and assigns, And to And with Every
of them by these presents Well and truly to pay or Cause to be paid unto the
Said Myndert Schuyler his heirs and assigns all the day and time above
mentioned And the said Myndert Schuyler for him Self his heirs
Execut$ and adminis doo hereby Covenant grant and agree to and with the
Said John Eckerson his heirs and assigns, that be the Said John Eckerson
his heirs and assigns, Shall from henceforth and for Ever hereafter
peaceably and Quietly have hold use occuppy possess and enjoy the hereby
granted Severall and Respective parts or Shares of all and Every the
afors$ Severall Lotts or parcell of land and premisses afores$ With
the appurtenances Without any the Least Lett hinderance Evcition trouble or
molestation of him the Said Myndert Schuyler his heirs Execut$ or adminis,
or of any person or persons Claiming or which might hereafter Claim by
from or under him, and the same & Every part & parcell thereof unto
him the Said John Eckerson his heirs and assigns Shall & Will Warrant &
for Ever by these presents Defend In Wittness whereof thes parties to
these presents have Interchangeably Sett their hands and Seals the day
& year first above Written
Sealed and Delivered in the presents of
Michel freymeyer junr.   Myndert Schuyler
In DeBeysten

H Cady
No 72

E100-48 A&B

141

Appendix B: Indenture Between Peter B. Vroman and Cornelius Vroman, 1770.
The original document is located in the Old Stone Fort. The following transcription is from a document found in the collection of Mildred Vrooman. There is some damage to the original manuscript; unreadable sections of the document are indicated by ( ) <u>For original document, see Fig. 10.</u>

At top of transcript:
Indenture from Col. Peter B. Vroman 1770 – 300 acres, a part of 18,000 acres granted to Michael Byrne of Kingsboro and others [John Johnson, Dan Claus, Guy Johnson, Jelles Fonda, Gilbert Tice) by George III 1768; and by them to Sir William Johnson and he to Vroman. The lands are between Schoharie & Middleburgh along Stony Brook. Peter B. Vroman, the grantor of this deed, had long been high in the confidence of Sir William Johnson He had been appointed captain and served during the French Wars; highly recommended by Sir William to Governor Colden to be promoted as major 1770, date of this deed.

This Indenture Made and Concluded This Twenty Second Day of February in the Tenth year of the Reign of our Sovereign Lord George the Third By the grace of god of great Britain france and Ireland king Defender of the faith &c and in the year of our Lord Christ one Thousand Seven hundred and Seventy Between Peter B Vroman (…) in the County of Albany and province of new york yeoman of The one part and Cornelius Vroman of the (…) County and province aforesaid yeoman of the other part Wittnesseth That the Said Peter B. Vroman for and a (Considera)tion of the Sum of fifty pounds Currant money of the province of new york aforesaid To him in hand paid by (the said Cor) nelius Vroman on the perfection hereof The Receipt whereof he Doth hereby acknowledge and Thereof and Every (…) Doth acquit and (…) him the Siad Cornelius Vroman his heirs Executors administrators and Assigns – (Grant) ed Bargained Sold (Assigne)d Remised Released for Ever Quit Claimed and Confirmed and By These presents Doth (grant) Bargain Sell Assign Remise release and for Ever Quit Claim and Confirm unto the Said Cornelius Vroman (in his actual possession now being by Virtue of a Bargain and Seal To him Thereof made by the Said Peter B. Vro- man for one whole year by Indenture Bearing Date the day next before the day of the date hereof and by force of the Statue for Transferring uses into Possession) and To his heirs all that one undivided Third part of all That part parcel or Lott of Land (Being part of a Tract of Land granted To Micheal Byrne and his associates by his majesties Letters Patent Bearing date the Twenty fifth day of march one Thousand Seven hundred and Sixty Eight Containing Eighteen Thousand acres and Since Legally Conveyed to Sir William Johnson and the Said Sir William Johnson Did by Certain Indenture of Lease and Release Convey To the Said Peter B. Vroman The above said parcel or Lott of Land) Contain- ing Three hundred acres Beginning at the End of Twenty Six Chains on a Line Running north forty Seven Degrees Ten minutes west as the Compass points which is the northerly Bounds of Said Vromans patent and Running along the west Bounds of Said Patent South Twelve Degrees fifty minutes west Sixteen Chains and Thence South Thirty Six Degrees fifty minutes west Twenty one Chains Thence north Sixty Three Degrees fifty minutes west Thirty Three Chains opposite the South west Corner of Peter Vromans Lott Thence north Eighteen Degrees west fifty Two Chains and fifty Links to Stony kill or Creek Thence along the Said patented Lands To the place of Beginning Situate Lying and Being in the Neighbourhood or nearly adjoining To Schohary in the County of Albany and province of new york and all the Estate Right Title and Interest of the Said Peter B. Vroman of in and To the Same TO have and To hold all and Singular The one Equal undivided Third part of the aforementioned part Parcell of Lott of Land Containing Three hundred acres unto the Said Cornelius Vroman his heirs and Assigns for Ever And The Said Peter B Vroman Doth hereby for himself his heirs Execution and administrators Covenant and promise To and with the Said Cornelius Vroman his heirs Executors administrators and Assigns That he the Said Peter B. Vroman hath now in himself good Right full power and Lawfull authority to grant Bargain Sell Assign Release and Confirm all The Said hereby granted Lands unto the Said Cornelius Vroman his heirs Executors administrators and Assigns in manner and form aforesaid And That it Shall and may be Lawfull to and for the Said Cornelius Vroman his heirs Executors administrators and Assigns Respectively peaceably and Quietly to hold uses occupy Possess and Enjoy the Said hereby granted Lands as his and Theirs Real Estate and inheritance according to the True Intent and meaning of these presents without The Lett Suit Trouble or Interruption of him the Said Peter B. Vroman his heirs Executors or administrators or any other person or persons whatsoever Claiming or To Claim by from or under him Them or any of Them AND That free and

Clear and freely and Clearly acquitted Exonerated and Discharged of and from all other gifts grants Bargains Sales Assignments Leases mortgages Judgments alienations Despositions and Incumbrances whatsoever (his majesties Tax or Crown Rent only Excepted) AND Further That he the Said Peter B. Vroman his heirs Executors and administrators Shall and will at all Times hereafter at the proper Cost and Charges of him the Said Cornelius Vroman when Required make and perfect UNTO him The Said Cornelius Vroman his heirs Executors administrators or Assigns all Such further or act or acts Deed or Deeds assurance or Assurances for the further Better and more Sure and Effectuall granting and Confirming The Aforesaid on Equal undivided Third part of the aforesaid Three hundred acres of Land unto him the Said Cornelius Vroman his heirs Executors administrators and assigns as by him or Their Council Learned in Land Shall be Reasonably advised Devised or Required In Wittness whereof The Parties aforesaid have hereunto Sett Their hands and Seals The day and year First above written.

(Signed)   Peter B. Vroman

SIGNED SEALED AND DELIVERED
IN THE PRESENCE OF US

John Valek
Jonas Vroman

Appendix C: Letter Written by Peter Vroman Requesting Tax Exemption for the People of Schoharie Because of Conditions Caused by the War and a Major Flood [n.d.]. Copied by Rufus Alexander Grider. Grider's *Albums*. New York State Library, Manuscripts and Special Collections. Transcribed by Berna Heyman.   <u>For original document see Fig. 12.</u>

That your Petitioners have Long Endured the Burden of a Distressed War and are of the greatest sufferers in the State of new york, By Reason of Living on the Very frontiers of the State, open to the Dayly incursions of a Cruel Enemy, and ~~having~~ are destroyed to the utmost Degree, the most of us not Left a Building to go in to keep them and families Dry from the waether, and no money to Erect Buildings again, the inhabitants of Tryon County are Exampted from paying Taxees, we think it right, and Rather more, we have understood that the District of Schohary was Left to the Subpervisors of the County of albany, you knowe Very well that men are apt to throw the Burden from their own Shoulders upon others.

Your Petitioners therefore applies to you as the grand inquest of this State for a Redress of grievances and Deeply indtrusted in the free Constitution of their County they beg leave to observe to your honorable houses, that if you are inclined to shew any favor <redress?>, to do it then [to] us, as a District and not Leave to the subpervisors again.

What great Loss your petitioners have sustained in their Land and Crops of grain in the ground in this Settlement almost from one End to the other by a thaw, which happened the Latter End of Last week and Likewse great Rain that fell Last Sunday which Together Raised Such a prodigius Quantity of water that overflowed almost all the flats in this Settlement on account of the River Being stopt up with Cakes of Ise to the Top of its Banks, which has happened by another thaw and Rain before, the Said Lakes (…?) with the water were frozen to Solid Ise, which ocasuned the over flowing of the flats, Several Dams of the Ise Still in the River and the water Still Running thru the Land, That whereby Several farms ~~are~~ almost intirely Spouyld, when the water Came Last Sunday night the people were a Bed But got aware of it, Some Drowned in their house were neer any water in that manner had Been Before. Some men women and Children Run thru the water Before it got too Deep to the mountains to Save their Lives, whole Stables with Cattle and horses were drowned your petitioners are apprehensive of Taxes Laid or will be Laid by your honors which we hope to be Exampted from if you Don't Beliefe us Send men that we have suffered as above mentioned, we pray your honorable houses to Send men where you may perhaps place more Confidence in as in us to Take a View of our Situation an Loses.

Appendix D: Petition for the rebuilding of the Low Dutch Reformed Church, 1785. Copied by Rufus Alexander Grider. Grider's *Albums,* New York State Library, Manuscripts and Special Collections. Transcribed by Berna Heyman. <u>For original document see Fig. 13.</u>

L.B.S. (Lector, Benevole, Saloc = Benevolent Reader Greeting)
Sine we of the Reformed Low, dutch Congregation of this Place … have been in Want for a public Building for the Service of God, from the Time our Church was burnt and laid into Ashes, until this Day. We thought it proper, that after Peace were made with Men we Should make peace with our God, which we have So cruaelly offended.

But, whilst we have been destroyed in Like Manner we found Ourselves too weak to the purpose; Therefore we thought it good to make this our humble Petition. To All and Every One, of the Welwishers of Christianity; to Assist us by their good Will, according to what they please to the Building of a New Church, And we will always give our most humble Thanks. For to receive such Benefits we have appointed the Bearers hereof: viz Hannes H. Becker and Martinus van Slyke.

In Expection of your Kindness we remain

Benevolent Readers

Schohary March 11th

1785   Your Dutiful & very humble Servants
                                                                       Ephraim Vroman

Albany 14th March 1785   Peter Vroman
Permission is Granted to Messrs   *Elders*
Hames H. Becker and
Martines Van Slyck to go in this
City pursuant to the above   Thomas Eckerson Jnr
Petition   Martines Vroman
    [In Tar?] Beeckman Mayor (Johannes Jacobse Beeckman)   Johannes Vroman

145

Appendix E: Peter Vroman Letter to Captain [George] Richtmeyer, 1779.

Schohary June 11th 1779

Sir / you will Remain at fort Dubois with the party un[der]
your Command and Take the nessacary Steps in defending that p[lace]
and keeping out nessacary Scouts — untell a further order f[rom]
me. the Continentel troops Stationed here are mostly march[ed to]
Schonectady and the Rest will Soon I Expect, I have Some
melitia now on Scout and are obliged to order more of them [to]
the forts, as Soon as the melitia from albany arrive here [I]
will have those of my Regiment now at Cobus kill und[er my]
Command belonging here in Schohary all Releave. I Remain —

Sir your humble [Servant]

Peter Vroma[n]

To Capt Richtmeyer

P.S. if there is any Danger of an appearance of the Enemy, [it will be]
Very Soon, as the troops are now on their marching the[refore]
keep a good Look out and be upon your gaurd

on publick Service

Capt
George Richtmeyer

Fort Dubois

146

Transcribed by Berna Heyman:

Captain George Richtmyer was in the 3rd Company of the 15th regiment of Militia of New York.

Schohary June 11th 1779

Sir/

You will remain at Fort Dubois with the party under your Command and take the nesacary steps in defending that post and keeping out nesacary Scouts – untell a further order from me. The Continental troops stationed here are mostly marched to Schonectady and the rest will soon I expect. I have some of our militia now on Scout and are obliged to order more of them in the forts, as soon as the militia from Albany arrive here I will have those of my Regiment now at Cobus kill under your command belonging in Schohary all Releaved. I remain ---

Sir your humble Scout

To Capt Richtmeyer

Peter Vroman Col.

PS if there is any Danger of an appearance of the Enemy, it will be very soon, as the troops are now on their march therefore keep a good lookout and be on your guard.

Appendix F. John N. Bleecker letter to Peter Vroman, September 21, 1792. *John N. Bleecker Collection.* 1792-1796. New York State Historical Society. Copy of the letter in the possession of Berna Heyman.

Page 1:

& next them with Water, boile it well, Stir it
so as to leave no Lumps, then Cut your paper
the Exact height of the Wall which is to be
Covered, lay the paper on a level table and
with a Clean painters brush or border rub the
paste over the paper, and every time before the paper
is put on, brush the Wall for about two
breadths of the paper with the glue prepared
as above — you may put some of the glue
water into your paste — from these directions
I suppose any person using some Exactness
may perform the business. When the paper is
placed on the Wall a Clean towel is used in
the hands to lay it smooth — when finished
with the hangings, place the borders on the
Edges of the Upper part, sides, & lower
part of the Room over the hangings

Page 3:

the Walls ought to be very dry & sweated
out before you attempt to proper them. —

I Mrs Bleecker is much in the
Same Situation as when you was here,
Except that the lump in her breast seems
Separated, & one part appears so loose
that Doctr Williams entertains hopes of
its Coming out soon, upon the Whole he
is Confident with the blessing of God
to perform a Compleat Cure. — I am

Dear Sir
Your most Hum: Serv
John N. Bleecker

N. B The paper & Glue is put
into a bag of mine Marked ₤NB which
Can be returned when your people Come down

Mr Peter Vroman

Appendix G.

A Dendrochronological Analysis of the "Peter Vroman House", Schoharie, Schoharie County, New York.

Dr. Edward R. Cook
William J. Callahan, Jr.

September 2017

Introduction

This is the final report on the dendrochronological analysis of a structure known as the "Peter Vroman House" (surname variably "Vrooman") which stands at 112 Covered Bridge Lane, Schoharie, Schoharie County, New York 12157 (42°40'47"N-74°18'05"W). The house and grounds are owned and occupied by Joseph & Berna Heyman, who carefully preserve the historical integrity of the property. The Heymans also maintain a house in Williamsburg, VA. For convenience, in this report the studied site will be known throughout as the "Vroman House".

In an effort to establish a more precise history of the building, the Heymans requested that dendrochronologists William Callahan and Dr. Edward Cook perform a tree-ring analysis of selected representative structural timbers. To that end, Callahan visited the site and collected samples for the dendrochronological analysis of the timbers on 11 & 12 September, 2017.

Of the 13 field samples taken, all 13 were deemed of sufficient quality for submission for laboratory analysis. Seven of the submitted samples were of oak (Quercus sp.), and six were of pine (Pinus sp.).

Every effort was made on site to locate bark or waney edges on the sampled timbers in order to ascertain the absolute cutting date, or dates, of the trees used in the construction. After this analysis, the core samples and their associated measurement series will be permanently archived at the Tree Ring Research Laboratory, Lamont-Doherty Earth Observatory, Columbia University, under the sample reference numbers as listed in Tables 1 & 2, column 1.

1.   Dendrochronological Analysis

Dendrochronology is the science of analyzing and dating annual growth rings in trees. Its first significant application was in the dating of ancient Indian pueblos of the southwestern United States (Douglass 1921, 1929). Andrew E. Douglass is considered the "father" of dendrochronology, and his numerous early publications concentrated on the application of tree-ring data to archaeological dating. Douglass established the connection between annual ring width variability and annual climate variability which allows for the precise dating of wood material (Douglass 1909, 1920, 1928; Stokes and Smiley 1968; Fritts 1976; Cook and Kariukstis 1990). The dendrochronological methods first developed by Douglass have evolved and been employed throughout North America, Europe, and much of the temperate forest zones of the globe (Edwards 1982; Holmes 1983; Stahle and Wolfman 1985; Cook and Callahan 1992, Krusic and Cook 2001). In Europe, where the dendrochronological dating of buildings and artifacts has long been a routine professional support activity, the success of tree-ring dating in historical contexts is noteworthy (Baillie 1982; Eckstein 1978; Bartholin 1979; Eckstein 1984).

The wood samples collected from the Vroman House were processed by Dr. Edward Cook following well-established dendrochronological methods. The core samples were carefully glued onto grooved mounts and were sanded to a high polish to reveal the annual tree rings clearly. The rings widths were measured under a microscope to a precision of ±0.001 mm. The cross-dating of the obtained measurements utilized the COFECHA computer program (Holmes 1983), which employs a sliding correlation to identify probable cross-dates between tree-ring series. In all cases, the robust non-parametric Spearman rank correlation coefficient was used for determining cross-dating. Experience has shown that for trees growing in the northeastern United States, this method of cross-dating is greatly superior to the traditional skeleton plot technique (Stokes and Smiley 1968). It is also very similar to the highly successful CROS program employed by, for instance, Irish dendrochronologists to cross-date European tree-ring series (Baillie 1982).

COFECHA is used to first establish internal, or relative, cross-dating amongst the individual timbers from the site. This step is critically important because it locks in the relative positions of the timbers to each other, and indicates whether or not the dates of those specimens with outer bark rings are consistent. Subsequently, one or more internally cross-dated series are compiled from the individual site samples, and these are compared in turn with independently established tree-ring master chronologies compiled from living trees and dated historical tree-ring material. All of the regional "master chronologies" are based on completely independent tree-ring samples.

In the Vroman House study, species specific, regional composite master chronologies from living trees and historical structures from New York, eastern and central Pennsylvania, Massachusetts, and New Jersey, and other near-lying regions were referenced primarily. All dating results were verified finally by subsequent comparison with other independent dating masters from surrounding areas. In each case, the datings as reported here were confirmed as correct.

Results and Conclusions

The results of the dendrochronological dating of the Vroman House timbers are summarized in **Tables 1 & 2** and **Figures 1 & 2**. A total of 13 samples (seven oak, six pine) were analyzed in the laboratory, with all 13 of the samples providing firm dendrochronological dates. To achieve these datings required attention during analysis to the previously recorded structural context of the samples (see **Tables 1 & 2**, column 3). The contextual association of samples from within the structure, the redundancy of the indicated relative cross-datings, and the eventual existence of bark/waney edges demonstrating cutting year, provides the essential constraints necessary for establishing cross-dating, both within a site and with absolute chronological masters.

The strength of the cross-dating of the samples is indicated by the Spearman rank correlations in the seventh column ("CORREL") of **Tables 1 & 2**. These statistical correlations, produced by the COFECHA program, indicate how well each sample cross-dates with the mean of the others in the group. The individual correlations vary slightly in statistical strength, but all are in the range that is expected for correctly cross-dated timbers from buildings in the eastern United States.

The outermost ring on a waney, bark-edged sample identifies the absolute cutting year. Absence of the bark edge (interchangeably called the wane) on a sample indicates that the outermost extant ring is not the year of cutting, but some identifiable year preceding the cutting. In the absence or loss of wane, field observations of wood anatomical factors often permit close approximation of the number of missing rings and thus estimation of the cutting date. In particular the presence of sapwood, a physiologically active wood found immediately within the bark on the outer portion of the trunk, is an indication that the original wane stood near.

Table 1. Dendrochronological dating results for the oak samples taken from the Peter Vroman House, Schoharie, NY. For WANEY, +BE means the bark edge was present and thought to be recovered at the time of sampling; -BE means that the bark edge was not recovered or was completely missing on the timber. If –BE, +SP refers to the likelihood that sapwood rings are present. If so, the outer date may be close to the cutting date. All correlations are Spearman rank correlations of each series against the mean of all of the others of the same site oak species. If the outermost recovered +BE ring is completely formed, it is indicated as "comp", meaning that the tree was felled in the dormant season following that last calendar year of growth, during late autumn/winter. "Incomp" means that the outermost ring was not fully formed, meaning that the tree was felled during the spring/summer growing season.

ID	SPECIES	DESCRIPTION	WANEY	RINGS	DATING	CORREL
VHSCNY 01	Oak	S cellar, joist beam, 1st from E wall	+BE?	228	1563 1790	0.51
VHSCNY 02	Oak	S cellar, joist beam, 3rd from E wall	-BE (BE at start, est. 3-5 r lost)	218	1569 1786	0.58
VHSCNY 03	Oak	S cellar, joist beam, 5th from E wall	+BE "comp"	213	1579 1791	0.39
VHSCNY 04	Oak	N cellar, joist beam, 1st from E wall	BE (note below)	253	1476 1728	0.53
VHSCNY 05	Oak	N cellar, joist beam, 2nd from E wall	+BE "comp"	249	1543 1791	0.51
VHSCNY 06	Oak	N cellar, joist beam, 4th from E wall	+BE "comp"	268	1524 1791	0.52
VHSCNY 07	Oak	Cellar, sill/lintel over central wall between N&S sections	-BE, +SP (BE est. close)	185	1606 1790	0.63

Note VHSCNY04 - Many outer rings unmeasureable because of extreme growth suppression, thus not recorded.

Table 2. Dendrochronological dating results for the pine samples taken from the Peter Vroman House, Schoharie, NY. For WANEY, +BE means the bark edge was present and thought to be recovered at the time of sampling; -BE means that the bark edge was not recovered or was completely missing on the timber. All correlations are Spearman rank correlations of each series against the mean of all of the others of the same site pine species. If the outermost recovered +BE ring is completely formed, it is indicated as "comp", meaning that the tree was felled in the dormant season following that last year of growth. "Incomp" means that the outermost ring was not fully formed, meaning that the tree was felled during the spring/summer growing season.

ID	SPECIES	DESCRIPTION	WANEY	RINGS	DATING	CORREL
VHSCNY 10	Pine	Attic, rafter, 4th pair from N wall, W side	+BE "comp"	115	1677 1791	0.56
VHSCNY 11	Pine	Attic, rafter, 7th pair from N wall, W side	+BE "comp"	115	1677 1791	0.62
VHSCNY 12	Pine	Attic, rafter, 8th pair from N wall, W side	+BE?, close	115	1676 1790	0.44
VHSCNY 13	Pine	Attic, rafter, 7th pair from N wall, E side	+BE "comp"	91	1701 1791	0.57
VHSCNY 14	Pine	Attic, rafter, 2nd pair from N wall, E side	BE?, close?	94	1692 1785	0.62
VHSCNY 15	Pine	Attic, rafter, 1st pair from N wall, E side	-BE, close?	88	1691 1778	0.59

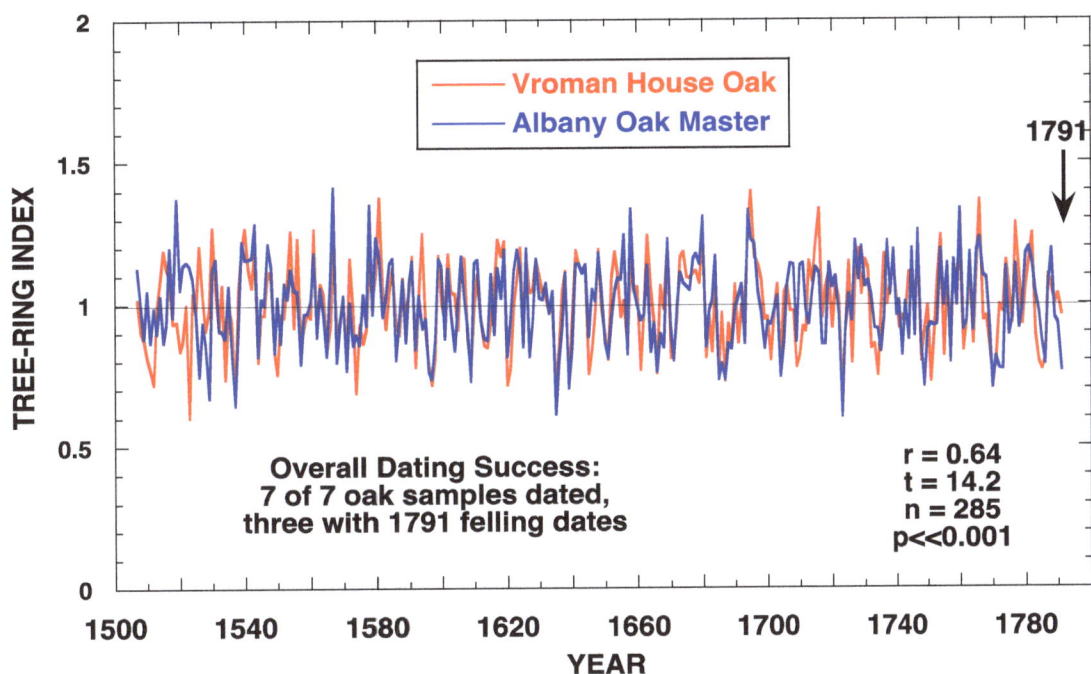

Figure 1. Comparison of the cross-dated, site compiled oak chronology for the Peter Vroman House against a historical oak dating master chronology for the Albany region. The Spearman rank correlation between the series (r=0.64) is highly significant (p<<0.001) with an overlap of 285 years and a t-statistic of 14.2.

The "r-factor" is the Spearman rank correlation coefficient, a measure of relative statistical agreement between two groups of measurements or data. It can range from +1 (perfect direct agreement) to -1 (perfect opposite agreement). The "t-value" is Student's distribution test for determining the unique probability distribution for "r", i.e. the likelihood of its value occurring by chance alone. As a rule, a t=3.5 has a probability of about 1 in 1000, or 0.001, of being invalid. Higher "t" values indicate exponentially increasing, stronger statistical certitude.

The t-statistics (t=14.2) associated with the correlation between the Vroman House oak series and the regional oak master chronology (r=0.64) is statistically very significant (p<<0.001) for a 285-year overlap. For that reason, there can be no doubt that the dates presented here for the sampled oak elements of the structure are robustly valid, and that the statistical chance of the cross-dates being incorrect is far less exponentially than 1 in 1000.

Pine Tree-Ring Dating Results For The
Peter Vroman House, Schoharie, New York

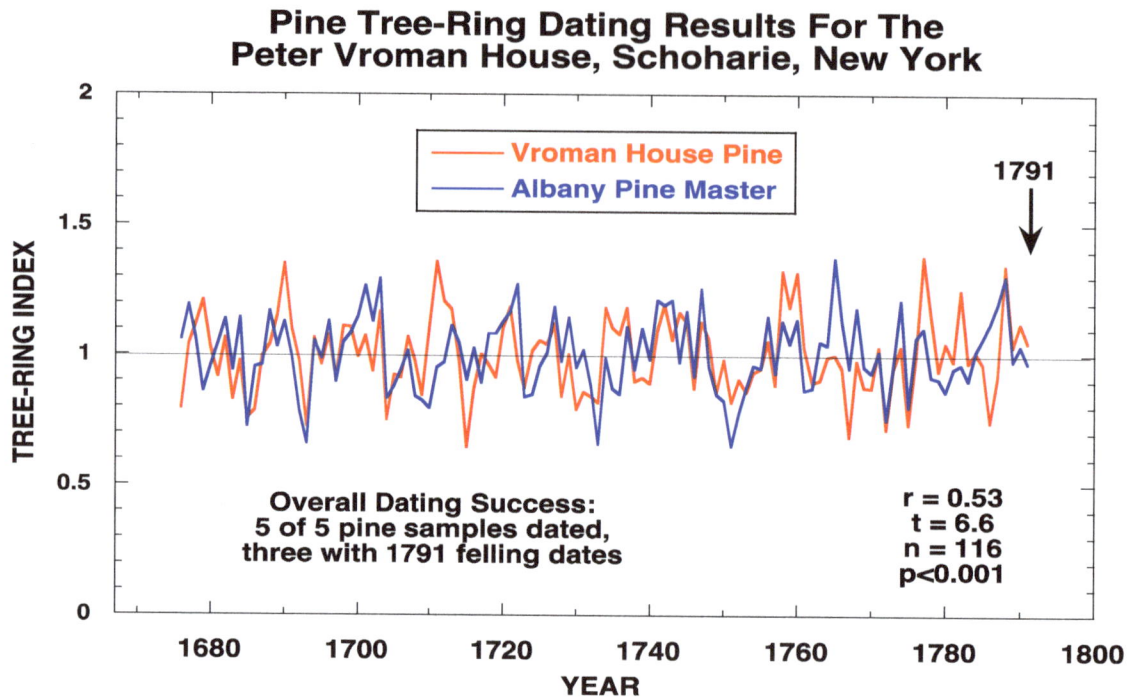

Figure 2. Comparison of the cross-dated, site compiled white pine master chronology for the Peter Vroman House against a historical white pine dating master for the Albany region. The Spearman rank correlation between the series (r=0.53) is highly significant (p<0.001) with an overlap of 116 years and a t-statistic of 6.6.

The "r-factor" is the Spearman rank correlation coefficient, a measure of relative statistical agreement between two groups of measurements or data. It can range from +1 (perfect direct agreement) to -1 (perfect opposite agreement). The "t-value" is Student's distribution test for determining the unique probability distribution for "r", i.e. the likelihood of its value occurring by chance alone. As a rule, a t=3.5 has a probability of about 1 in 1000, or 0.001, of being invalid. Higher "t" values indicate exponentially increasing, stronger statistical certitude.

The t-statistics (t=6.6) associated with the correlation between the Vroman House pine series and the regional pine master chronology (r=0.53) is statistically very significant (p<<0.001) for a 116-year overlap. For that reason, there can be no doubt that the dates presented here for the sampled pine elements of the structure are robustly valid, and that the statistical chance of the cross-dates being incorrect is far less exponentially than 1 in 1000.

Of the 7 oak samples that cross-dated well between themselves, and also dated well against the local historical oak dating master (see **Table 1**, column 6), three (VHSCNY03, 05, 06) had field verified bark edge at the time of sampling. Evidence of sapwood remained on all of the non-wane samples, strengthening a reasoned evaluation of the cutting date for the structural unit as a whole. Of the six pine samples that cross-dated well between themselves, and also dated well against the local historical pine dating master (see **Table 2**, column 6), three (VHSCNY10, 11, 13) had field verified bark edge at the time of sampling. In several BE cases for both species bark surviving on the tested timbers was removed just prior to sampling.

For both the oak and pine samples, analysis of the degree of development of the outermost wane rings indicates that cutting of the bark-edged timbers occurred during the regional period of winter dormancy following the end of the growth season, i.e. cutting took place during approximately November to February when no wood growth occurs (see **Tables 1 & 2**). The outermost extant ring on any of the analyzed oak samples is 1791; these oak beams employed in the construction of the cellar were harvested during dormancy between 1791/1792. The outermost extant ring on any of the analyzed pine samples is likewise from 1791; these pines employed in the construction of the rafter system were harvested during dormancy between 1791/1792.

Initial usage of the materials took place not long after harvesting, for *in situ* inspection of the timbers indicated that most if not all were worked soon after cutting, in keeping with historical woodworking and carpentry techniques. Although not strongly suggested by any of the timbers analyzed in this project, other construction phases prior or subsequent to the dates identified by this investigation cannot be empirically supported or discounted. The slight variance in the dates of two pine rafters (VHSCNY14, 15) may indicate materials gathered from another structure or harvested at an earlier time, though neither has the certain evidence of wane edge to absolutely date the outermost extant ring, nor do they pre-date the other associated timbers by many years. Subsequent re-use of the timbers in other construction phases, although not evidenced in the materials, cannot be excluded absolutely and must be considered when developing the site's construction history. However, given the uniformity of the dating of the majority of the tested oak and pine timbers, selected as structurally representative after deliberate inspection, it is likely that the dates are demonstrative of the original construction of the existing building.

The degree of chronological congruency in the collective set of datings of the selected cellar oak and attic pine timbers indicates that a significant construction phase for the Vroman House began with the laying down of the cellar oak timbers, conceivably performed during the clement weather months of calendar year 1792, or if delayed during 1793 at the latest. Moreover, the corresponding cutting dates of the cellar beams and the roof rafters demonstrate that the construction was thoroughly planned and organized, and that deliberate preparatory work for timbering of the structure as a whole was conducted during the very late autumn of 1791 or the winter of 1791/1792, i.e. that specific timber harvesting occurred in advance of an intended construction. It seems reasonable to suppose that the structural carpentry continued apace, though of course final construction efforts may have continued for some few years afterwards.

MODERN/HISTORICAL OAK CHRONOLOGIES
REGIONAL LOCATIONS OF SAMPLES

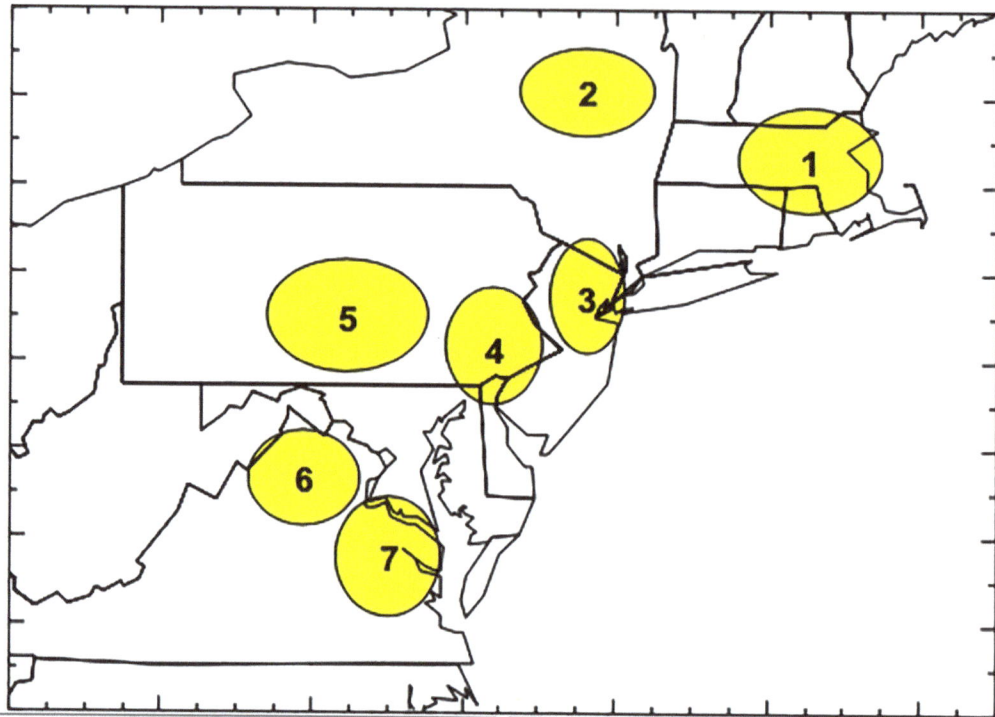

MODERN/HISTORICAL OAK TREE-RING CHRONLOGIES

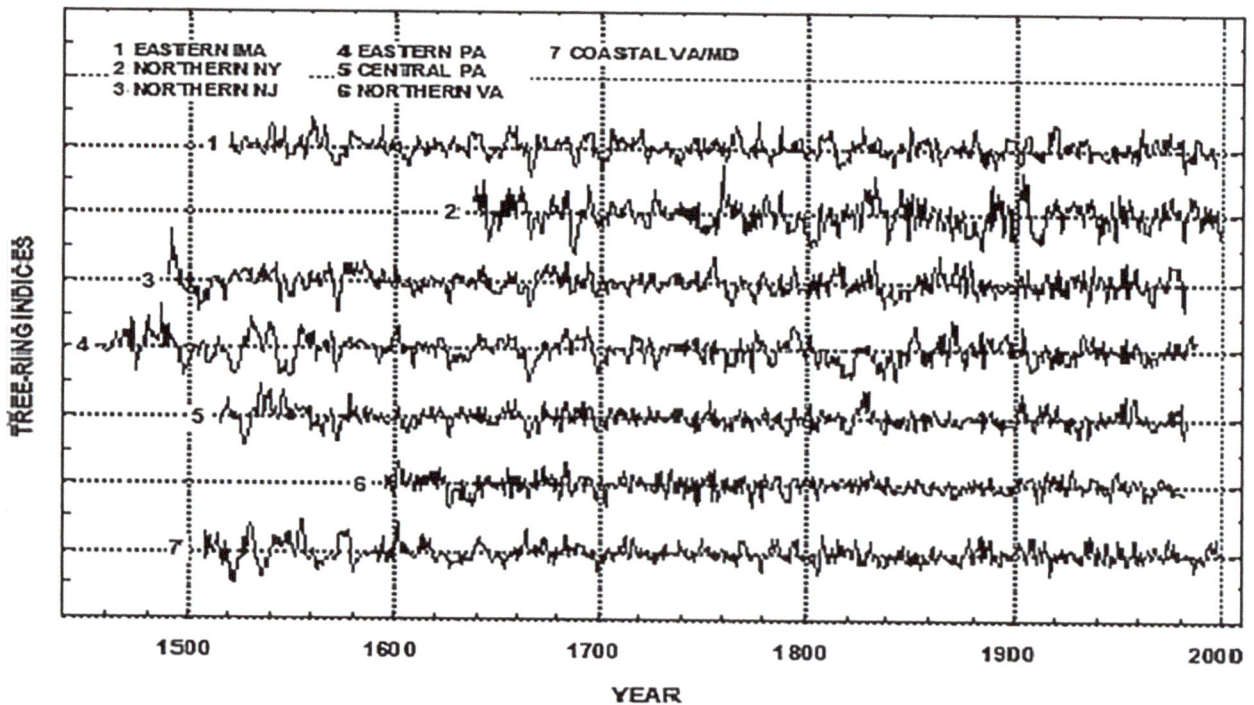

1 EASTERN MA   4 EASTERN PA   7 COASTAL VA/MD
2 NORTHERN NY   5 CENTRAL PA
3 NORTHERN NJ   6 NORTHERN VA

TREE-RING INDICES

YEAR

Some Selected References

Baillie, M.G.L. 1982. *Tree-Ring Dating and Archaeology*. Croom Helm, London and Canberra. 274 pp.

Baillie, M.G.L. 1995. *A Slice Through Time: Dendrochronology and Precision Dating*.B.T. Batsford, Ltd., London

Bartholin, T.S. 1979. "Provtagning för dendrokronologisk datering och vedanatomisk analys." *Handbook i archeologiskt fältarbete, häfte 2*. 1-15 Riksantikvarieämbetets dokumentationsbyrå, Stockholm.

Cook, E.R. and Callahan, W.J. 1987. *Dendrochronological Dating of Fort Loudon in South-Central Pennsylvania*. Limited professional distribution.

Cook, E.R. and Callahan, W.J. 1992. *The Development of a Standard Tree-Ring Chronology for Dating Historical Structures in the Greater Philadelphia Region*. Limited professional distribution.

Cook, E.R., Callahan, W.J. and Wells, Camille 2007. *Dendrochronological Analysis of Rural Plains, Mechanicsville, Hanover County,Virginia*. Limited professional distribution..

Cook, E.R. and Callahan, W.J. 2008. *Dendrochronological Analysis of Freer-Low House,Huguenot Street, New Paltz, Ulster County,NewYork*. Limited professional distribution.

Cook, E.R. and L. Kariukstis, eds. 1990. *Methods of Dendrochronology: Applications in the Environmental Sciences*. Kulwer, The Netherlands.

Douglass, A.E. 1909. Weather cycles in the growth of big trees. *Monthly Weather Review* 37(5): 225-237

Douglass, A.E. 1920. Evidence of climate effects in the annual rings of trees. *Ecology* 1(1):24-32

Douglass, A.E. 1928. Climate and trees. *Nature Magazine* 12:51-53

Douglass, A.E. 1921. Dating our prehistoric ruins: how growth rings in trees aid in the establishing the relative ages of the ruined pueblos of the southwest. *Natural History* 21(1):27-30

Douglass, A.E. 1929. The secret of the southwest solved by talkative tree-rings. *National Geographic Magazine* 56(6):736-770.

Eckstein, D. 1978. Dendrochronological dating of the medieval settlement of Haithabu (Hedeby). In: *Dendrochronology in Europe*, (J. Fletcher, ed.) British Archaeological Reports International Series 51: 267-274

Eckstein, D. 1984. *Dendrochronological Dating (Handbooks for Archaeologists, 2)*. Strasbourg, European Science Foundation.

Eckstein, D. and Bauch, J. 1969. "Beitrag zur Rationisilerung eines dendrokronologischen Verfahrens und zur Analyse seiner Aussagesicherheit." *Forstwissenschaftliches Centralblatt* 88, 230-250.

Edwards, M.R. 1982. Dating historic buildings in lower Maryland through dendrochronology. In: *Perspectives in Vernacular Architecture*. Vernacular Architecture Forum.

Fritts, H.C. 1976. *Tree Rings and Climate*. Academic Press, New York. 567 pp.

Holmes, R.L. 1983. Computer assisted quality control in tree-ring dating and measurement. *Tree-Ring Bulletin* 43:69-78

Krusic, P.J. and E.R. Cook. 2001. *The Development of Standard Tree-Ring Chronologies for Dating Historic Structures in Eastern Massachusetts: Completion Report*. Great Bay Tree-Ring Laboratory, May 2001.

Stahle, D.W. and D. Wolfman. 1985. The potential for archaeological tree-ring dating in eastern North America. *Advances in Archaeological Method and Theory* 8: 279-302.

Stokes, M.A. and T.L. Smiley. 1968. *An Introduction to Tree-Ring Dating*. University of Chicago Press, Chicago 110 pp.

Edward Cook was born in Trenton, New Jersey, in 1948. He received his PhD. from the Tucson Tree-Ring Laboratory of the University of Arizona in 1985, and has worked as a dendrochronologist since 1973. Currently director of the Tree-Ring Laboratory at the Lamont-Doherty Earth Observatory of Columbia University, he has comprehensive expertise in designing and programming statistical systems for tree-ring studies, and is the author of many works dealing with the various scientific applications of the dendrochronological method.

William Callahan was born in West Chester, Pennsylvania, in 1952. After completing his military service he moved to Europe, receiving his MA from the University of Stockholm in 1979. He began working as a dendrochronologist in Sweden in 1980 at the Wood Anatomy Laboratory at the University of Lund, and returned to the United States in 1998. A former research associate of Dr. Edward Cook at the Tree-Ring Laboratory of Lamont-Doherty, he has extensive experience in using dendrochronology in dating archaeological artifacts and historic sites and structures.

Some regional historical dendrochronological projects completed by the authors:

Abraham Hasbrouck House, New Paltz, NY
Allen House, Shrewsbury, NJ
Belle Isle, Lancaster County, VA
Bowne House, Queens, NY
Carpenter's Hall, Philadelphia, PA
Charpentier House, Philadelphia PA
Christ's Church, Philadelphia, PA
Clifton, Northumberland County, VA
Conklin House, Huntington, NY
Customs House, Boston, MA
Daniel Boone Homestead, Birdsboro, PA
Daniel Pieter Winne House, Bethlehem, NY
Ditchley, Northumberland County, VA
Ephrata Cloisters, Lancaster County, PA
Fallsington Log House, Bucks County, PA
Ferris House, Old Greenwich, Fairfield County, CT
Fawcett House, Alexandria, VA
Gadsby's Tavern, Alexandria, VA
Garrett House, Sugartown PA
Gilmore Cabin, Montpelier, Montpelier Station, VA
Gracie Mansion (Mayor's Residence), New York, NY
Grove Mount, Richmond County, VA
Hanover Tavern, Hanover Courthouse, VA
Harriton House, Bryn Mawr, PA
Hills Farm, Accomack County, VA
Hollingsworth House, Elk Landing, MD
Indian Banks, Richmond County, VA
Indian King Tavern, Haddonfield NJ
Independence Hall, Philadelphia, PA
John Bowne House, Forest Hills, NY
Kirnan, Westmoreland County, VA
Linden Farm, Richmond County, VA
Log Cabin, Fort Loudon, PA
Lower Swedish Log Cabin, Delaware County, PA
Lummis House, Ipswich MA
Marmion, King George County, VA
Martin Cabin, New Holland PA
Menokin, Richmond County, VA
Merchant's Hope Church, Prince George County, VA
Millbach House, Lebanon County, PA
Monaskon, Lancaster County, VA
Monaskon, Lancaster County, VA
Morris Jumel House, Jamaica, NY
Frederick Muhlenberg House, Trappe, PA

Nottingham DeWitt House, NY
Old Barn, Madison VA
Old Caln Meeting House, Thorndale, PA
Old Parsonage, Kinderhook NY
Old Swede's Church, Philadelphia, PA
OTB House, West Nyack, NY
Panel Paintings, National Gallery, Washington, DC
Pennock House & Barn, London Grove, PA
Penny Watson House, Greenwich, NJ
Podrum Farm, Limekiln, PA
Powell House, Philadelphia, PA
Pyne House, Cape May, NJ
Radcliff van Ostrade, Albany, NY
Reese's Corner House, Rock Hall, MD
Rippon Lodge, Prince William County, VA
Rochester House, Westmoreland County, VA
Rockett"s, Doswell VA
Rural Plains, Hanover County, VA
Sabine Hall, Richmond County, VA
Shirley, Charles City County, VA
Sisk Cabin, Culpeper VA
Stiles Cabin, Sewickely PA
Spangler Hall, Bentonville, VA
Springwater Farm, Stockton, NJ
St. Peter's Church, Philadelphia, PA
Strawbridge Shrine, Westminster, MD
Sweeney-Miller House, Kingston, NY
Thomas & John Marshall House, Markham, VA
Thomas Grist Mill, Exton, PA
Thomas Thomas House, Newtown Square, PA
Ticonderoga Pavilion, Ticonderoga, NY
Tuckahoe, Goochland County, VA
Tullar House, Egremont MA
Updike Barn, Princeton, NJ
Varnum's HQ, Valley Forge, PA
Verville, Lancaster County, VA
West Camp House, Saugerties, NY
Westover, Charles City County, VA
White Plains House, King George, VA
Wilton, Westmoreland County, VA
Yew Hill, Fauquier County, VA

ENDNOTES

To 1714 -- The Mohawk Iroquois Nation (pp.1-2)

1. Arthur C. Parker, "Archaeological History of New York," *New York State Museum Bulletin* (1922): 693.

2. David K. Schafer, *Cultural Resources Reconnaissance Survey Report of PIN 9125.05.121, Routes 30/30A Intersection and Vroman Corners Intersection, Town of Schoharie, Schoharie County, New York.* (Prepared for the New York State Dept. of Transportation by the New York State Museum. Albany, 1995): 50.

3. Christina B. Rieth, *Cultural Resources Site Examination Report of The Vroman I Site ... and The Vroman II Site ... Schoharie County, New York.* (Albany, NY: Division of Research and Collections, New York State Education Department, 2015): 6.

4. Ibid.: 61.

1714-1752 Myndert Schuyler and Others (The Old Schoharie Patent) (pp. 3-5)

5. Governor Hunter also granted a 1,000 acre patent to Adam Vroman in 1714. This patent was along a creek flowing into the Schoharie. Since Vroman had established a mill in Schenectady, he presumably expected to do the same with the patent grant. The Adam Vroman land became known as Vroman's Land.

6. Jeptha Root Simms, *The Frontiersmen of New York.* (Albany, NY: George C. Riggs, 1882): 146

7. William E. Roscoe, History of Schoharie County, New York. (Syracuse, NY: D. Mason & Co, 1882): 28.

8. *Gazetteer of the State of New York.* (Syracuse, NY; R. Pearsall Smith, 1860): 602.

1752-1785 John (Johannes) Eckerson; Thomas Eckerson (pp. 6-11)

9. Ray Eckerson, *The Eckersons of the Schoharie Valley* (Los Angeles, 1939 with additional information added 1984): 7.

10. "John Eckerson 1752 Land Deed Schoharie Stone Fort Property," digital images, ancestry.com (accessed 28 March 2017). Transcription of handwritten land deed.

11. Solomon Sias, *A Summary of Schoharie County.* (Middleburgh, NY: Press of Pierre W. Danforth, 1904): 79.

12. John M. Brown, *Brief Sketch of the First Settlement of the County of Schoharie.* (Schoharie, 1823): 4.

13. Rufus Alexander Grider (1817-1900) created numerous pen-and-ink sketches and watercolors of places and objects related to New York State history. Many of his works are contained in nine albums of drawings and sketches housed in the Manuscripts and Special Collections of the New York State Library. Volume 8 (created 1887-1888) primarily relates to Schoharie history. Many maps and documents copied by Grider are the only versions now available. He intended the volume as a "collection of illustrations old and new and of objects possessed by inhabitants of that region ... of what exists and what formerly existed there." He drew landscapes and Indian relics and then traced rare documents making a "complete duplicate of the original." His works were invaluable to this book.

14. An 'oyl' (oil) mill is a grinding mill designed to crush oil-bearing seeds, such as cottonseed or soybeans or other oil-rich vegetable materials to extract their oil.

15. Claude Joseph Sauthier and William Faden, *A Chorographical Map of the Province of New-York in North America* (London, 1779). (accessed May 31, 2017); available from the Library of Congress. https://lccn.loc.gov/74692657

16. Paul B. Mattice, "Old Grist Mills Along the Schoharie," *County Historical Review – Schoharie County Historical Society*, v. 12, no. 1, (May 1949): 6.

17. Ibid.: 4.

18. Roscoe, *History of Schoharie County:* 405.

19. Jeptha Root Simms, *History of Schoharie County and the Border Wars of New York* (Albany, NY: Munsell and Tanner, 1845): 418.

20. Roscoe, *History of Schoharie County*: 375.

21. Nelson Greene, ed. *History of the Mohawk Valley*, v.2 (Chicago: S.J. Clarke, 1925): 1028.

22. The Treaty of Paris was signed in 1783.

23. *Survey of Historical Sites in MVLA Area.* (n.p., n.d.) Typescript.

1785-1793 Adam B. Vroman, Colonel Peter Vroman (pp. 12-51)
The Vroman Family Early Year (pp.12-14)

24. Massacre at Schenechtady [in Dutch]. [Government document]. At: The Gilder Lehrman Institute of American History. GLC03107.01990. Available through: Adam Matthew, Marlborough, American History, 1493-1945. (Accessed October 25, 2018). http://www.americanhistory.amdigital.co.uk.proxy.wm.edu/Documents/Details/GLC03107.01990.

25. [Vroman Family Reunion], typescript, 1983?

26. "DEC Acquires Vroman's Nose Parcel in Schoharie County." *DEC News Release*, December 18, 2017. (Accessed Oct. 2, 2017). https://www.dec.ny.gov/press/112186.html

27. Sanford H. Cobb, *Story of the Palatines*, (NY: G. P. Putnam's Sons, 1897): 223.

28. John M. Brown: 13.

29. Some of the background information on the Vroman family is from Henry Cady's Schoharie County, New York Families. He collected the information from various sources but did not include citations. The records are found in the Old Stone Fort Library.

30. "Abstracts of Wills on File in the Surrogate's Office, City of New York," *Collections of The New-York Historical Society for the Year 1899*, v. 8 1771-1776 (1900): 39.

Peter B. Vroman — Early Military Career (pp. 15-17)

31. A. B Gregg, "'Pull-Foot' Vroman and the Massacre in Vroman's Land," *The Enterprise Altamont* (March 11, 1949), Section 2: 7.

32. Sir William Johnson. *The Papers of Sir William Johnson.* v.3: 59.

33. Ibid., v.3: 65.

34. Wies Erkelens translated Vroman's Account from the Dutch.

35. Vroman was among the over 3,500 men Brigadier General John Prideaux and Sir William Johnson (the British Indian agent who commanded Iroquois and Colonial militia forces) led from Fort Oswego to battle at Fort Niagara.

36. Lt. Col. Michael Thody was shot in the leg.

37. The Colonel in Chief was Col. John Johnson.

38. Frida was Brigadier General John Prideaux, who was killed when a shell fragment from one of his own guns hit him.

39. Ohio is the Ohio Valley, also known as western Pennsylvania.

40. Captain Pouchot surrendered Fort Niagara.

41. Volkert Petrus Douw is considered the founding father of Colonial Albany. He was vice president of the First Provincial Congress, mayor, captain of the Colonial Militia, first judge of County Court and state senator.

Peter B. Vroman — Pre-Revolution (pp. 17-19)

42. *Documentary History of the State of New York*. Albany: Weed, Parsons & Co., 1849. v.2.: 959. https://archive.org/details/documentaryhisto02ocal/page/959 [Accessed Nov. 1, 2018]

43. [Indenture from Col. Peter B. Vroman 1770 to Cornelius Vroman]. Typescript originally in the possession of Mildred Vrooman, now owned by the author.

Colonel Peter Vroman — Revolutionary War Years (pp. 20-22)

44. Peter Vroman is referred to as 'Esquire' in several documents. In colonial America that might mean he was an office holder or current or former justice.
45. *American Loyalist Claims, 1776-1835*. Series II. Kew, Surrey, England: National Archives of the United Kingdom, Kew, Surrey, England, piece 012.
46. Ellsworth Vrooman. *Schoharie Valley Lore: Tales of the Days When the Old Stone Fort Was Young*. St. Petersburg, FL, 1924?: 19.
47. *Annual Report*, New York Historical Society, v.51, no.5, 1967: 29.
48. Capt. Barent Ten Eyck had a checkered military career. He was passed over for a more senior position in 1776 and labeled a "drunkard." After promising to reform, he was given another senior position but was later transferred to a different Battalion and served at Valley Forge. In 1778, he wrote to General Washington asking to be discharged for health reasons.
49. *Minutes of the Albany Committee of Correspondence, 1775-1778* – Digital Edition. Albany: University of the State of New York, ?? v.1 :264. https://archive.org/details/MinutesOfThe AlbanyCommitteeOfCorrespondence1775-1778Vol1/page/n285 [Accessed Nov. 1, 2018]
50. Ibid., v.1: 978.
51. Ibid., v.1: 585.
52. Ibid., v.1: 586.
53. Ibid., v.1: 784.
54. Ibid., v.1: 815.
55. "Feeding the Garrison of Fort Defyance," *2017 Season Guide: 240ᵗʰ Anniversary of the Battle of the Flockey*. Schoharie County Historical Society, 2017: 50.
56. *The Papers of George Washington Digital Edition*. Charlottesville: University of Virginia Press, 2008: 112.
57. Ibid.: 148.
58. *Albany New York Evening Journal* (September 14, 1893): 8.
59. Simms, *History of Schoharie*: 410.
60. Ibid.: 408.
61. Roscoe, *History of Schoharie County*: 201.

Colonel Peter Vroman — After the Revolution (pp. 22-23)

62. Louise S. Vrooman, "The Home of Colonel Peter Vrooman," *The Quarterly Bulletin – Schoharie County Historical Society* 6, no. 3 (July 1942): 4.
63. *Gazetteer and Business Directory of Schoharie County, NY*, 1872/73: 80.
64. Rufus A. Grider Albums, 1886-1900. Manuscript, New York State Library, Manuscripts and Special Collections, v.8, no.4.
65. Roscoe: 367.
66. Simms, *History*: 434.

Colonel Peter Vroman — Church (pp. 23-27)

67. The Low Dutch Reformed Church of Schoharie is a different church than the Old Stone Fort. The Old Stone Fort was not burned or damaged during the Revolution.
68. Grider, Albums, v.8, no.119.
69. Roscoe, *History of Schoharie County*: 201.

Colonel Peter Vroman — Native Americans (pp. 27-29)

70. George Rogers Howell and Jonathan Tenney, *Bi-centennial History of Albany*. v.1. (New York: W. W. Munsell & Co.,1886): 409.

Colonel Peter Vroman — Governance (pp. 29-30)

71. Julia K. Smith. *The Forging of a Constitutional Government on the Frontier in New York's Schoharie Valley*. (New York: Schoharie County Historical Society, 1990): 6.

72. New York (State). Legislature. Assembly. *Journal of the Assembly of the state of New-York, at their first meeting of the seventh session, begun and holden at the city-hall in the city of New-York, on Tuesday the sixth day of January, 1784*. (New York City, New York: Printed by E. Holt, printer to the state, 1784): 36.

73. Clarence E. Miner, *The Ratification of the Federal Constitution by the State of New York*. (New York: Columbia University, 1921): 92-93.

74. Linda Grant De Pauw, *The Eleventh Pillar: New York State and the Federal Constitution*. (Ithaca, NY: Published for the American Historical Association by Cornell University Press, 1966): 247.

75. *The Documentary History of the Ratification of the Constitution Digital Edition*, ed. John P. Kaminski [and others]. Charlottesville: University of Virginia Press, 2009: 2500. http://rotunda.upress.virginia.edu.proxy.wm.edu/founders/RNCN-01-23-01-0003-0004 [accessed 20 Sept 2018]

76. *Albany Gazette* (April 18, 1791): 2.

77. Franklin B. Hough, *Historical and Statistical Record of the University of the State of New York During the Century from 1784 to 1884*. (Albany, NY: Weed, Parsons & Co, Printers, 1885): 146.

78. *Albany Gazette* (April 8, 1790): 1.

79. *Albany Gazette* (April 16, 1792): 6.

Colonel Peter Vroman — Hero or Not? (pp. 31-33)

80. William W. Campbell. *Annals of Tryon County*. (New York: J. & J., 1831): 141-142.

81. William L. Stone. Life of Joseph Brant. (New York, 1838): 354-355.

82. Simms. *History*: 377.

83. Ibid.: 377.

84. Ibid.: 401.

85. Simms, *History*: 407.

86. Ibid.: 400.

87. Pusillanimous, a lack of courage or determination.

88. Simms, *History*: 214.

89. Sias: 84.

90. Alfred W. Abrams, "Schoharie in the Border Warfare of the Revolution" *Proceedings of the New York State Historical Association*, v. 7 (1907): 35.

Colonel Peter Vroman — Possessions (pp. 33-37)

91. Label for foot warmer displayed in the Old Stone Fort Museum, Schoharie, NY.

92. Nina Fletcher Little, "Itinerant Painting in America, 1750-1850," *New York History* v.30, no.2 (April 1949): 206.

Colonel Peter Vroman — Slavery (pp. 38-39)

93. Paul Wilson Blood Herring. *"Selected aspects on the history of the African-American in the Mohawk and upper Hudson Valley, 1633-1940*. (SUNY at Binghamton, 1992): 4.

94. *Roscoe, History of Schoharie County: 31.*
95. Storm Becker was also of Dutch descent.
96. Hal Von Linden, "If Ghosts Walk, They Step Softly in Vroman House," *The Knickerbocker News* (June 23, 1959): 3B.

Colonel Peter Vroman — House (pp. 39-45)

97. Edward R. Cook and William J. Callahan, Jr., "A Dendrochronological Analysis of the 'Peter Vroman House," Schoharie, Schoharie County, New York. n.p., 2017: 7.
98. Peter Vroman. Account memorandum book: manuscript, 1759-1792. New York State Library.
99. John N. Bleecker letter to Col. P. Vroman. John N. Bleecker Collection. 1792-1796. New York State Historical Society.
100. Catherine Lynn. Wallpaper in America .(NY: W.W. Norton, 1980): 89.

Colonel Peter Vroman — Death and Memorials (pp. 45-51)

101. Grace Vrooman Wickersham and Ernest Bernard Comstock. *The Vrooman Family in America*. [n.p.] 1949: 72.
102. Roscoe, *History of Schoharie County*: 361.
103. "Old Stone Church and Its Cemetery," *Canajoharie Radii* (July 31, 1873): 1.
104. Minutes, Memorial Fund Committee, Schoharie Chapter, D.A.R., Dec. 10, 1912, Jan. 14, 1913, April 29, 1913.
105. *Cobleskill Index* (Oct. 23, 1913): 6.
106. Frances B. Spencer, *Vrooman Family of Schoharie County* (1982): 72.
107. Sias: 31.
108. Arthur U. Stevenson, "Colonel Peter B. Vrooman," *The Quarterly Bulletin of the Schoharie County Historical Society*, v.6, no.2 (July 1942): 5.
109. A. W. Clark, "Reminiscences of Schoharie County," *Jefferson Courier*, v.23, no.40, (Nov. 29, 1894).

1793-1832 Angelica Vroman and her husband, Peter A. Vroman; Katie Vroman and her husband, Adam D. Hager (pp. 52-57)

110. "Homes of the Early Settlers in Schoharie Valley." Typescript. [possibly by Ellsworth Vroman, 1915?].
111. Dow Beekman, "The Defenders of the Frontier," *Schoharie Republican* (June 10, 1937): 8.
112. Simms: 410.
113. "Major Vroman's Certification," *Albany Centinel* (Albany, NY) April 13, 1802: 2.
114. "State Department Receives Addition," *Montgomery Advertiser* (Montgomery, Alabama, Aug. 12, 1921).
115. Roscoe, *History of Schoharie County*: 365.
116. State of New York Supreme Court, Jackson, ex dem. Synder and Snyder v. Lawrence. 1814: 191-192.
117. Josiah Priest. *Stories of the Revolution.* (Albany: Hoffman & White, 1836): 9.
118. Louise S. Vroman, *The Home ... Peter Vrooman*: 4.
119. *Homes of the Early Settlers*, 1913? Typescript.
120. Louise S. Vroman: 4.
121. Simms, *History*: 354.
122. Hal Von Linden: 3B.
123. Spencer, *Vrooman Family*: 117.
124. Ibid.: 178.

1832-1844 Jacob Fisher (pp. 58-60)

125. Deed of Sale from Peter Vroman … & his wife Anna … to Jacob Fisher, May 4, 1832. (County Recorder's Office, Schoharie, New York). Book O: 409.

126. Roscoe, *History of Schoharie County*: 375.

127. "For sale," *Albany Argus* (September 18, 1843).

1844-1860 John P. Griggs; Benjamin Griggs (pp. 61-65)

128. Joseph R. Brown, Jr., *Schoharie County Miscellany*. Transcribed and submitted by Roger Smith (accessed Sept. 18, 2016); available from http://www.rootsweb.ancestry.com/~nyschoha/miscell.html

129. Roscoe, *History of Schoharie County:* 381.

130. Roscoe, *History of Schoharie County*: 413.

131. "Another Fatal Occurrence," *Albany NY Argus,* (June 27, 1849).

132. *Bi-centennial History of Albany: History of the County of Albany, NY, from 1609 to 1886.* Edited by George Rogers Howell and Jonathan Tenney. (New York : W. W. Munsell & Co., 1886). v.4: 862.

133. 1858 Land Deed between John P. Griggs and Simon Griggs and Benjamin P. Lake. (County Recorder's Office, Schoharie, NY), Book 34: 192.

134. A hoop pole is a straight slender length of green sapling wood (usually white oak or hickory) that was used to make barrel hoops.

135. A stave is a vertical wooden post or plank used in buildings.

1863-1879 Samuel B. Stevens (Stephens) (pp. 67-79)
1879-1912; Charles B. Stevens

136. Smith Youngs was a farmer who lived in Schoharie in 1840, according to the United State Federal 1850 Census. No land transactions have yet been found concerning a transfer between Simeon Fairlee and Smith Youngs.

137. Marian S. Lynes, *Water-powered Grist Mills of Schoharie County* (Cobleskill, NY: Times-Journal, 1988).

138. Grandmother Cady is likely Martha Stevens Cady (a daughter of Samuel B. Stephens) who married John H. Cady.

139. Louise S. Vrooman: 4.

140. David K. Schafer, *Cultural Resources*: 33.

141. *Schoharie NY Union* (1866).

142. Paul B. Mattice, *Grist Mills*: 8.

143. *The Gilboa Monitor* (April 10, 1879): 3.

144. *The Gilboa Monitor* (April 17, 1879): 3.

145. *The Plattsburgh Republican* (May 29, 1886).

146. *The Gilboa Monitor* (September 8, 1898), 3.

147. Schoharie Drive-About," *Schenectady Gazette* (Oct. 5, 1989).

148. D. B. Vroman might have been David B. Vroman, identified as a farmer in the 1872/3 Gazetteer and Business Directory of Schoharie.

149. "Runaway in Schoharie," *Gilboa Monitor* (June 14, 1900): 3.

150. "Charles B. Stevens," *Cobleskill Index* (Dec. 23, 1915): 1.

151. Ibid.: 1.

1912-1945 Louise (Stevens) Vrooman (pp. 80-84)

152. "Auctions," *Schoharie Republican and County Democrat* (November 1918).

153. Louise S. Vrooman: 4.

154. The Gilboa Monitor (September 8, 1898): 3.

155. "Village Notes," *Schenectady Gazette* (Jan. 5, 1928): 14.

156. "Wild Bullet Misses Housewife By Inches," *Albany New York Knickerbocker News* (August 16, 1938).

157. "Banker Wins in Heart Balm Suit for $50,000," *Albany Evening News* (June 19, 1930): 3.

158. "Notice," *Schoharie Republican* (August 18, 1938).

159. Louise S. Vrooman: 4.

1945-1956? Charles S. Vrooman (pp. 85-86)

160. "Dr. and Mrs. G. L. Jones Move to Schoharie," *Schenectady Gazette* (Oct. 28, 1950): 17.

2013-   Joseph and Berna Heyman (pp. 92-93)

161. Bill Buell, "Two local sites nominated for National Register," *The Daily Gazette – Schoharie County* (Dec. 8, 2018): C1-2.

162. Buell: C1.

163. Buell: C2.

Adjacent Property (pp. 94-98)

164. Louise S. Vrooman: 4.

165. "Schoharie Loses Public Spirited Citizen," *Schoharie Republican and County Democrat* (Feb. 15, 1919).

166. "Necrology," *New York Genealogical and Biographical Record*. v.51 (April 1920): 129.

167. *Plans for Reconstructing a Portion of the Schoharie-Middleburg Highway and a Portion of the Gallupville-Vrooman Highway*. FARC 54-33. New York State Department of Transportation: 78.

Vroman House Description and Features (pp. 99-139)

168. "The Cora Vrooman Home," *The 1975 Drive-About*. Presented by the Schoharie Colonial Heritage Association. Oct 11, 1975.

Known House Alterations (pp. 133-135)

169. Historic American Buildings Survey. Colonel Peter Van Vrooman House, Schoharie, NY. HABS NY 48-SCHO, 8. Note: the house is incorrectly identified as Van Vrooman, rather than Vrooman or Vroman.

170. Hal Von Linden: 3B.

BIBLIOGRAPHY

Articles/Books/Manuscripts

Abrams, Alfred W. "Schoharie in the Border Warfare of the Revolution." *Proceedings of the New York State Historical Association*. 7 (1907): 30-41.

"Abstracts of Wills on File in the Surrogate's Office, City of New York," *Collections of The New-York Historical Society for the year 1899*. 8, 1771-1776 (1900): 39.

American Loyalist Claims, 1776-1835. AO13. Kew, Surrey, England: National Archives of the United Kingdom.

Annual Report, New York Historical Society, v.51, no.5, 1967: 29.

Bi-centennial History of Albany: History of the County of Albany, New York, from 1609 to 1886. Edited by George Rogers Howell and Jonathan Tenney. New York : W. W. Munsell & Co., 1886: v.4, 862.

Bleecker, John N. *John N. Bleecker Collection*. 1792-1796. New York State Historical Society. <Archival material>
Letter, signed John N. Bleecker, dated Albany, September 21, 1792, to Peter Vroman, listing the materials he has sent for papering the walls, and gives instructions as to the mixing of the glue and hanging of the paper. Copy In the possession of Berna Heyman, current owner of the Colonel Peter Vroman House.

Brown, John M. *Brief Sketch of the First Settlement of the County of Schoharie, by the Germans: Being an answer to a circular letter, addressed to the author by 'The Historical and Philosophical Society of the State of New-York.'* Schoharie: Printed for the author by L. Cothbert, 1823.

Cady, Henry. *Early Settlers of Estates*. Retrieved from NYGenWeb Site, http://www.rootsweb.ancestry.com/~nyschoha/cady.html. [Accessed June 1, 2017]

Cady, Henry. *Genealogy Schoharie County New York*. Copied by Charlotte Taylor. Albany, NY: Luckhurst?, 1922.

Campbell, William W. Annals of Tryon County; or, the Border Warfare of New York During the Revolution. New York: Printed by J. & J. Harper, 1831.

Cobb, Sanford H. *The Story of the Palatines: An Episode in Colonial History*. New York: G. P. Putnam's Sons, 1897.

Cook, Edward R. Cook and William J. Callahan, Jr., *A Dendrochronological Analysis of the 'Peter Vroman House,' Schoharie, Schoharie County, New York*. [n.p.], 2017.

"The Cora Vrooman Home," *The 1975 Drive-About*. Presented by the Schoharie Colonial Heritage Association. Oct 11, 1975.

Danforth, Elliot. *Old Schoharie. Address Delivered Before the Schoharie County Historical Society at Schoharie*, NY, April 12, 1892. Albany, NY: James B. Lyon, Printer, 1893.

De Pauw, Linda Grant. *The Eleventh Pillar: New York State and the Federal Constitution.* Ithaca, NY: Published for the American Historical Association by Cornell University Press, 1966.

"DEC Acquires Vroman's Nose Parcel in Schoharie County," *DEC News Release,* December 18, 2017. https://www.dec.ny.gov/press/112186.html [Accessed Oct. 2, 2017]

Directory and Reference Book of Schoharie County. By Mallery & Danforth. Middleburgh, NY: Pierre W. Danforth Printer, 1899. (Cover title: *The Schoharie County Directory 1899 and Ready Reference Book*).

The Documentary History of the State of New York Digital Edition. Arranged under the direction of Christopher Morgan by Edmund Bailey O'Callaghan. Albany: Weed, Parsons & Co., 1849. http:// https://archive.org/details/documentaryhisto02ocal/ [Accessed Nov. 1, 2018]

The Documentary History of the Ratification of the Constitution Digital Edition, ed. John P. Kaminski [and others]. Charlottesville: University of Virginia Press, 2009. http://rotunda.upress.virginia.edu.proxy.wm.edu/founders/RNCN-02-23-02-0003-0003-0004 [Accessed July 6, 2018]

Eckerson, Ray. *The Eckersons of the Schoharie Valley.* [Los Angeles, CA, 1984?]

"Feeding the Garrison of Fort Defyance," *2017 Season Guide: 240th Anniversary of the Battle of the Flockey.* Produced by the Schoharie County Historical Society, 2017: 50.

Gazetteer and Business Directory of Schoharie County, NY for 1872-73. Compiled by Hamilton Child. Syracuse: Printed at the Journal Office, 1872.

Gazetteer of the State of New York. Compiled by J. H. French. Syracuse, NY: R. Pearsall Smith, 1860.

Gould, Jay. *Border Wars of New York: Containing a Sketch of the Early Settlements in the County, and A History of the Late Anti-Rent Difficulties in Delaware, With Other Historical and Miscellaneous Matter Never Before Published.* Roxbury: Keeny & Gould, 1856.

Greene, Nelson, ed. *History of the Mohawk Valley: Gateway to the West 1614-1925: Covering the Six Counties of Schenectady, Schoharie, Montgomery, Fulton, Herkimer, and Oneida.* Chicago: S. J. Clarke, 1925.

Gregg, Arthur B. "Tales of Old Fountain Town." *Schoharie County Historical Review,* (May 1954): 5-9.

Grider, Rufus Alexander. *Albums, 1886-1900.* [Manuscript] New York State Library, Manuscripts and Special Collections.

Hagan, Edward A. *War in Schohary, 1777-1783.* [n.p.]: Middleburgh News Press, 1980.

Hendrix, L. E. and A. W. Hendrix. *Sloughter's Instant History of Schoharie County, 1700-1900.* Schoharie, NY: Schoharie County Historical Society, 1988.

Herring, Paul Wilson Blood. *Selected Aspects on the History of the African-American in the Mohawk and Upper Hudson Valley, 1633-1940.* PhD diss., State University of New York at Binghamton, 1992.

Heyman, Joseph. *An Egg-straordinary Folk Art Museum: The Amazing Creations of Mildred Vrooman*. Schoharie, NY: Covered Bridge Books, 2019.

Heyman, Joseph and Berna Heyman. *The Mildred Vrooman Easter Egg Collection*. {n.p.} 2014.

Historic American Buildings Survey, Creator. *Colonel Peter Van Vrooman House, Schoharie, Schoharie County, NY*. New York, Schoharie, Schoharie County [ca. 1940] Documentation Compiled After 1933. Photograph. Retrieved from the Library of Congress, https://www.loc.gov/item/ny0755/. HABS NY-3125 [Accessed May 08, 2017]
Note: the house is incorrectly identified as Van Vrooman, rather than Vrooman or Vroman.

Homes of the Early Settlers in Schoharie Valley. Unpublished typescript manuscript from the collection of Mildred Vrooman.
Likely written ca. 1915, based on the author dating the Vroman house at 1785 and then taking into account the author stating the house had stood for 130 years. Possibly written by Ellsworth Vrooman.

Hough, Franklin B. *Historical and Statistical Record of the University of the State of New York During the Century from 1784 to 1884*. Printed by authority of the Legislature. Albany : Weed, Parsons & Company, Printers, 1885.

Howell, George Rogers and Jonathan Tenney. *Bi-centennial History of Albany: History of the County of Albany, from 1609 to 1886.*. Vol. 1. New York: W. W. Munsell & Col, 1886: 409.

Johnson, William. *The Papers of Sir William Johnson*. Albany: The University of the State of New York, 1921-65: v.3. Hathi Trust Digital Library https://hdl.handle.net/2027/hvd.32044024402901 [Accessed Nov. 1 2018]

Knittle, Walter Allen. *Early Eighteenth Century Palatine Emigration; A British Government Redemptioner Project to Manufacture Naval Stores*. Philadelphia: Dorrance & Company. 1937.

La Cerra, Jr., Charles Edward. *The Role of the Aristocracy Active in New York State Politics During the Period of Confederation, 1783-1788*. New York University, Ph.D., 1969. Ann Arbor, MI: University Microfilms, 1970.

Little, Nina Fletcher. "Itinerant Painting in America, 1750-1850." *New York History*, v.30, no.2 (April 1949): 204-216. URL: http://www.jstor.org/stable/23148215 [Accessed 5 July 5, 2018].

Lynes, Marian S. *Water-powered grist mills of Schoharie County*. Cobleskill, NY: Times-Journal, 1988.

Lynn, Catherine. *Wallpaper in America From the Seventeenth Century to World War I*. New York: W. W. Norton, 1980.

Massacre at Schenectady [in Dutch]. [Government document]. At: The Gilder Lehrman Institute of American History. GLC03107.01990. Available through: Adam Matthew, Marlborough, American History, 1493-1945. http://www.americanhistory.amdigital.co.uk.proxy.wm.edu/Documents/Details/GLC03107.01990 [Accessed October 25, 2018].

Mattice, Paul B. "Old Grist Mills Along the Schoharie." *County Historical Review – Schoharie County Historical Society* 12 no. 1 (May 1949): 3-9.

Miner, Clarence E. *The Ratification of the Federal Constitution by the State of New York,* New York: Columbia University, 1921.

Minutes of the Albany Committee of Correspondence, 1775-1778 Digital Version. Prepared for publication by the Division of Archives and History, James Sullivan. Albany: University of the State of New York, 1923. 2 vols. https://archive.org/details/MinutesOfTheAlbanyCommitteeOfCorrespondence1775-1778Vol1/ [Accessed Nov. 1, 2018]

National Register of Historic Places, Col. Peter B. Vroman House, Schoharie, N.Y. Prepared by Berna Heyman, edited by William Krattinger. New York State Division for Historic Preservation, 2018.

"Necrology." *New York Genealogical and Biographical Record.* v.51, (April 1920): 128-9.

New York (State). Secretary's Office, *The Documentary History of the State of New-York,* arranged under direction of Christopher Morgan, Secretary of State, by E.B. O'Callaghan (Albany, NY: Weed, Parsons & Co.), vol. 1-3, 1849-1851.

New York (State). Legislature. Assembly. *Journal of the Assembly of the state of New-York, at their first meeting of the seventh session, begun and holden at the city-hall in the city of New-York, on Tuesday the sixth day of January, 1784.* New York City, New York: Printed by E. Holt, printer to the state, 1784. Readex: Readex https://infoweb-newsbank-com.proxy.wm.edu/apps/readex/doc?p=ARDX&docref=image/v2:0F2B1F-CB879B099B@EAIX-0F2FD4B9C6F55388@-0FA80259CCF926D8@95. [Accessed August 12, 2018]

New York (State) Supreme Court. *Reports of Cases Argued and Determined in the Supreme Court of Judicature by William Johnson.* Vol. 11. New York: Banks & Brothers, 1873. Jackson, ex dem. Snyder and Snyder v. Lawrence. Construction of Exception in Deed – Natural Mill-seat. 1814. https://books.google.com/books?id=5Po2AQAAMAAJ&pg=PA160&dq=peter+vroman&hl=en&sa=X&ved=0ahUKEwj3opz31b-fXAhWjiFQKHTUTCak4ChDoAQgyMAI#v=onepage&q=peter%20vroman&f=false [Accessed Nov. 11, 2017]

New York State Census of the Town of Schoharie, Schoharie County, New York: 1855, 1865, 1875, 1885, 1895, 1905, 1915, 1925.

Noyes, Marion. F. *A History of Schoharie County.* Richmondville, NY: Printed by the Richmondville Phoenix, 1964.

The Papers of George Washington Digital Edition. Charlottesville: University of Virginia Press, 2008. http://rotunda.upress.virginia.edu.proxy.wm.edu/founders/GEWN-03-16-02-0165 [Accessed July 7, 2018]

Parker, Arthur C. "The Archaeological History of New York Part 2," *New York State Museum Bulletin,* Nos. 237-238. (1922): 692-693. http://nysl.cloudapp.net/awweb/guest.jsp?smd=1&cl=all_lib&lb_document_id=54818 [Accessed Oct. 20, 2017]

Priest, Josiah. "Intrepidity of Colonel John Harper, related by Judge Hager of Schoharie." *Stories of the Revolution.* Albany: Printed by Hoffman and White, 1836.

Proper, Kathleen. "Restoration of the Col. Peter Vroman House at Schoharie." *Schoharie County Historical Review* 25, no. 1 (Spring-summer 1961): 17.

Randall, Lora Vrooman. *Josiah B. Vrooman (Vroman): his ancestors and descendants.* El Paso, Tex. : C. Hertzog, 1946.

Record of Wills and Administration, 1787-1922. New York. Surrogate's Court (Montgomery County); http://ancestry.com [Accessed by Aug 4, 2016]

Rieth, Christina B. *Cultural Resources Site Examination Report of The Vroman I Site (NYSM #10146 and 10148) and The Vroman II Site (NYSM #10147 for PIN 9125.05.121 Routes 30/30A Intersection and Vroman Corners Intersection, Town of Schoharie, Schoharie County, New York.* [Albany, NY]: Division of Research and Collections, New York State Education Department, 2015. http://www.nysm.nysed.gov/common/nysm/files/crsp-vol6_0.pdf

Roscoe, William E. *History of Schoharie County, New York with illustrations and biographical sketches of some of its prominent men and pioneers.* Syracuse, NY: D. Mason & Co, 1882.

Schafer, David K. *Cultural Resources Reconnaissance Survey Report of PIN 9125.05.121, Routes 30/30A Intersection and Vroman Corners Intersection, Town of Schoharie, Schoharie County, New York.* Prepared for the New York State Dept. of Transportation by the New York State Museum. Albany, 1995.

Schoharie Chapter, D.A.R. *Minutes ... Memorial Fund Committee.* Dec. 10, 1912, Jan. 14, 1913, April 29, 1913. [manuscript]

Schoharie County Miscellany. Compiled by Joseph R. Brown, Jr. Transcribed and submitted by Roger Smith. http://www.rootsweb.ancestry.com/~nyschoha/miscell.html [Accessed Sept. 18, 2016]

Sias, Solomon. *A Summary of Schoharie County, giving the organization, geography, geology, history.* Prepared at the request of the County Teachers' Association. Middleburgh, NY: Press of Pierre W. Danforth, 1904.

Simms, Jeptha Root. *The Frontiersmen of New York: Showing Customs of the Indians, Vicissitudes of the Pioneer White Settlers and Border Strife in Two Wars.* Albany, NY: George C. Riggs, 1882.

Simms, Jeptha Root *History of Schoharie County and the border wars of New York.* Albany, NY: Munsell and Tanner, printers, 1845.
Simms work is the closest to a contemporary account of Colonel Vroman. Although it was published about 50 years after Col. Vroman's death, it does include information Simms gathered from Vroman's daughter, Angelica, and others who were alive during the Colonel's lifetime.

Smith, Julia K. *The Forging of a Constitutional Government on the Frontier in New York's Schoharie Valley.* [n.p.]: Schoharie County Historical Society, 1990.

Souvenir of Schoharie. Middleburgh, N.Y. : Pierre W. Danforth, Publisher, 1904.

Spencer, Frances B. *Vrooman Family of Schoharie County.* 1982.

Stevenson, Arthur U. "Colonel Peter B. Vrooman." *The Quarterly Bulletin - Schoharie County Historical Society.* (July, 1942): 5,10.

Stone, William L. *Life of Joseph Brant—Thayendanegea the border wars of the American Revolution and sketches of the Indian campaigns of generals Harmar, St. Clair, and Wayne …* New York, George Dearborn and Co., 1838.

Sullivan, Mark. "Lt. Peter B. Vrooman, New York Provincial, 1759," *Schoharie County Historical Review.* (Spring-Summer 1995).

Survey of Historical Sites in MVLA Area. [n.p., n.d.] Typescript in vertical file at Old Stone Fort Library with note: taken from the Summer issue of the Schoharie County Review for 1962.

Taylor, Eleanor. *Schoharie County in Legend and History: Commemorating its one hundred and fiftieth anniversary.* Schoharie, NY: Published by The Chamber of Commerce, 1947.

United State Federal Census of Schoharie County, New York: 1790, 1800, 1810, 1820, 1830, 1840, 1850, 1860, 1870, 1880, 1890, 1900, 1910, 1920, 1930, 1940.

Vroman, Adam B. [*Will of land deeded by Adam B. to his son, Peter A. Vroman*] New York, Wills and Probate Records, 1659-1999 [online database] http://ancestry.com [Accessed March 11, 2018]

Vroman, Peter. *Account Memorandum Book: manuscript, 1759-1792.* . [New York State Library, Manuscripts and Special Collections]
Blotter of debit-credit accounts kept by Col. Peter Vroman. Also includes narratives describing the battle at Niagara in July, 1759, and his journey from Oswego to Three Rivers from October 10 to October 29, 1759, both of which relate to the French and Indian War.

Vroman, Peter. [*Quit Rent Payment Certifications, 1787*]. Manuscript in the possession of Berna and Joseph Heyman, Schoharie, NY

Vrooman, Ellsworth. *Schoharie Valley Lore: Tales of the Days When the Old Stone Fort Was Young.* St. Petersburg, FL, 1924?
Contains historical matter used in histories published by Simms, Roscoe, Gould, Stone and Campbell and other writers. The pamphlet does not include citations so cannot identify the source of his stories.

Vrooman, John J. *Forts and Firesides of the Mohawk Country, New York: the Stories and Pictures of Landmarks of the Pre-Revolutionary War Period Throughout the Mohawk Valley and the Surrounding Countryside, Including Some Historic and Genealogical Mention During the Post-War Period.* Philadelphia, PA: E. E. Brownell, 1943.

Vrooman, John J. "The Johnson-Brant Raid of 1780." *Schoharie County Historical Review* 17, no. 1 (May 1953): 3-8.

Vrooman, Louise S. "The Home of Colonel Peter Vrooman." *The Quarterly Bulletin – Schoharie County Historical Society* 6, no. 3 (July 1942): 4.

Vrooman family. *Vroman Family Papers, 1720-1879.* New York State Library. [Archival material]

Wickersham, Grace Vrooman and Ernest Bernard Comstock. *The Vrooman Family in America: Descendants of Hendrick Meese Vrooman who came from Holland to America in 1664.* [n.p.] 1949.

Deeds
• "A Deed from Myndert Schuyler to John Eckerson for Lands att Schoharie, 1752" https://www.ancestry.com/media/viewer/viewer/e0350fb8-0de6-4032-9a08-d4325cf51e6c/40985206/19561168478 [Accessed March 28, 2017]
Transcription of handwritten land deed.
• [Deed from Thomas Eckerson to Adam Vrooman, 1785]
Listed in an 1899 donation inventory of items given by Henry Cady to the Old Stone Fort. [missing]
(Thomas Eckerson was the son of John Eckerson)

Deeds -- Schoharie County, New York Land Deeds
Colonel Peter Vroman House
• 1844 Land Deed between Jacob Fisher and John P. Griggs. Book 9, p.206.
• 1845 Land Deed between Jacob Fisher and John P. Griggs. Book 10, p.164.
• 1847 Land Deed between Jacob Fisher and Cornelius P. Vroman.
• 1856 Land Deed between John P. Griggs to Benjamin Griggs and Hiram Hunt. Book 30, p.545.
• 1857 Land Deed between Benjamin Griggs and John P. Griggs. Book 37, p.245.
• 1858 Land Deed between John P. Griggs and Simon Griggs and Benjamin P. Lake. Book 34, p.192.
• 1860 Land Deed between Hiram Griggs and Benjamin P. Lake, assignees of John P. Griggs to Simeon Fairlee. Book 37, p.315.
• 1863 Land Deed between Smith Youngs to Samuel B. Stevens. Book 42, p.91.
• 1877 Land Deed between Samuel B. Stevens and Charles B. Stevens. Book 83, p.415.
• 1884 Land Deed between Mary M. Handy, Pamelia Stevens, Martha H. Cady and Giles Stevens to Charles B. Stevens. Book 95, p.609.
• 1912 Land Deed between Charles B. Stevens and Louise S. Vrooman. Book 161, p.161.
• 1945 Land Deed between Louise Vrooman and Charles S. Vrooman. Book 238, p.545.
• 1949 Land Deed between Charles S. Vrooman to Augustus Von Linden. Book 257, p.83.
• 1950 Land deed between Charles S. Vrooman to Augustus Von Linden. Book 261, p.83.
• 1956 Land deed between Charles Vroman foreclosure sale to Cora W. Vroman and Mildred G. Vroman. Book 275, p.230.
• 1972 Land deed between Cora W. Vroman to Mildred G. Vroman. Book 953, p.218.
• 2013 Land deed between Mildred Vrooman deceased, executor Hawley Zwahlen to Joseph S. Heyman and Berna L. Heyman. Book 953, p.218, document no. 646733.

Adjacent Property (Dietz House)
• 1828 Land Deed between Peter M. Vroman and Adam Vroman Junior. Book J, p. 131.
• 1828 Land Deed between Peter M. Vroman and Maria Vroman, the wife of Adam Vroman Junior. Book J, p.133.
• 1828 Land Deed between Peter Vroman & his wife Anna and Peter M. Snyder. Book J, p.204.
• 1832 Land Deed between Peter Vroman of Glen & his wife Anna, Adam Vroman Junior and his wife Nancy; Jacob L. Vroman and his wife Lydia; David Dietz and Julia Ann his wife and Jacob Fisher. Book O, p.409.
• 1832 Land Deed between Peter M. Snyder and Jacob Fisher.
• 1845 Land Deed between Jacob & Sophia Fisher and Lorenzo Huff. Book 10, p.260.
• 1848 Land Deed between Lorenzo & Jerusha Huff and Paul Haverly. Book 15, p.159.
• 1853 Land Deed between Paul & Maria Haverly and Jacob H. Deitz. Book 25, p.383.
• 1866 Land Deed between Jacob H. & Sarah E. Dietz and Adam D. Hagar. Book 48, p.242.
• 1883 Land Deed between Henry & Kate Cady and Charles B. Stevens. Book 93, p.295.

- 1908 Land Deed between Charles B. and Ida Stevens and Nancy C. Smith. Book 146, p.373.
- 1916 Land Deed between Nancy C. Smith and John C. Wilber. Book 168, p.73.
- 1923 Land Deed between John C & Luella Wilber to Lloyd S. Guernsey. Book 180, p.479.
- 1926 Land Deed from Lloyd S. & Mary Guernsey and Carey & Elizabeth Mattice. Book 189, p.415.
- 1938 Land Deed from Carey & Elizabeth Mattice and Fred Westfall, Jr. & Evelyn R. Westfall. Book 221, p.307.
- 1946 Land Deed from Fred & Evelyn Westfall to Fred, Evelyn, and Walter R. Westfall. Book 243, p.38.
- 1959 Land Deed from Fred and Walter R. Westfall and Arthur E & Inger F. Jenner. Book 291, p.77.
- 1997 Land Deed from Arthur Edward Jenner, prelim executor of Inger Frances Jenner, deceased and Mildred Vrooman. Book 614, p.57.

Maps

(1714) *Survey of Land for Myndert Schuyler et al.* Retrieved from the New York State Archives, Survey maps of lands in New York State, Series A0273-78, map #613. http://digitalcollections.archives.nysed.gov/index.php/Detail/Object/Show/object_id/37131 [Accessed March 5, 2018]

(1731?) Cockburn, Will. *Map of the Lands Mentioned in the Diferent Releases.* [Vromansland: 1716-1731]. Copied by Rufus Grider from a map in possession of A. B. Richmond, Canajoharie, 1888. Rufus Alexander Grider Albums, v.7, 154 oversize.

(1758) *Map of the Northern Parts of New York.* [1758?] Map. Retrieved from the Library of Congress, https://www.loc.gov/item/73691805/ [Accessed April 27, 2017]

(1778 – copied 1888) Gray, William. *A Map of Schohara: drawn by Capt. Wm. Gray, Oct. 1778 while with Genl. Sullivans Expedition to the Indian Country.* Copied by Rufus Grider in 1888. Rufus Alexander Grider Albums, v.8, 132 oversize.
(Original publication: *Journals of the Military Expedition of Major General John Sullivan Against the Six Nations of Indians in 1779 with Records of Centennial Celebrations.* Prepared by Frederick Cook, Secretary of State. Auburn, NY: Knapp, Peck & Thomson, 1887, p.288).

(1779) Sauthier, Claude Joseph, and William Faden. *A chorographical map of the Province of New-York in North America, divided into counties, manors, patents and townships; exhibiting likewise all the private grants of land made and located in that Province.* London, 1779. Map. Retrieved from the Library of Congress https://www.loc.gov/item/74692647/ [Accessed April 27, 2017]

(1802 – copied 1888) Machin, Thomas. [Map – *supposed to be part or all of a patent granted to Myndert Schuyler and commonly called the Old Schoharie Patent.* Copied March 1888 by Rufus Grider. Rufus Alexander Grider Albums, v.8, 136.

(1856) Wenig, E, Wm. Lorey, and Robert Pearsall Smith. *Map of Schoharie Co., New York.* Philadelphia: Published by R.P. Smith, 1856. Map. Retrieved from the Library of Congress, https://www.loc.gov/item/2008620859 [Accessed April 27, 2017]

(1866) Beers, S. N. and D. G. Beers. *New Topographical Atlas of Schoharie Co., New York* From Actual Surveys by S. N. Beers & D. G. Beers and Assistants. Philadelphia: Stone and Steward, 1866. (Original copy in New York State Archives)

(1900) Historic USGS Maps of New England & New York, Schoharie, NY Quadrangle, Northeast Corner, 1900. Retrieved from University of New Hampshire Library Digital Collections. http://docs.unh.edu/ NY/scho00ne.jpg [Accessed August 24, 2017]

(1914) *Plans for Improving the Schoharie-Middleburg State Highway. SH 5444.* New York State Department of Transportation.

(1943) *USGS 7.5 min Schoharie Quadrangle.* Washington, DC.. Rev. 1994. http://ia802301.us.archive. org/13/items/usgs_drg_ny_42074_f3/o42074f3.tif [Accessed Feb. 22, 2019).

(1954) *Plans for Reconstructing a Po*rtion of the Schoharie-Middleburg Highway and a Portion of the Gallupville-Vrooman Highway. FARC 54-33. New York State Department of Transportation.

(1977) *NYS DOT 7.5 min Schoharie Quadrangle.* New York State Department of Transportation.

(1995) Schafer, David K. *Cultural Resources Reconnaissance Survey Report of PIN 9125.05.121, Routes 30/30A Intersection and Vroman Corners Intersection, Town of Schoharie, Schoharie County, New York.* Prepared for the New York State Dept. of Transportation by the New York State Museum. Albany, 1995. Many of the early maps were copied from this document -1914, 1943, 1954, 1977)(2002) Plat of the Colonel Peter Vroman Property. Surveyed for Mildred G. Vrooman, April 16, 2012.

Newspaper Articles
Note: most of the newspaper sources came from the following Internet databases:

- Early American Newspapers Series (subscription only service)
  Albany Argus (Albany, NY) 1813-1825

- New York State Historic Newspapers. http://nyshistoricnewspapers.org
  Altamont Enterprise (Altamont, NY) 1892-1958.
  Cobleskill Index. (Cobleskill, NY) 1864-1945.
  Gilboa Monitor. (Gilboa, NY) 1878-1918.

- Old Fulton NY Post Cards   http://www.fultonhistory.com/fulton.html
  Albany Evening News (Albany, NY)
  Albany Gazette (Albany, NY)
  Albany New York Evening Journal (Albany, NY)
  Amsterdam Daily Democrat & Recorder (Amsterdam, NY)
  Canajoharie Radii (Canajoharie, NY)
  Cobleskill Index (Cobleskill, NY)
  Jefferson Courier (Jefferson, Schoharie Co., NY)
  The Knickerbocker News (Albany, NY)
  The Plattsburgh Republican (Plattsburgh, NY)\
  Schenectady Gazette (Schenectady, NY)
  Schoharie Republican and County Democrat (Schoharie, NY)

"$125,000 Suit Dropped by Stipulation." *The Schoharie Republican.* March 22, 1934: 1.

Albany Gazette. April 8, 1790: 1.

Albany Gazette. April 18, 1791: 2.

Albany Gazette. April 16, 1792: 6.

Albany New York Evening Journal. September 14, 1893: 8.

Amsterdam NY Daily Democrat & Recorder. June 2, 1926: 2

"Another Fatal Occurrence," *Albany NY Argus*. June 27, 1849.

"Auctions." *Schoharie Republican and County Democrat*. November 1918.

Balme, Robert. "Why Didn't Vrooman Vote on Ratifying the Constitution?" *The Mountain Eagle* (March 24, 1987): 8B.

"Banker Wins in Heart Balm Suit for $50,000." *Albany Evening New,* June 19, 1930: 3.

Beekman, Dow. "The Defenders of the Frontier," *Schoharie Republican*, June 10, 1937: 8.

Buell, Bill. "Two Schoharie Sites Nominated for National Register." *Daily Gazette – Schoharie County* (December 8, 2018): C1-2.

"Charles B. Stevens," *Cobleskill Index*, Dec. 23, 1915: 1.

Clark, A. W. "Reminiscences of Schoharie County," *Jefferson Courier*, v.23, no.40, Nov. 29, 1894.

Cobleskill Index, Oct. 23, 1913: 6.

"Dr. and Mrs. G. L. Jones Move to Schoharie," *Schenectady Gazette,* Oct. 28, 1950: 17.

"Fires," *The Plattsburgh Republican,* May 29, 1886.

"For sale," *Albany Argus,* September 18, 1843.

The Gilboa Monitor, April 10, 1879: 3.

The Gilboa Monitor, April 17, 1879: 3.

The Gilboa Monitor, September 8, 1898: 3.

Gregg, Arthur B. "'Pull-Foot' Vroman and the Massacre in Vroman's Land." *The Enterprise Altamont,* (March 11, 1949): Section 2: 7.

"Major Vrooman's Certification," *Albany Centinel* (Albany, NY) April 13, 1802: 2.

"Notice," *Schoharie Republican*, August 18, 1938.

"Old Stone Church and Its Cemetery," *Canajoharie Radii*, July 31, 1873: 1.

"Runaway in Schoharie," *Gilboa Monitor*, June 14, 1900: 3.

"Schoharie Drive-About," *Schenectady Gazette*, Oct. 5, 1989.

"Schoharie Loses Public Spirited Citizen: Henry Cady passes away at the age of 71 years," *Schoharie Republican.* Feb. 15, 1919.

"State Department Receives Addition," *Montgomery Advertiser* (Montgomery, Alabama) Aug. 12, 1921.

"Take Notice," *True American* (Schoharie, NY), January 30, 1820: 3.

"Village Notes," *Schenectady Gazette,* Jan. 5, 1928: 14.

Vogel, Carol. "Creating Decorative Illusions with Borders of Wallpaper." *New York Times* (April 7, 1983). https://www.nytimes.com/1983/04/07/garden/creating-decorative-illusions-with-borders-of-wallpaper.html [Accessed May 29, 2018]

Von Linden, Hal. "If Ghosts Walk, They Step Softly in Vroman House: Historic Schoharie Mansion Recalls Stirring Days of Revolution." *The Knickerbocker News* (Albany, NY). June 23, 1959: 3B.

Vrooman, Ellsworth. "Holland Record of the Vrooman Family." *The Cobleskill Index*, June 27, 1929: 9.

"Wild Bullet Misses Housewife By Inches." *Albany New York Knickerbocker News*, August 16, 1938.

Collections
Albany Hall of Records, Albany. Deed Books
Middleburgh Library, Middleburgh, New York
New York Historical Society, New York City
New York Public Library, New York City. Vrooman Family Papers
New York State Archives, Albany.
New York State Library, Manuscripts and Special Collections, Albany, New York
Schoharie Free Library, Schoharie, New York
Swem Library, College of William and Mary